A THRILLING NOVEL

SURGICAL STRIKE

A THRILLING NOVEL

SURGICAL STRIKE

ISH KUMAR GANGANIA

PRABHAT
PAPERBACKS

Published by
PRABHAT PAPERBACKS
An imprint of Prabhat Prakashan Pvt. Ltd.
4/19 Asaf Ali Road,
New Delhi-110002 (INDIA)
e-mail: prabhatbooks@gmail.com

ISBN 978-93-5521-302-0
A THRILLING NOVEL SURGICAL STRIKE
by Ish Kumar Gangania

Edition
First, 2022

Price
₹ 300 (Rupees Three Hundred Only)

Printed at
Sanjay Printers, Sahibabad

Dedicated
To the sacrifices of the martyrs of Pulwama
and
the struggle of their families

Foreword

A dialogue with time

There is no doubt about the origins of world literature; perhaps from stories. We believe that the rise of narrative literature became possible with story writing. The novel has emerged in the face of emergence of excellent story writing. There need not be any confusion in understanding the difference between a story and a novel. The tale analyses a particular part of life and society. Ernest A Baker, while defining the novel, describes it as the best means of interpreting life and culture through proselytising storylines.

Also, the use of prose in literature has been a sign of an accurate depiction of life. Through a novel, simple colloquial language makes it easy for the author to directly relate with his characters, their problems, ideas, and the broader background of their lives.

Ish Kumar Gangania has published a storybook Intuition, three collections of poetry and a dozen books on literary criticism and essays in Hindi before the novel Surgical Strike. Gangania has dared to have a meaningful dialogue over time, prioritising the art of novel writing in presenting a comprehensive depiction of the anomalies of life in his novel. So, his attempt to write a story is not spontaneous.

His insistence on reality is entirely new; it is not His insistence on reality is not at all new. It has been on par with his poems and essays. Prima facie, the platform of the novel, seems to be political, but its contents have left no aspect of man's life untouched. He has made the surrounding landscape a subject of his novel. Beyond the world of mere imagination, his book will undoubtedly attract readers living beyond the world of a castle in the sky; that's my belief. Though the number of characters in this novel is limited, the canvas of the ideological surface is quite extensive.

The ideology of Baba Sahab Ambedkar has been presented and questions raised about his thinking. There are heated discussions, and dialogues on all issues. The characters in the novel represent every aspect of society, whether political or social anomalies, religious upheaval, mainstream literature, or Dalit writers' associations and research activities. There is no lack of space for the natural development of the characters and no sign of interference by the novelist in the natural evolution and portrayal of the characters. I may say that the novelist has a strong urge to think differently under many circumstances, but the lack of prejudice behind it underscores authoritative integrity. It leads to justice in the novel's area of concern and the characters.

In a nutshell, the storyteller is far from the world of fantasy. He keeps it anchored in the world of reality, so the admissibility of the novel presented increases. There is no need for unnecessary flights beyond the absolute periphery, nor does the storyteller make any disproportionate effort. The reality of the novel helps keep the readers connected.

The emergence and development of his book is after-story writing mean honing his skills in portraying the individual and society. It is a rational and practical view document of a new approach to life's problems. In the end, it would not be an exaggeration to say that the storyteller's way of thinking plan is not just intellectual. The novelist's art of writing brings out the problems of society's problems firmly and has a solid ability to tread on spread the path of broader social awareness. The novel presented has an artistic presentation of the gradual development of social and political consciousness and expression.

Most authors believe that a broad and all-around picture of life is not available in any other form of literature other than in the novel. I have no hesitation in saying that the book lives up to this expectation. In fact, for the novelist, the story is merely a means, not an ultimate end. His aim is not just to entertain the readers; it enables them to think and consider solving society's problems through multiple layers of issues. It encourages the person to discharge his responsibilities towards the present circumstances. This art of the storyteller leads to honesty in writing.

T P Singh 'Tej'

Author's Note

Humble Submission

I am fond of the democratic fabric of the nation; hence, I couldn't stay silent at any visible threat to its sovereignty; obviously, no conscientious citizen must tolerate it. Recently, I realised some chaotic elements were trying to shatter it with unbridled enthusiasm; the novel Surgical Strike is the outcome of such apparent intimidation. Without caring for any specific language, art or skill, I found it one of the best ways for dialogue with the readers.

Though the novel's background stands at the foundation of the terrorist attack in Pulwama, the canvas of its aftermaths forced me to peep into the dark domain; an underworld where the empire was in its whole spirit. However, there was no trace of the don. This sphere of influence was foreign to enforcing agencies; they were in deep slumber or working under the invisible don. The public at large, as I observed, had turned into a mindless crowd no better than the pets in houses or wild beasts of a circus, faithfully obedient to the ringmaster.

The characters in my story try to pierce through the dense darkness to expose the frenzied elements getting beyond the law. They expose the terrorist attacks, caste and religious hostility, aiming to crush the social fabric and the overall blame games played by the political masters to win the election, the new trend of crooked politics. And the constitutional institutions on ventilators for life support, and the media as if they were teams of Indian Media Premier League (IPML), batting for the new masters instead of strengthening the state.

Worst of all, I hit upon the explosion of the crowds on roads and public places. It fills the sky with smog to pave the way for opportunistic politics to crush the socio-political structure of the nation. The protagonist of the novel, Aajivak Babu, is a genuine person whose agonised cries die down unheard under the anarchic environment.

Even though his cries die down, still unheard, the protagonist doesn't lay down his arms. He fights back hard to find out the root causes of the corruption responsible for the total collapse of the system. His journey takes us on a post-mortem of the contemporary society and its socio-political environment, and also analyses the Indus Valley civilisation, precisely focusing on the period of Lord Buddha.

Finally, I would like to convey my gratitude to Prof. Mukesh Manas and Dr R S Chandel for extending their support and worthy suggestions for writing the book. I express my sincere thanks to Mr T P Singh 'Tej' for sparing time to write the book's foreward and his involvement in several discussions at regular intervals.

***

The background of the novel is a terrorist attack in Pulwama, and the timing covered in the book from the second half of February to 18 May 2019, is a fact. The content and characters are fictitious and have nothing to do with reality. The resemblance to a person, feature, organisation, institution, political party, etc., is a coincidence and has nothing to do with fact. The information related to history and social media is authentic and is available on record.

— Ish Kumar Gangania

CONTENTS

ONE

It is Valentine's Day, and there is no bang-bang on the TV screen. It was strange but a genuine source of comfort for Aajivak Babu. Love could not be described in a single way. The public parks, bushes, tree trunks, hedge of grasses, footsteps of huge stones and rocks, and solitary shelters were well-occupied. Young couples were taking every liberty, as usual, making use of every opportunity they had. They were trying to hold on to time, making every second count.

Although they had no privacy, everything else was invisible to the loving couples. They could only see each other and nothing else. They enjoyed their wonderful dreams, whether they materialised or not; there was no time to even think. The passion for love was breaking all barriers. No one was there to keep tabs on them and question as to whether there was any embracing, kissing, flirting, or intimate touching. There might be talk of undying loyalty and fidelity and promises of eternal love apart from the stories of fetching stars from the sky and making any supreme sacrifice for their love to each other. The peace seemed to have no threat this year.

Strange! It was extraordinary for Aajivak Babu as the activities of the Romeo brigade were missing. Its hullabaloo, that had been a standard feature these days, seemed to be missing from the scene. Had the new regime won the battle to keep Indian culture free from all threats? The question was intact, but the air in the region did not support it. Since long, for the first time, the festival of love seemed to be Valentine's Day. No tears! No cries! No begging!

The new democratic monarchs held the reins of criminal elements to achieve its hidden agendas like *Gau Raksha*, *Ghar Vapsi* and Love *Jihad*. Valentine's Day was one of the popular programmes for the new regime to remain in the limelight. The lovers, sometimes, had to pay a hefty price. Panic was entwined with love like thorns with flowers. The hypocrites had turned into self-declared custodians of culture and society to treat the youth they way they wished to, in the name of religion.

It would be far from the truth to say that Indian culture was neglected before this regime. The value system had never collapsed. It was well taken care of at the family and society level. The youth in love had never been out of reach of the social fabric. Checks and balances were there, and wrongdoings were never acceptable. But no private army of goons was patronised by political masters so viciously. This Valentine's Day took Aajivak Babu to his early youth when he studied in Delhi University. Shalini's father had caught Aajivak Babu and Shalini together once. Shalini had to face a volley of questions at the family level and counselled as a child of family and society, but not like the custodians and political masters of today. It gave an inner bliss and an evident smile to Aajivak Babu's lips but didn't last long.

The peace of Valentine's Day was strangely suspicious to Aajavak Babu. Aajivak Babu suspected if he might have got the dates wrong. So, he confirmed it meticulously. Newspaper and mobile screens were checked and it was found that both the witnesses agreed with the calendar. Where could the wind flow if not from the North Pole to the south? So he was pretty sure that the date was 14 February. He was sure he had not got the dates wrong. Was it the same 14 February, Valentine's Day? Why was there no uproar? However, the current situation didn't give Aajivak Babu any peace of mind. The needle of suspicion turned to the other side. Has the power in rule changed? In his mind, the question flashed for a moment and disappeared the next moment. He knew no regime could change without elections, even in the present-day autocratic way of ruling, no way less than a monarchy.

But to return to the conclusive fact, what he saw puzzled him. There were no mikes-on-the-go in the streets. There was no distribution of alcohol and money to the voters. There were no rallies.

There had been no *tu, main* among the political workers and no political rallies and street fights for votes. There was no issue of police and courts. No one came to ask in a small majority, and there was no threat or intimidation from political musclemen . Nothing like that had happened. Aajivak Babu dismissed the election picture and returned to the TV screen. Aajivak Babu's return to the world of TV screens was like a return to the world of reality from the gloomy world of contemplation.

Aajivak Babu still could not focus on the TV. The date was 14 February, and it was Valentine's Day. The emperorship of the rulers was also intact. But the peace wasn't getting easier to assimilate. Everything seemed determined to spoil the romantic climate—the persistent drizzling, the sudden fall in temperature, and change in the season's mood. But the love birds were fluttering their wings with no bounds to cover the limit of the sky. Anyway, this changed climate was proving to be an uninvited but welcome guest to enhance the temperature of love. The love-stricken birds were enjoying the tenderness of the season, for which they waited the whole year to cherish their dreams.

Aajivak Babu was a little different in this case. He observed Valentine's Day, Mother's Day, and Father's Day the same way. He didn't need to wait for a 'special day' to show gratitude, respect and love. Every day should be a special day for expressing love. Any 'Valentine' is no more an exception to this criterion. He felt if one had to love one's

'Valentine', and desired to present them with a gift, why wait for a 'special day'? When desire sprouts wings to flutter and fly, why wait for anything else and for what? Why make a public show or any announcement to show evidence of your emotional outburst?

Today, 'Valentine's Day' was not romantic for Aajivak Babu. It did not seem to be a normal day like other days as well. In fact, it was not going well with Shalini, his Valentine. He was busy in his drawing room with a WhatsApp chat on his mobile after his morning walk; mindless of the fact that he was drenched in sweat.

"Don't have time to change your clothes?" Shalini questioned.

"You are drenched in sweat; you will catch a cold. Are you hearing me?" The words were a little softer this time. It did not reach his mind, engrossed in the phone, and the passive ears had no interest in listening to anything now. Aajivak Babu was away from the ringing bells of love and the call of any Valentine's Day.

"You seem lost in your mobile since the morning." Shalini's tone was slightly louder this time; it seemed to issue from the bottom of her throat. However, her words did not reach the ears it was intended for.

"What is happening? You will fall ill and then learn what sitting in wet clothes in winter means. This mobile phone and your morning walk will not help you from catching a cold."

When the ice in the drawing room did not melt, the imprisoned emotions had to come out. The temperature of the drawing room was bound to rise. It was enough to raise Shalini's temperature. She was greeted with dead silence. Aajivak Babu was still engaged in the mobile world.

"Wear this, wear that, cover up this way or that way, or you will fall ill, will catch cold and what not, you keep on reciting the same raga the whole day. And you are sitting badly drenched in sweat. Do these instructions have any sense to you? Are all the instructions meant just for me and have nothing to do with you?"

The words were harsh enough and were beyond Shalini's control, it seemed. The suppressed emotions were making their way out to meet their target.

I agree that suppressed emotions are damaging. The emotions always scramble to come out, stir up turmoil, and increase agitation. The longer they stay buried, the more force with which they come out. They stay latent and relaxed, but when they come out, they challenge the peace of the concerned to raise the body's temperature.

Suppressed emotions or a person's injured feelings mean pain and treachery.

The peace-loving people preferred to stay away from all such prisons, as they ought to be. The privileged goons under the protection of their political masters, gave vent to their emotions through mob-lynching and killing the innocent. Under the present regime, Aajivak Babu, a victim, felt that peace lovers had no channels for the outflow of their mind. I think nothing is as simple as it has been for long.

Shalini's outburst did not let Aajivak Babu make his point. She continued her tirade. "All the records are being broken this winter. Is it only me or are you aware of it too? Can't you do this vital work of yours a little later?"

There was a reasonable emphasis on her every word. Now the words were not issuing from the throat, but as a direct transmission of heat from the brain.

"What's about my green tea, Madameji?" Aajivak Babu asked while peeping out of the world of WhatsApp.

Now, the words 'Madamji' had become pet words to deal with his wife, Shalini. The word 'Madam' to Aajivak Babu seemed foreign and dictatorial, or remote. But he liked it too. So he had formed a strong alliance of 'Madamji' by linking 'ji' with 'Madam'. It looked like an unbreakable alliance like an Indian marriage that remains intact for seven births. Now the word 'Madamji' was very close to his heart. So, he used this word liberally for his wife. He also realised that the term 'Madamji' was also of great use for the gesture of love.

When he saw Madamji talking with her eyes and not with her lips, Aajivak Babu realised that the matter was serious. He knew that the language of the eyes, whether it is of love or anger, is always more effective than mere words of any language. So Aajivak Babu put the mobile aside and said, "Let me know what's happened? Why are you glaring at me like this, Madamji?" Finding no change in the climate, Aajivak Babu reiterated with a bit of humility, "What happened? If you tell nothing, how shall I understand?" He looked into her eyes after a pause.

"I've been talking for a long time, but you have no time to listen. If you don't listen, how will you understand?" Scornfully, Shalini continued, "If you take your eyes away from the phone, only then will you listen to anyone, and when you listen, then only can you understand." Shalini was speaking with her eyes as well.

It was not a healthy sign. The bitterness was no longer about Aajivak Babu getting wet or sitting in his sweaty clothes. It had gone a little beyond saving Aajivak Babu from the cold. This resentment was due to his neglect of Shalini. If a wife is too concerned about her husband, such negligence naturally can terrify the weather. The situation was had turned bitter like bitter gourd and was nourished by the neem tree.

The challenge was now double. Aajivak Babu had to save both him and mobile Babu as well. Aajivak Babu made Shalini sit next to him on the sofa and asked her to look at the mobile screen. "Look at this message for a couple of minutes, then you are free to react the way you like. Okay? When someone sends such a message to say good morning, naturally, the focus is inevitable. The answer to 'good morning' shouldn't be 'bad morning' anyway, Madameji? Just read the message for a minute; just for a minute and then..." Before Aajivak Babu finished, Shalini took over the mobile and looked at the message...

'yoon asar dala hai

Imposed an impact in such a way

matlabi duniya ne logon par

On the people by the selfish world

pranam bhi karo to

Even when you wish them, then

log samajhte hain ki jaroor koi kam hoga

The people think that there might be some work

ham bhi lagav rakhte hain

We have a concern

par bolte nahin

But do not express

kyonki ham

Because we

rishte nibhate hain, tolte nahin.

Don't judge but nurture the relations.

Shalini had relaxed a bit, but her eyes were still talking simultaneously. Aajivak Babu's eyes were also responding in chorus with Shalini. Words turned worthless while the eye to eye dialogue was going on. At last, Shalini smiled, and her smile was the signal as if it was the declaration of a white-flagged ceasefire.

Aajivak Babu too smiled with a sigh of relief; the ceasefire was one of the outstanding achievements of this morning. Ultimately, Shalini commented, smiling, "Change your clothes; otherwise, you will get catch cold. Just take care of your health; you are too careless about it."

"It was just that, Madamji! It was all about changing my clothes to avoid getting a cold. Your frown frightened me this morning. How could you do this with such an 'innocent guy' like me?" It was an old habit of Aajivak Babu to call himself an innocent guy to cover up his negligence of Shalini's sentiments. Shalini always rejected Aajivak Babu's self-acquired certificate of an innocent guy wrapped in a grin. But Aajivak Babu never forgot to produce this certificate to see a smile on Shalini's face.

There had been no change in the scene today, too. Words wrapped in a smile spurted from Shalini. She spoke, "I know how innocent you are. Don't talk unnecessarily." Now Aajivak Babu let out a peal of loud laughter, and in exchange, Shalini smiled first, and then broke into laughter.

Shalini returned to the world of her kitchen. The storm between them had passed, causing no damage to their peace. Valentine's Day didn't create any new controversy, and no one was there to disturb the pleasure they both were enjoying.

The message was still in front of Aajivak Babu and the sender in his memory; the man's robust, fresh and alluring smile, his addressing Aajivak Babu as 'sir', a genuine gesture of respect. Aajivak Babu couldn't forget his eye to eye contact while talking. Cautiously selected vocabulary and its articulation in a profound way, collectively gave shape to a forty-year-old personality known as Manish Kumar Shukla, M K for Aajivak Babu.

Usually, Aajivak Babu addressed him as M K, not Manish Kumar Shukla. He often preferred to call a person by his original name and avoid calling him by his surname. Aajivak Babu believed that calling a person by the surname is popularising and promoting the caste identity and system. He thought that the virus of castes has made Indian society mentally crippled, an ugly stain on the face of the community and the nation. Here, the caste-based surname represented the individual with its caste hierarchy. A person's noble thoughts, actions, and achievements turn futile, and a man merely taking birth in the so-called upper caste had a sense of superiority.

Aajivak Babu observed the caste dominance minutely in day-to-day life as a middleman in human relations. The country's electoral process had become a detestable game of casteism. It was an ugly stain on the face of democracy. Aajivak Babu was simply a soldier in the battle fought by those who were willing to wash away the disgusting stains of casteism. He continued to fight against it through dialogues and literature. H stayed associated with some social and literary organisations too.

Aajivak Babu felt delighted with the victory of Sneha of Vellore, Tiruvattra district. After a nine-year court struggle, she got a certificate with 'no-caste' and 'no religion'. The court's verdict made Aajivak Babu more optimistic about vigorously fighting against caste and religious prejudices.

He did not follow any religious beliefs and never failed to attack the evil practices of caste and spiritual superiority in personal dealings. However, he couldn't bring himself to follow Buddhism. But it was a strange coincidence that the ideological expediency of Aajivak Babu is still more among the peers responsible for ensuring the virus of casteism gets growing .

M K Shukla was a Brahmin by caste. He was a teacher and had a PhD in history. But, amazingly, Aajivak Babu and M K had solid ideological commitments on the same issues. They never compromised on any wrongdoing. Once they confronted someone on an issue, they didn't retreat. Who was in the front, what would be the consequences of the confrontation—such questions were always pointless to them. The only thing that dominated the relationship was a fusion of absolute values and principles with no compromise.

Aajivak Babu realised that M K Babu was gentle and sincere enough. There must be a solid reason to send a message about a 'selfish world'. He knew well enough not to post a message to upset anybody's morning instead of wishing them a 'good morning'. Aajivak Babu, too, knew well that M K Babu was an emotional person; he might expect a logical comment on human relations and their breakdown in the contemporary world. Present-day issues of society and the nation were always the pivots of their discussions to focus.

Aajivak Babu realised he could infer nothing more from the message. So, he responded in the same tone to keep holding the belief of positivity. However, the matter demanded a detailed discussion, which was possible only by sitting face-to-face.

'abki Harsu ajib tufan-sa hai

There is a strange storm-like situation Harsu

aangan mera jyun aasman-sa hai

The courtyard of mine is like a sky

dam ghuta ja raha hai jazbaton ka mere

I am getting emotionally choked

har gali-kooncha jyun pareshan-sa hai

Every street seems to be bothered

chiragh-e-roshan gul khilaega jaroor

The bright lamp shall bring some hope

har nazar mujhko aisa guman-sa hai

At each view, I do have such a pride'

❑

TWO

14 February, Valentine's Day, is always the same as any other day of the year. The day does not have any unusual feature or sparkle to make it extraordinary. However, the day provides a platform for lovers to shower their love on their Valentines. It has become a special day to raise the pike of love and rob the kite of love. Still, it is not different from the other days of the year. This day does not encourage the beloved ones alone but buzzes the market's pulse. Today, simple folk sitting on the footpaths with their flowers get a slight boost. It was natural to see the uncrowned kings of the world of gifts with high-flying flights.

The restaurant is like a breath-taking garden. Here, the lissome youths blossom, chatter and swing around each other's necks to whisper their blissful notes. The body language of the teens drunk in love, their tantrums and surrender to each other take the onlookers to the days to their earliest youth. And nobody wishes such a melodious song to lose its sparkle to the time immortal. But it has to go, and one has to return to the world of reality.

Money is one aspect of coins, but another one falls more massive on the element of love and livelihood. Yes, not knowing which parties, forces, and organisations wait for this day. They do all love, but to be a pet of their masters and fulfil their hidden agendas. They love bullying others and get a perverse pleasure in inflicting pain on the innocent. Suddenly, the Indian culture gets endangered under the present political mindset. And something has automatically found its security and patriotic tenders in the grip of the stray chaotic street elements.

The list of endless items creating turmoil in Aajivak Babu's mind made him uneasy. Under the umbrella of the existing regime, these fundamentalists had no fear at all. But it was beyond Aajivak Babu's understanding as to how the guardians of Indian culture had forgotten the day and date of Valentine's Day. If it wasn't so, had they gone to sleep consuming a quarter or a half bottle of country alcohol? Or had the so-called patrons of Indian culture gone on a more important cultural and patriotic mission? These questions guided Aajivak Babu's mind to call it a peace that we observe before a terrible storm.

Were the curators of culture at peace now? Had they have achieved the plan of protection of culture? Had they had a change of heart? Had they stopped being the bonded labourers of their masters? Were their masters no longer needed to achieve their political and religious aspirations? Was Indian culture no longer an under any threat? Such questions troubled Aajivak Babu. How would they become headlines of TV channels and newspapers if that were to happen? How would the organisations, private armies and autocratic unions survive and the empire of the domineering stay intact? How would their descendants and heritage survive?

Gau Mata (mother cow) can no longer survive her illegitimate children. The sick pet herself was homeless, forced to fill her stomach with filth, to roam in the fields. As a stray cow, she had to face the bamboo sticks of farmers, not knowing what she had to eat for her survival. Poor cow, the *Gau Mata.* How could she feed many organisations, armies, associations, and captains? She could have survived somehow if they had not crowned her as *Gau Mata*.

The temple-mosque brand bait to exploit communal sentiments of the people had lost its catalytic property. The people did neither agitate to vomit venom nor shed any blood. It was no longer a profit-making product for communal politics. Still, it was being served by the 'pet' TV channels without the fresh bait provided by their political masters. In a nutshell, it was better to say that they were making all the efforts to give life to the dead carcass of temple-mosque but in vain.

Aajivak Babu had closed his eyes over all this, but the peace of Valentine's Day was beyond his understanding. In the state of contemplation, these lines flashed in his mind:

'sarahadon par kuchh tanav hai kya?

Is there any tension at the borders?

pata to karo kaheen chunav hai kya?

Find out if there is an election?'

He knew that election and bloodshed came together these days. When there was an election, the air in the border would get heated or communal riots break out in any part of the country. Or any film became the ethnic or religious mantle. Such instances were a common feature of the political parties, synonymous with patriotism, and become a reliable tool for power-grabbing.

Aajivak Babu was chasing the cause of peace, when suddenly the news of the terror attack flashed on the TV screen. 'Terrorist Attack in Pulwama. Feared Huge Loss of Life and Property'. The echo and scream of the attack shook Aajivak Babu squarely. The relief of Valentine's Day, Rahat Indori and his poetry, everything vanished from Aajivak Babu's mind, and his eyes suddenly popped out. He could watch the TV anchors' nostrils, faces, and their body language. The eyes were no less than missiles, and the anchors' tongues turned into machines which fired ammunition nonstop.

The media's patriotism was not ready to accept anything less than the total ruin of the enemy. The TV screen had turned into a live battlefield. The anchors had become everything—the voices of the hurt victims; the view of the country, the army and the government. The anchors could win the battle brilliantly sitting in their studios. There was a feeling that terrorists, their bosses, and their country would not survive anymore.

The media now did not have to use the pretext of Valentine's Day; the guise of a terrorist attack was a better chance to outshine. It was to win the heart of their political masters and the poor masses. The battle of Valentine's Day was small, as the enemies were the country's youth. It did not require powerful missiles. But with a terrorist attack, the media was privileged to use all its ammunitions openly. Now the media, as well as the Romeo brigade, had got the job done. They were doing everything in the country; namely, sabotage, arson, and demonstration, and opportunism set a record of patriotism with its rhetoric. It was enjoying the autocracy; nonstop.

What better opportunity for the media to woo its bosses and show its loyalty? It was a matter of its choice. So the devoted media did not care about their hunger and thirst to settle the score with the opponents. There had been no limits of hypocrisy for the media to cross. But this pretence was not a matter of interest for Aajivak Babu. For him, it was very dull and tiring, but as it was the question of the country, he could not switch off the TV. He needed a cup of tea to relieve his fatigue. It was a strange coincidence when suddenly, Shalini came out with a tea tray.

"How did you know I was craving tea?" said Aajivak Babu, smiling.

"Telepathy, dear, it is called telepathy. I have been living with you for thirty years, after all. I know that much." Shalini didn't want to lose such a chance to pat herself on the back; she smiled, happy with her presence of mind, and the two sipped their tea together.

"Don't you get bored hearing the same thing for hours?" she asked.

"Yes, I do! The smile you saw on my face is because of this tea which will wash away the agony I am going through. This Indian media is making much more than the present crisis. The issue is of the country's security; it is a question of the life of fifty soldiers. And the serious issues are the security of the nation and the political will to tackle it. The busting of the conspiracy behind the terror attack is one of the biggest challenges. So, I am trying to get a genuine picture of the whole episode. That is why I am changing channels occasionally. It is a time-consuming process." While Aajivak Babu was explaining this, Shalini observed a strange pain and helplessness on his face.

"If that didn't happen, would you still be glued to the TV?" Shalini remarked, picking up the tray in such a way as if she couldn't bother to know the answer. Or she might want to know but had little concern.

"You're right, but…?" Aajivak Babu switched off the TV and lay down, keeping his eyes closed.

His eyes were closed, and he made an effort to relax, but the situation didn't help. Ultimately, Aajivak Babu had no option but to switch on the TV once more.

The war was still being fought with no rest. Aajivak Babu kept changing the news channels to gauge the pulse of the situation; whether the Indian media had settled the account with the enemies. He wanted to see if there was any news of the enemies' surrender; an apology or any final picture. Or, confirmations from a superpower like the US as 'the enemies are completely routed, so India should now ceasefire'.

But the situation was not so merciful so that a consoled Aajivak Babu could heave a sigh of relief. Still, he understood that only the free patriotic channels and anchors were in full command of such a terrible war. The patriotic fever was so sky-scraping that no army, government and people were needed. The rest of the news channels looked at it as news, not like a battlefield in TV studios.

There was no significant change in their body language. There was a strange control in the anchors. These TV channels and their anchors were not participating in the war. Perhaps they were less patriotic or not patriotic at all. Maybe they had left the issue with the army and the government to decide. There may be trouble for the unintended fatwas and oratory on the TV. They played their role differently by transmitting only information.

The war, which broke out inside the country, was probably not going to end soon. The enemies from across the border had waged a corresponding threat war, allowing the patriotic media to be more aggressive. It was making it more provocative by setting fire to fuel. Finally, the aggression of the press resulted favourably by the evening of 15

February. The crowd of the children, men and women filled the roads and streets with tricolours, banners and boards of slogans and a roar of slogans. The streets and roads were a new battleground, and a slogan battle was going on. What happened to the cross-border war was far from known. But the country's media had won by its decisive action.

Aajivak Babu witnessed the media getting more potent, being the mouthpiece of their political masters. There was no change in its tone and tantrums even on the second day of the terrorist attack. Aajivak Babu browsed Facebook to get away from the battle of the Indian media and judge the common masses' mood. He found many vocal tongues here. It would probably have been colossal if such a sound immediately after the attack. And the titles of a traitor ship would itself have been arson to stick to persons in question. It would have been an easy job for the crowd to bloodshed and threaten lives. Mob-lynching could have given air to the fray, and the consequences could have been beyond the expectations.

The sponsors and the architect of the mob-lynching syllabus deserved appreciation for the achievement of new patriotic gestures. The terrible rescue of a mother cow and the temple-mosque episodes had taught the people to remain tight-lipped and self-possessed. Mob-lynching made people an excellent judge of time and its temperature. The Dalits had become wiser and a particular group of the minority had learnt a lot. So, they were trumpeting their patriotism in such a way that no one could suspect them—not even the self-labelled patriots.

There was also a section of people apart from the blind crowd who was no longer silent. Possibly they were not part of the irrational mob. The people of this section were quite vocal, and on Facebook, gave their opinions. The magic of mainstream media was no longer working on this section. Aajivak Babu found a different picture here. It looked at terrorism, martyrs, media, politics and the government reasonably.

Why did a hypocrite, who gives a prediction on India every morning on the TV channel, not predict a terror attack?

Modiji's life is at risk! They reported it to the intelligence, but not the news of a horrific attack like Pulwama? It is bizarre and ironic.

A FEW DAYS AGO, the US said India could face riots before the Lok Sabha elections. Something similar appeared after the Pulwama attack. The sanghis created havoc. The vehicles were blown up. Then, people could be instigated in the name of patriotism and nationalism. The Muslim community could be targeted. And to win the elections, they could throw the country into a war with Pakistan. Moderation is needed, not to be drifted in feelings.

Sniffed beef in Akhlaq's freezer but didn't sniff 350 kg RDX?

Vehicles carrying cow's meat are caught day after day, but 200 kg of explosives are not seized. There is something suspicious.

Hindu organisations, which spread terrorism within the country, should be sent to the border, including their leaders.

It may be a conspiracy of murder because whenever the Lok Sabha elections in India come to a close, why do terrorists target only India for terror?

The PM held four election meetings after the terror attack but did not attend an all-party meeting on the issue. Electoral lust? At whose behest is such negligence? Now, will you contest on this basis?

When the terror attack occurred at 3:37 p.m. yesterday, Modi from Uttarakhand, Yogi from Kerala at 5:45 p.m., Shah 8 (live) from Karnataka, was there Valentine's party? The country will never forgive them.

A big bang and # Rafel disappeared, #unemployment disappeared, # rising prices disappeared, #corruption disappeared, #200-point roster disappeared, #casteism disappeared, and surely there is a brain behind all this disappearance. Though the Photo of Dated 15/2/2019, happiness is remarkable. # 56-inch #Ban EVM.

Thank you, Pakistan people, that Modiji is in power now. If he were in opposition, Pakistan would have been shattered.

There are about 6 lakh troops stationed in Kashmir, and the search is on; then, how did it come to 350 kg RDX in Kashmir?

It is an issue of sadness; Bharat Ratan Atal Bihari Ji had stopped the pension of paramilitary forces while retaining retirement benefits. Today the widows of 40 martyred soldiers under the NPS will not get any help for their livelihood instead of this sacrifice. However, the newly appointed MLA's family will get it when he passes away.

Indian Muslims. The biggest protests against the Pulwama attack are by Muslims, and they have to give the most patriotic evidence after partition. Yet, they have viewed a particular ideology of the country with suspicion. After separation, Indian Muslims have been considered second-class citizens, whether in India or Pakistan. Such a mentality has been that of the Hindu-Muslims who wanted to divide the country. Even today, the same mindset is present.

For Aajivak Babu, this terrorist pageant was not new; it was an everyday spectacle. It is one show that took place every day. It was a little more explosive. A little bigger. He believed that there were hardly 10–15 per cent of the people in the country who were not a part of the crowd. Aajivak Babu considered those people a 'mob', 'group' or blind followers. He sometimes called them a bunch of fools.

He believed that there was no difference between the crowd and the sheep (bheed and bhed in Hindi). The group (bheed has 'ee' suffix with 'bh', while bhed has 'e' instead of 'ee' and 'd' is common in the end. 'bh' short-form run the crowd and the sheep 'bhay' in Hindi and 'fear' in English. The master is the shepherd, and with crowds, the central figure may be a so-called religious leader or a well-known politician.

The business had become more or less the same. Nowadays, crowds and sheep had become personal property for shepherds, religious leaders or politicians. So, there was no difference between the two in their use and exploitation. Aajivak Babu was disturbed by this.

He was disturbed because the crowd were like products on sale, giving boundless rights and supremacy to the master players of this game. Under this new regime, the business of sale and purchase was flourishing with no limits. The commoner and the media, bureaucracy, politics, and even the courts had become easy targets to the vicious cycle of sale and purchase.

There seemed to be a competition of becoming part of the crowd or sheep. Large constitutional institutions were also part of this. Aajivak Babu knew that the mob also had a role in any war. Crowds were part of battles. Aajivak Babu considered this unreasonable and sponsored crowd a significant threat to society and the nation.

❑

Three

Aajivak Babu witnessed and understood the invisible war on different fronts. However, there was silence on the border after the terror attack. There was a hue and cry and a painful wound that seemed not to heal so quickly. There was heart-wrenching mourning at the homes of the terror attack victims. Many men who were not directly present on the war front were also not unaffected by this battle. They were going through a parallel struggle. Some were fighting illness. Some were struggling for their livelihoods. Some were fighting to meet every day needs.

Yes, they too were fighting against the crowds, the traffic and the smoke emitted in long traffic jams. They were fighting against the helplessness that the present circumstances had created. And significantly, the most decisive battle was the one they were fighting within themselves. Arguably, they were sailing their boats out of the midstream against the fierce storm encountering them. A decisive action it was.

In this war-like situation, Aajivak Babu found himself utterly isolated. It was not like that he was not fighting any combat. Indeed, he had to take decisive action. The current campaign was not new to Aajivak Babu. Such conflicts had been part of his life since he had been a student in school. These battles had become an integral part of his life. Earlier, the actions were double-handed, discharging family responsibilities and meeting educational needs without economic resources.

When Aajivak Babu was a ninth-class student, his father lost his job, the only source of income to the family. There was an economic crisis in the family. He could neither quit schooling nor ignore the onus that befell the family. The family had no land to cultivate and no other ways to generate income except two buffaloes to meet the needs of a family of seven members. The milk of these two buffaloes was not enough to meet the family's needs. They somehow managed to buy one more buffalo, and the family joined hands to bear this additional responsibility without any great change in their lifestyle or the children's studies.

Aajivak's mother and father had other duties apart from looking after their children. His mother would pluck the grass from the fields and farmlands. It was not enough to feed the buffaloes. Besides, an unused factory had some wild grass growing near it. Aajivak Babu's family used this as fodder.

Aajivak Babu had voluntarily taken the responsibility of cutting fodder and carrying it for about one kilometre on his head.

Part of his job was to carry the fodder to his home. The second part was hard work as he cut the hay on a hand-held grass cutting machine. Similarly, he cut dry pearl millet and maize which grew on the roof of his house. Aajivak Babu's brothers also helped him. The three brothers used fodder machines to do their work alternately and sometimes together in the mornings. This was their physical exercise; a by-product of the work making them sweat, nostrils inhaling the dry dust of the fodder.

They added fodder to the already soaked *khali* to make the fodder palatable for the buffaloes and then the buffaloes ate it. The buffaloes got three meals like breakfast, lunch and dinner as Indian masses do. Through this process, the family got milk twice a day, in the morning and evening. Milking was also done mainly by Aajivak Babu. His brothers also used to milk the buffaloes at times. The family had to be satisfied with small quantities of milk. They sold the rest of the milk to a milk supplier who carried all the liquid in his drum.

The family thus produced milk at minimal cost and sold it. Not only that, when it was the season of wheat harvest, each member supported the family in his own way. What grains they harvested in those 10–12 days, they used as rations for six months. This had been the legacy of Aajivak Babu. Luckily neither did the five siblings have any significant obstacles to their education, nor did the family ever sleep on an empty stomach. Tackling the situation had become Aajivak Babu's sole passion. Thus, Aajivak Babu got the energy to fight new challenges from this legacy.

Today, he might have to fight new battles. The major purpose behind this was to fight for dignity; an identity. To stand up against social evils had become his passion, as a responsible citizen of the country. Aajivak Babu knew very well that this fight would never end. But Aajivak Babu was neither dejected nor weak. He was not among those who quit the struggle. He was not a loser; he was prepared to fight nonstop.

His current battle was not to become a part of the mob. He had to fight against cowering weaknesses and fleeing from responsibilities. This fight was against forcibly carrying the outdated ideals of the past to the present. The argument was against glorifying blind beliefs and stupid traditions, flattery and opportunism, a fight for truth against deceit and conspiracy. The idea was against the false demonstration of honesty through shrewdness. I say it in one voice, 'we domesticated this battle of none but by Aajivak Babu himself, and it is to stand by his conscience, the only heritage of Aajivak Babu'.

Aajivak Babu was being severely neglected by the writers' fraternity. He was losing many friends because of this fight for his principles. It was all because of his determination not to compromise on his principles. He had no access to mainstream media, nor did he have any plans for the same.

He never bothered to build personal relationships with editors. He used Facebook though it was not free from factionalism or politics. He did not care to be a pet of any newspaper. It would be not far from wrong to say that he was a little backward in the so-called working world, the world of compromise.

Aajivak Babu found a terrifying picture of the Pulwama episode on Facebook, which presented a picture contrary to that of the mainstream media. It is a fact that Facebook is the platform where everyone can share his pleasures, sorrows and even frustrations. This post made Aajivak Babu's wounds bleed. It was about the undue glorification of astrology; it was being made part of the curriculum of universities and converted into dignified employment to the privileged classes. He wanted to ask these questions—why they should betray the society in the name of astrology? What kind of a science is this? What culture is it?

He had some more questions for astrologers. When natural disasters like storms, landslides and floods take innocent lives, why doesn't astrology come out of its slumber to predict these disasters before these calamities take place? When terrorists infiltrate the country, attack soldiers and the innocent masses, blowing everything to pieces, where do astrology and its beneficiaries keep on hiding their faces? His caravan of encountering queries dies down but sparks out. When there were difficulties in politics, economics and the markets, on what critical assignments are the astrologers and their wicked masters engaged? Though astrology is the super boss, why not raise the question over this criminal nexus? Why shouldn't the hands of victims of traumatic deaths and multiple sufferings reach out to grab the collars of the conspirators? And why not expose the conspiracy that fools the country publicly on every platform?

Aajivak Babu wanted to know how terrorists reached the spot with such a large amount of explosives undetected. Where did the sniffer dogs and the fringe elements who sniffed beef in Akhlaq's fridge and killed him for no reason, go? Where did they go—those who passed judgement on others and the one who claimed to bring ten heads from the enemy countries in return for one? Where did the faithful sons of *Gau Mata go*? Why not take revenge on the martyrdom of our brothers? If the media converted the innocent masses into mindless mobs to sabotage, set fire to public and personal property and suppress the question of safety lapses, why couldn't the government and the media's sycophancy be questioned?

Aajivak Babu wanted to know why the anchors made the media houses, war rooms. Why were the sentiments of the innocent public being played with? Why was the country being made an 'idiot's paradise'? Why were the families of the martyrs in mourning being abused by chanting about their loved ones, the martyrs? Martyrs were martyrs—they did not benefit from anything; there was nothing like a martyr family pension. Why were they making the deaths of soldiers a weapon, a means of winning the election? Why?

Aajivak Babu's mind boggled. He was not sure if he should ask these questions to the crowd or the sheep.

Should he ask these questions to the army of goons and their uncrowned monarchs? Should these questions be proposed to the media houses who turned the intelligent public into mindless beings or to 'pet' anchors who screamed for no reason on TV channels? Aajivak Babu was well aware of the answers to all these questions. They would be stereotyped. "You are traitors, you are hand in hand with the enemies, you are agents of Pakistan, and there is no place for traitors in India."

It was the pet answer of those who issued the certificate of patriotism; the criterion was clear: the mindless crowd were patriots. The rest who raised questions were traitors. If you didn't treat cows as mothers and didn't support or stay mum on the issue of mob-lynching, you were a traitor. If you opened your mouth against the gangsters and the ones who trolled, you were a designated traitor with no scope of any change.

Aajivak Babu, too, was terrified of being labelled a traitor; the fear was inevitable. No one would like to be a branded a traitor only by opening his mouth for a few seconds, without being heard in any court of law. However, the authorities who issued the certificates of patriotism had become ongoing courts in the country. The self-proclaimed sovereign and uncrowned emperors had become everything in this political era. But Aajivak Babu was not afraid of these hoodlums; the mobile courts were auto-authorised to give verdicts on patriotism. He dared to be an inheritor of the Indus Valley civilisation. It came from being a follower of Charvak and Lokayat culture and to be an Aajivak; And ultimately, he was a responsible citizen of the country.

There was also a heart-warming story behind being 'Aajivak' and being renamed 'Aajivak Babu'. Aajivak Babu's original name was Deepak Kumar. He was from a Dalit society with hundreds of castes under the Dalit identity. He was like a bone stuck in the throat of the privileged Indian society—it could neither be swallowed nor vomited.

He was undermined and it turned into a symbol of hatred and melancholy. Aajivak Babu considered caste to impede the peace and progress of the society and the nation. For the Dalit community had to face thorny challenges at each step; it had become their destiny to stay wounded with the social stigma of caste.

Aajivak Babu tried his best to come out of this disgrace of caste, but the ghost of caste chased him at every nook and corner to threaten his sense of worth. The lust for self-esteem made Deepak Kumar a writer and Aajivak Babu for the literary world. In turning Deepak Kumar to Aajivak Babu, Dr Kamal Kant had a significant role. He had been a bureaucrat in the Gujarat cadre. Once, Dr Kamal Kant attended an event organised by 'Caste Annihilation Literary Forum' (CALF) at ISI, Lodhi Colony, Delhi. During the personal conversation, he said, "Why don't you work on 'Aajivak'... the identity with historical evidence... I mean identity with dignity?"

He paused a little and then advised further. "For this, you must go through the book written by A L Basham, *History and Doctrines of the Aajivak (A Vanished Indian Religion).* Read it; I am sure you will enjoy it and bring out something remarkable."

"Why do you feel like I could do something remarkable on this subject?" Aajivak Babu intentionally asked this question so that he could hear some praise. It was his first meeting with Dr Kant. He was very impressed with what he had contributed to the literary world.

"I've read your articles... You're associated with Professor Ajit Singh and his popular journal of literary criticism, *Times Review*. I have read your articles in that magazine."

"Right, sir... I was the one associated with *Times Review*. If you think I can do something on this subject, I will do something. I won't let you down, sir." Deepak spoke gratefully and assured him that he would work on the 'Aajivak' philosophy.

"I am always there with you. If you need any support, ask me without hesitation. Take my card; you can call me directly or email me, no issue at all." Dr Kamal Kant shook his hand and patted his back, smiling.

Fire and fuel were already present in Aajivak Babu. Dr Kamal Kant's counselling and encouragement gave it the much needed push. Aajivak Babu didn't look back and carried out 'Mission Aajivak'. He read so zealously for two or three months so that he could put his point of view on 'Aajivak' in the next issue of *Times Review* decisively. He announced that the Dalits had their inheritance with the Saindhav civilisation.

Hence, they were the aboriginals of this country; the follower of the Lokayat and Charvak philosophy means they are the 'Aajivakas'. So, they should designate themselves as 'Aajivak'. There can be no better alternative but to replace Dalit with Aajivak to make Aajivak literature a symbol of identity. There were a lot of reactions to this matter. A vital letter came to the editor of *Times Review* from Dr Durga Prasad. He had been one of the genuine thinkers and has held many important administrative and political positions.

But after this letter, his voice was silenced or we can say, suppressed. One of the main reasons for this was Dr L K Nigam, who couldn't have been a part of the campaign. Mr Nigam edited and published a magazine *Dalitottan*, which means the upliftment of Dalits. As a result, everything, whether writing, sitting, laughing, singing, and whatever was possible in human life, he did under the umbrella of the word 'Dalit'.

Nigam *Sahab* had assimilated himself with Dalit and had nothing left to say or breathe except 'Dalit'. But Dr Durga Prasad was his blind follower and dared not go against him. To a significant extent, he had imprisoned Dalit literature under the ambit of the word 'Dalit' and was still there today. Perhaps the self-announced protagonists don't dare peep out of the periphery for any new ideas.

Dalit inheritors were like the fundamentalist Hindus who are unwilling to give up the word 'Hindu' imposed on them. They had launched several campaigns to make India a 'Hindu nation' for its glorification. More or less, this was the case with the promoters of Dalit literature. They were neither willing to think beyond nor had the courage to cross the boundary line. Raising questions and following a diverse track by Aajivak Babu became such a big crime that Dalit writers had issued an undeclared fatwa to boycott him. So, they called Deepak Kumar 'Aajivak Babu' to upset him. However, Deepak Kumar was not bothered by this new title and accepted it as a challenge. Deepak Kumar had become 'Aajivak Babu', a villain in the fraternity of Dalit literature today with no gazette notification.

Aajivak Babu's role as a villain was a part of the identity battle. He considered it a compliment and a by-product of Dr Kamal Kant's influence on Aajivak Babu. Dr Kamal Kant had become a villain because of his controversial remarks against women. Dr Kamal Kant had not always been against women but now crossed all limits

Dr Kamal Kant had been soft by nature and a charming person. He was a very earnest, curious and learned person; he was blessed to shine in the literary world of Hindi. Dr Kamal Kant had also been writing poems of love and was in the habit of humming songs. He was in love with a woman from a higher social hierarchy because of his merits but was deceived. This betrayal was so overwhelming in his life that now the very sight of a woman dismayed him. This hatred grew so intense that his family could not stay away from the flames of his failure in love.

It was not as though he would have sacrificed his life because he had failed in love. In his passion for doing something new, he first talked about the founding of 'Dalit religion' and then came to a standstill on the 'Aajivak' topic. The Aajivak, as is claimed, was associated with the Dalit society. But the community was in the Hindutva camp or Buddha's under the influence of Dr Ambedkar. To set up his religion, he first attacked Buddha and Ambedkar to influence the intellectuals. He planned to bring the rest of the society under the same umbrella of Aajivak through them.

Dr Kamal Kant wanted to consider women as subordinates. It was his way of dealing with the frustrations of his love. The campaign against Buddha and Ambedkar put Dr Kamal Kant in such a position that he could neither be dear to Buddha nor Dr Ambedkar. As a result, he became the sole target of women's contempt; simultaneously, the concept of his Aajivak religion faced adversaries like in the form of women's protests.

He, too, tried to make Saint Kabir his shield to debate against women to avoid being called a villain. But it didn't work because there was a flood of writers in Kabir's support. Dr Kamal Kant could not succeed in his mission but did not give up the gender-bias agenda. He took refuge in 'Aajivak', his only hope about recovering the damage. He also organised a devoted team of followers, brought out a magazine and launched an aggressive campaign.

Under this project, 'Aajivak' as a religion, he made himself an undeclared 'promoter of the religion' to justify his prejudice against women on the lines of other faiths. To make the Aajivak philosophy a religion and establish himself as the founder of the religion Aajivak, Dr Kamal Kant attacked below the belt to target Buddha and Buddhism. He left no stone unturned to disgrace Ambedkar, the new god of the Dalit community. He claimed that he only had the community's interests in his mind, while carrying out his ambitious plans to become a god by replacing Dr Ambedkar. Significantly, whatever name and fame he had attained through critical thinking and literature were washed away. His selfish ambitions showed him to be a villain.

Aajivak Babu suffered because of Dr Kamal Kant's villainy. Everybody was irritated by the mere mention of the word 'Aajivak' and its philosophy because of Kamal Kant's foul play. Aajivak Babu was also bound to reap the crop of hatred in the name of Aajivak as there was a time when Aajivak Babu was working on Aajivak philosophy. Kamal Kant would talk for hours from Gujarat. It confused him that Aajivak Babu was also working under his direction like his other followers. He treated himself as the warlord of the writers and addressed each one as 'Aajivak'. He talked enthusiastically but never opened his cards.

Dinesh Gautam from Banaras was also working on Aajivak. His work was to be published soon. He often took a role in exploring his studies and writings with Aajivak Babu and encouraged him. It was not possible to have a discussion without dragging Buddha and Ambedkar into it, and passing offensive remarks. Aajivak Babu did not appreciate it, but it would always be a part of the discussion. Aajivak Babu followed Buddha and Baba Sahab more significantly.

Dinesh Gautam also considered Kabir to be a living tradition. He appreciated his work and enjoyed it but didn't forget to mention that his work would take time. He was also doing a serious study of Kabir. Kabir was an important link in the Aajivak tradition. It was important to understand Kabir to understand the Aajivak tradition.

Aajivak Babu also accepted this view but wasn't in favour of using Kabir against women. He avoided the disputed issues. One day, Aajivak Babu lost his patience, and he made his stand clear.

"No, I don't believe that Kabir is a part of the chain in 'Aajivak' tradition. As far as your views regarding women are concerned, it is all beyond my comprehension."

"No, it isn't. How can you jump to such a conclusion? You can talk to Dinesh Gautam about this. Concepts may be clearer then. Aajivak and Kshatriya Buddha are dead opposite poles. Would you agree to this point? Would you like to see Buddha as an 'Aajivak'?" Kamal Kant lost his temper at this point.

"No, I am not against Buddha anyway, nor do I consider Buddha to be anti-Aajivak. I consider him an associate in the Aajivak tradition." Aajivak Babu was firm in stating his point of view.

"It makes no sense. How can Buddha be an associate?" Aajivak Babu's refusal to associate Buddha in the Aajivak tradition left him somewhat agitated.

Aajivak Babu spoke without losing his restraint, “I have strong evidence of it, and you will see it later . It is too early to comment on this issue right now.”

Aajivak Babu’s remarks had shattered the foundations of Dr Kamal Kant’s future dreams. That’s why it was natural for Dr Kamal Kant to lose his temper. He had no other choice but to patiently wait for Aajivak Babu’s work to be made public. He said, “What do you have to say about the Aajivak religion? Please explain. It would be better if you let me know about it.”

Aajivak Babu said, “No, I don’t even find it a religion. I consider it to be a lifestyle which should keep on changing to suit the needs of the individual, society and the nation. It should lend itself to change. It is based on scientific temperament and shall naturally remain experimental. Therefore, I consider ‘variability’ in the vital tradition as a permanent element.”

Having made his stand clear, Aajivak Babu knew Kamal Kant’s reaction. Aajivak Babu kept on saying, ‘Hello! Hello! Hello!’ but there was no response from the other end. Aajivak Babu knew what Dr Kamal Kant might have done. Dr Kant had hung up on Aajivak Babu’s non-acceptance of ‘Aajivak’ as a religion. He didn’t even bother to listen to the latter.

Similarly, Aajivak Babu faced the same issues with Dalit literature. It is as if no writings of the Dalits were possible without the word 'Dalit'. Similarly, for Kamal Kant, 'Aajivak' meant nothing other than as a religion.

That's why Kamal Kant was going to be shocked. There was nothing unusual in it. Perhaps he understood that Aajivak Babu was no longer of any use. So, he did not think it was necessary to continue telephonic conversations with him anymore. After this communication was over, Aajivak Babu wrote two books on 'Aajivak'. He began a separate monthly publication of a magazine *Asmita Vahini* to make the vital philosophy easier to reach people and dispel the confusion. He dispatched all its published issues to Kamal Kant, but no response. Finally, Aajivak Babu received one last call from him.

"You are deviating from the 'Aajivak' movement using a well-thought-out strategy. You are creating problems for me." His voice was resounding. There was pain, frustration and a slight threat of the bureaucratic mindset.

"You are a superior officer, a great writer and a popular one; make your point the way you like. I am making my point the way I feel appropriate. It is not a question of the present but the future; I hope you understand. I think there should be no question of antipathy. Now the ball is in the reader's court and let the readers decide. The one who presents better views and arguments will be accepted; otherwise, it is for the readers to decide. One more important thing I wish say right now, which I had never thought to share, I will let anyone dictate to me as to what to write. I did never compromise on what I believe in and don't have any such intentions in future."

Aajivak Babu paused a little to know Kamal Kant's reaction, but it was of no use. Ultimately, he lost him because of his stand.

Aajivak Babu, a free bird, could never be a part of Kamal Kant's camp. Because Dr Kamal Kant misappropriated the subject, opponents still lashed out at the Aajivak ideology. Meanwhile, a book to counter Aajivak ideology came into the market. All the articles targeted eradicating Charvak and Lokayat culture and Aajivak instead of Dr Kamal Kant. Now Kamal Kant had lost his followers. The battle between Aajivak Babu and the rest had become a standard feature. The flames had swallowed 'Aajivak' ideology. Aajivak Babu was open to facing challenges, but it was not clear what shape it would take in the days to come.

❑

FOUR

Aajivak Babu could not muster the courage to face the deafening screams of bogus nationalism. There were candle marches and flag marches in every part of the country. There were crowds in the streets shouting the slogans 'Pakistan Murdabad', claiming to teach the enemy a lesson, and wipe it out from the world map. Apart from this, the stupidities of politicians and TV anchors had become the monopoly. It was to keep the environment agitated in favour of the existing regime. Aajivak Babu did not want to get stressed and raise his blood pressure. He knew well that his troubles could exaggerate the problems of his family. Hence, Aajivak Babu had closed his doors to avoid hearing the street-to-street roaring slogans and kept his TV switched off. Despite all the precautionary measures, Aajivak Babu found his comfort zone regularly threatened; his peace of mind gone.

There was a strange battle from the platform of the luxurious tents to allure the poor people during the election meetings. Glorification, or rather, emotional blackmail was being done in the name of martyrdom, martyrs and the families of the martyrs for looting the people's votes. The government was making efforts to take credit for the historical gallantry of the armed forces. Ammunition, missiles and bombs were being uploaded to the minds of the common masses. The political masters addressed security issues to the country and the public as if they had won the war forever, but the real picture was different; it was to cover the failure of a serious security lapse.

The country's bright future was thus free of any doubts or failure. After all, everything the crowd needed was being shared with incredible generosity. Interestingly, even what the political masters didn't have was being distributed liberally. Every political podium had turned into King Vikramaditya's magic throne—where one had the wisdom to settle all issues. It was hypocrisy and stupidity which the state's history had never witnessed even in dreams.

The scenario was terrific, and in return, only blessings were being sought from the public, only once, that too on election day. Probably, they did not need it on other days. Just once in five years. Just once! When the citizens had turned into a 'crowd', there was nothing complicated in getting their blessings. The 'crowd' would do its duty, wouldn't it? Shouldn't it be done? These questions were whirling in Aajivak Babu's mind and didn't leave him undisturbed.

The alliance of this election and the internal war-like situation of the state worried Aajivak Babu. The mode of streets-free war was full of the election, and the election atmosphere was the whole war. So he did not care to step out of his house; entering the world of TV was an agonising proposition. He had just completed Rabindranath Tagore's novel *Gora*. The fact was that Aajivak Babu's mental state did not allow him to read or write anything new.

Suddenly, Aajivak Babu found that Gora, the protagonist of Rabindranath Tagore's novel, resembled the superstar of current Indian politics and his team full of newly defined nationalism. In *Gora*, a 'hard Hindu' had been the helmsman of Bharatvarsha, India. The present-day architects of nationalism had the same denomination as the protagonist Gora enjoyed. The 'hard Hindu' and 'Bharatvarsha' are merged into the blonde. The same way the existing fundamentalist Hindu monarch and India, the great architect of nationalism and a handful of his people, seems compounded.

Aajivak Babu's concern was not the amalgamation of anything and anybody. His sole concern was about the falsification. The protagonist Gora was neither a Hindu nor an Indian; he was the son of an English couple. He was parented by a Brahmin couple, Krishnadyal and Anandamayi. At the end of the novel, the real identity of Gora gets exposed. It became a hoax, and then there was no Hindu fundamentalism, no superiority of caste that Gora inherited as he had been looked after by a Brahmin couple. The lofty dreams about Bharatvarsha, India, had no significance, and finally, Gora seemed to be a different creature of the new world. Having shed his identity of caste superiority, his authentic self, emerged as an elite and responsible citizen of the society and the country. This end was as comforting as applicable.

That's what Aajivak Babu found—a glimpse of fabrication in the current patrons of nationalism, and the team that followed them blindly. He perceived the reflection of Gora in the protagonist of existing politics. But he was afraid to find no possibility of any change as the novel envisaged. On the contrary, the situation was getting worse and more frightening. Aajivak Babu was not able to get rid of his fears. So, he was petrified inside. Aajivak Babu was not scared of himself; he was not afraid of India alone; he was fearful of India and Pakistan.

He was frightened that somewhere a colonel, a fighter pilot, may not be Colonel Paul Tibbetts. He was afraid that the media and the autocratic political masters might not turn to be Harry Truman, Churchill and Chiang Kai Sheik and blindly give orders to drop the nuclear bomb to take credit and to outshine in history. He didn't even want to imagine the scenario if any cities of India and Pakistan had to face the consequences as the two cities, Hiroshima and Nagasaki of Japan, had to. He was grappling with this horror that suddenly his mobile snapped his horrible chain of thoughts. Dr Tarun Singh was on the phone line.

"Are you at home or somewhere else...?"

Before Dr Tarun finished, Aajivak Babu said, "Yes, I'm at home; what happened?"

"I'm coming; there's some work."

"What happened?" Aajivak Babu asked.

Dr Tarun didn't respond, just cut the phone.

These few words put Aajivak Babu in a strange upheaval. Not even a hello? No information, no mention of the reason for coming? Just a peculiar announcement! Great haste! All the queries remained unanswered, and Aajivak Babu didn't understand anything.

For several days, he was not keeping good health. He thought that he might want to go to a hospital. Was he thinking of taking him for help? Aajivak Babu started preparing for this. He turned the water heater on.

Meanwhile, he started getting out of his sweaty clothes. In half an hour, Aajivak Babu was 'ready to move'. But right now, there was no trace of Dr Tarun. Waiting for someone for a long time had never been easy for Aajivak Babu. For him, such a waiting was similar to a kind of punishment. But Dr Tarun was an exception in this case, and he couldn't even think of disappointing him.

Once, he called Dr Tarun. The phone was ringing but there was no response. Now he had no other option left but to turn on the TV. As soon as he saw the breaking news, he was shocked. His eyes were wide open, and he couldn't blink for a while. Only one question flashed in his mind. Surgical strike, again a surgical strike! Did that mean a bumper victory for private channels? It was a more significant achievement for the sycophancy: anchors, media houses, state champions, and credit seekers. That's not what Aajivak Babu was expecting to hear at all. But he knew well that tiny voices never reached the big ears and the heartless.

Aajivak Babu changed channels to see authentic war scenes. It seemed as if the TV anchors of Indian media had got a new tonic to settle a score. They had a strange passion and competed to make the figure of death bigger to woo the crowd and the political masters. It was a brilliant race to make the death toll even to the relatives of the so-called masterminds of the terrorist attack and, of course, to make the death figures more sensational.

They seemed to have gone mad and acted as hired ponies. Indian media had forgotten that the surgical strike was just for some seconds, for a few minutes. It was a rainy night and there was no way to count and identify the corpses. Even if the counting could be possible, it would have been at the military level, not at the level of media and opportunistic political leadership.

But the mainstream media was adamant about justifying its actions the way we keep explaining all the acts as the acts of God. God's laws are perfect, beyond question and arguments. Consequently, corpses were counted and identified without caring for the adverse damage caused to the country's image. The political environment was being influenced to please their political masters.

The crowd was in no way different in its character. The media houses and political opportunists had already captured the group to their heads, not letting them peep out of the coffin of the fake patriotism. Surprisingly, how did this surgical strike remain outside the purview of the satellites? There was not even a single photo as proof. Probably, it was not released at all to keep the shroud over the whole of the controversy and create confusion.

Thankfully, the doorbell rang suddenly. and Aajivak Babu got a break. It was a break in a gradual rise in the temperature of the skull that the climate of anchoring caused to boost. Aajivak Babu opened the door. Aajivak Babu was surprised to see Dr Tarun in seeming good health. Aajivak could not stop himself from asking, "Is everything okay, *Miyan* or...?"

"Will you let me come in or want to see me off at the door, *Miyan*?"

Dr Tarun emphasised the word '*Miyan*'. They both smiled at each other, probably to relieve the stress that both of them were undergoing due to the existing situation. This momentary smile resulted from the new word '*Miyan*' coined in the conversation for each other. Dr Tarun put his bag on the sofa, put a round pillow on the bed in the drawing room as usual and sprawled on it.

Dr Tarun's lounging on the sofa in such a comfortable manner was a sign that he was in no hurry. He probably intended to spend the day here. The long relationship between the two had taught him so much that it was no longer necessary to ask questions to answer some issues.

The TV anchors were still on the war front and were bombarding everyone with the same old-worn out linguistic ammunition. Aajivak Babu had not turned off the TV in his haste to open the door. As soon as Dr Tarun looked at the TV, his first reaction was, "Stop, these bastards, they're barking hysterically. I have fled from them, but here also, everything is the same. Just a new spectacle! The old pageant of the surgical strike."

Aajivak Babu was shocked at the word 'bastards'. He had never heard of words like 'bastards' before. But ignoring it, he switched off the TV and explained, "I turned on the TV, to pass the time while I was waiting for you. Anyway, there are only two options left to pass the time, either a TV or a smart mobile phone. I had to kill time while you were coming here. Let's drink some water first." While talking, Aajivak Babu had brought water from the kitchen.

"Did you already know of this 'surgical strike'? I don't even switch on the TV these days. I just see the newspaper headlines. There was nothing in the newspaper about this 'surgical strike'. If the TV had not been on, I would not have known. Anyway, I was busy reading a novel."

Dr Tarun interrupted before Aajivak Babu could complete his sentence. "I, too, don't even watch TV nowadays. Rajat Paswan's email revealed all this. He asked me to write an article about the war. So I turned on my TV to learn about the war. It was discovered a long time ago. The 'surgical strike' case is new, and the rest of the spectacle is the same old one. Learning something new, I had to face the torture of these TV anchors. I thought I would visit you in the hope of finding some comfort, away from this media terror."

"Why did it take so long… was there any traffic jam on the way?"

"Nothing like that, but old age is in itself an endless traffic jam. It's going to grow more now. No hopes of it slowing down." While revealing this fact, a gentle smile passed across his face.

Aajivak Babu smiled back. "When could these traffic jams of age stop you? The glow on your face still gives a complex to the youngsters. Just these white hairs..."

Before he could complete his sentence, Dr Tarun said, "Just stop, and don't push me to climb on the bush. If my limbs are broken falling from the bush, they are not going to fix them in this old age." The two smiled at this. Aajivak Babu generally called Dr Tarun 'Singh *Sahab*' or Dr *Sahab* as he was 8–10 years older. But the emphasis on the word *Miyan* was a little more as it was new in their dealings today.

Aajivak Babu put forth his concern in a humorous way. "What was today morning about? You did a surgical strike on me on the phone like the political bosses. I was a little nervous thinking that you were in trouble. So I'm sitting well prepared to face any urgent calls."

"When the atmosphere is conducive to surgical strikes, why should I lag behind?"

"I'm frightened just looking at the current situation. The country and world may be in a severe crisis if the border tension is not addressed in India's looting of the general election. In any case, there is no etiquette left in these madcaps. They neither have any conscience nor any ethics! What if war broke out?" Aajivak Babu shared his concern.

"I had written in one of my articles months ago that these madcaps could cause communal riots during elections. This was the same concern expressed by the US just a few days ago. Massacres may be there in the name of temples and mosques. A civil war-like situation may be there. The US, too, felt the need to express such an apprehension. Just take a look at the current circumstances! Now, we are heading in that direction. In any case, people are gradually beginning to understand the politics of the riots. Now let's see what happens ahead." Dr Tarun made his remarks.

"It means you do believe that anything can happen. As our neighbouring country also possess nuclear weapons, anything is possible. It may lead us to a world war-like situation. I have seen the aftermath of nuclear bombs on Hiroshima and Nagasaki, two cities of Japan. It was extremely terrible. Hiroshima's temperature rose to three to four thousand degrees Celsius in seconds. There was massive evaporation. Suddenly, a mushroom-shaped figure appeared in the sky. Broken and melted glasses of the buildings occupied several kilometres. The damage to hospitals and office buildings, failure of power and communication system, scorching of the trees—it is difficult to talk about the extent of losses." Aajivak Babu suddenly stopped and could not say anything further. Probably, the agony of the sufferings of the calamity had chocked his throat completely.

Dr Tarun was listening breathlessly and without any reaction. Perhaps he wanted Aajivak Babu to conclude. Aajivak Babu swallowed some water from the glass on the table and mustered some courage to continue. The current situation had forced him to let his flight of thoughts travel in that direction where there was nothing else but agonising shrieks.

"Seven thousand people were killed in the blaze. And the survivors' skin was scorched. Some had their skin hanging down from the body. Their eyes melted, and fluid ran away to leave hollow eye sockets. Pregnant women had miscarriages, and there were severe respiratory problems. People even lost their power to think. The body organs failed. The old scars bled, and fresh injuries would never heal. Later, children were born with multiple deformities. Even after so many decades, everything is not normal there."

Singh *Sahab* couldn't control his emotions while imagining the calamity that had befallen the Japanese masses. His restlessness was peeping out through his facial expression and body language. "Today, the capacity of the nuclear bombs is even more deadly," he said. "If..."

He left his words unarticulated after 'if', evident in his emotional outburst. He covered his ears with his hands and nodded his head as if he was not ready to listen and say anything more over this tragedy. Aajivak Babu had never seen Dr Tarun in such a state of emotional distress.

Profound silence occupied everything between them and the environment as well. None of the two could muster the courage to break the silence. Aajivak Babu got up with a heavy heart and said, "Singh *Sahab*, shall we have a cup of tea?"

"Yes, I too was expecting it. The issue is too serious. Even thinking about it is terrible. But remember, I have my tea without sugar."

"Absolutely not or...?"

"No... Nothing at all; there is no point in even a little when I am trying to avoid it. Yes, it is your choice. You can add as much as you want to in your cup of tea."

"Oh, sir, in this era of crisis, there is nothing to think that way. I will also take it without sugar with you. Anyway, there must be something we ought to do for the sake of *sabka sath sabka vikas*' which means 'together with all and development for all."

Dr Tarun Singh smiled a little. It was a remedy to support both to break the chain of thought, the cause of silence in the atmosphere.

Aajivak Babu had forgotten to offer tea to his guest as he was upset with the surgical strike and the threat of the nuclear bomb. The silence helped him to resolve his mistake; he went straight to the kitchen and carried out the 'tea' mission. In the absence of Shalini, his wife, it was no less than a mission for Aajivak Babu to manage the kitchen and carry it out appropriately. But the magnitude of the current situation was too high for Aajivak Babu to keep his mind free from thoughts. The ghost of the problem was there in the kitchen as an uninvited guest.

One couldn't say anything confidently about how authentic or fabricated this video was. But this video was very frightening. The video, released by an Indian emigrant Amit Mishra in France, was playing in Aajivak Babu's mind, in a loop. The three giants of politics dealt with a terror attack from an unknown person. Frequently, they said, "There is nothing wrong in carrying out a terrorist attack to win the election. It all happens in elections. Everything is fair in love and war. In the same way, in politics, everything is justified. Elections are also a form of conflict. The army has to sacrifice their lives in battles. And there is nothing wrong if the soldiers are sacrificed to win the elections. Whatever the job, it is part of their duty and a destiny to be martyrs. They also get recruited in the army for martyrdom."

"But...?" a woman's voice was heard in the conversation but was cut out without being articulated. A heavy sound suppressed it. "But…? Stop all ifs and buts. No more argument at all, okay?"

"Talk of the kernel and forget what is inside. Stop peeling it or...? If you don't, any of your brothers will do it. Such an opportunity does not come every day. What should we say, approve the deal or...?"

"Okay." Nothing else was said except 'okay'. The deal was settled.

Aajivak Babu had seen a lot of deals on human lives by smugglers and gangsters in films. But it was the first time that bargaining of soldiers' lives were made for politics in life. Whether it was true or false, he was not sure. But this bargain was very scary. Even if it wasn't the screen of a movie, it was on YouTube. But it was shocking. It was a bargain with the lives of soldiers. How close and far it was to reality, undoubtedly, it wasn't easy to say.

But both situations were of great concern to the authority and sovereignty of the country. The temperature of Aajivak Babu's thoughts was getting higher. Still, he had to return to 'Mission Tea'.

While sipping tea, Aajivak Babu shared his dilemma with Dr Tarun by saying, "Nowadays, social media seems to be somewhat more reliable and fairer as compared to the so-called mainstream media. Some issues are not as clear as they are on social media. Recently, a post surprised me. This dialogue was between a milkman and his customer.

A customer complained, "Brother, the milk that you are supplying is a little dilute nowadays."

The milkman said, "What are you saying, sir. You're blaming the mother cow, depressing her morale." He added further, "It insults the mother cow and will lead to sin. Please don't say such things, *Babuji*."

Both of them laughed. Meanwhile, Aajivak Babu said, "Singh *Sahab*, I too have read it. Talking of this, I have also read another post conveying such persistence. Maybe you've also read?"

Dr Tarun showed interest to know of it.

"It is a dialogue between a defiant son and a father. It is as follows."

The father said, "Son, your results are going to be declared; how was it?"

The son replied, "You will be proud of me; I've topped college, Dad."

"Well, oh, wow. You have done wonders. Now show me the mark sheet so that I can be proud of my son's achievement."

"Dad, you are questioning the reputation of the college. You are pointing fingers at my hard work." He continued further, saying, "You are demoralising the university. You are destroying the image of academia."

"Show me your mark sheet once. What is demoralising in showing what you achieved?"

"The mark sheet was stolen. Whatever, I am telling you, you must trust it to be accurate."

"Both the posts show lovely satire. Tell me if you have any such examples in mainstream media to describe the current situation in such a straightforward manner?" Dr Tarun added.

"Not at all, Singh *Sahab*; however, both the posts expose the hypocrisy of the mother cow and patriotism episodes. I do not see another example of such dramas. Still, it is being spread in the country in the name of mother cow and patriotism." Aajivak Babu took a deep breath while making this statement.

"I think we're getting accused in the country and the world. These hypocrite cow lovers and nationalists are not aware of the decline of human values. The government has direct involvement in this booming and ugly situation. There is a saying: 'If a house is on fire, rats get alerted first to run free.' But contrarily, we struggle with an unusual type of rat which sets fire to ruin everything. Those who have the onus to trap them, blindfold their eyes with communalism and corruption to let fundamentalism boom, which is essential for stabilising their power and politics. These rats, the lifeline of the existing regime, hollow out the foundation of the nation and humanity. Arguably it's the dark era of corruption. If it's stretched out for long, everything will be ruined; there will be nothing left behind to survive."

"It's not okay to be so pessimistic, Aajivak Babu. Just see, every problem has a solution, and the dark cloud of the existing situation will not remain for long . We must be optimistic."

"Hey sir, I too wish to keep on holding the rope of optimism. But the grip is slipping like sand from the hands. What is the point in holding on? These days, the opportunistic media houses have become the mouthpieces of the ruling parties and don't let us hope anymore. The media conducts daily trials of intellectuals, opposition parties, representatives of different castes and religions who differ from the government, ideologically. If you don't raise slogans like *Vande Mataram* and *Gau Mata ki jai*, if you don't chorus with hooligans, you're a traitor, and a fatwa to send to Pakistan is issued. Will patriotism come from the recitation of the national anthem in the cinema hall or from raising slogans of *Vande Mataram* and *Gau Mata ki jai*?" He continued further in a flow, "Patriotic spirit exists in the heart, in mind, and how can any opportunist know of it? A person never happens to be a patriot simply by raising slogans on the behest of any stupid guy or a hooligan. If Azhar Masood, a terrorist, shouts slogans like *Vande Mataram*, *Bharat Mata ki jai*, or Gau Mata ki jai, then will he be a patriot? Most of the self-acclaimed patriots in this country don't know the real spirit of a patriot and patriotism. Rather they can't understand it at all." Dr Tarun didn't interrupt him, so that the volcanic eruption would settle down.

Finding the fire settle down in Aajivak Babu now, Dr Tarun spoke calmly, "Just be patient; why are you getting so impatient, *Miyan*? When did I say that patriotism is something to be shown on a TV or in the cinema hall? I believe that patriotic spectacles are the gimmicks of fooling the country's people. Under the guise of patriotism, a conspiracy ensures votes. It is to teach a particular ideology in the minds of the people of the country. I also believe that it is mischievous to treat anyone as a traitor for anything else. It is part of the conspiracy. But still..."

Aajivak Babu lost patience, and he could not wait for Dr Tarun to sum up his views. Dr Tarun learnt that some remains of the volcanic emission were still struggling to come out. Perhaps it was the pain of staying locked in the room and hearing the deafening roar of slogans of fake patriotism in the streets. There could be an unholy nexus between media houses and their political masters, which crossed all limits of cheapness and shrewdness and deprived him of watching TV news.

"Singh *Sahab*, I also find this shouting of slogans a part of hypocrisy. The louder the noise, the farther it takes us from reality and truthfulness. If there is some constructive work going on, what is the need to tell it through slogans? Today, slogans mean to set an equilibrium in preaching and practice. They use various pitches of slogans to befool the public by glorifying something which doesn't have a gleam. This business is flourishing under the present regime. It feels like fake patriotism. It's a gimmick to cover the lapses and failures. It is to implement its secret plan to convert the public into a mindless crowd, a tool to keep everybody in the dark." He took a deep breath and carried on with his outburst. "The cow and Hindu-Muslim episodes are nothing but a cover for hidden agendas under the slogans of patriotism and religious insecurity. Similarly, shouting slogans in name of the gallantry of the soldiers, uninterrupted hue and cry by the ruling party in power is but to mute the voices that expose the state's worthlessness and tightfistedness. I don't see anything but a conspiracy to keep the people and everything in the dark and nothing else."

Dr Tarun had a serious look on his face. He did not interrupt him. Instead of speaking, he took the glass of water from the table and slowly started sipping. Aajivak Babu understood that he had not yet decided to state his view . So Aajivak Babu said, "Dr Sahab, how deadly it can be to use the army... what it means for the general public? Perhaps it is beyond the comprehension of these crazy politicians. They shouldn't have misused the army. By inculcating bogus patriotism in public, the government can make the opposition parties and intellectuals speechless who disagree. Power can be taken over, but what could be the consequences of using the army repeatedly to serve the personal interests? Perhaps they don't know. What may happen if India's military and political power become our neighbouring country Pakistan is bound to have? Will there be any independent existence of India's democratic government? Are we ready to accept too many power centres? Are we ready for military rule as Pakistan has, time and again? Whatever is to happen is destined in the womb of the future. So, the feeling of optimism doesn't comfort me anymore now. You know very well that an accountable citizen has minimal options to counter the prevailing situation. Still, you..."

"Hey brother, where's my disagreement with you? You seem to be losing your temper like the blind trolls of the regime. They are always raging. I feel as if I have become a victim of a troll today."

Dr Tarun took out his lunch box from his bag and said, "It seems my lunch has become a victim of a surgical strike today." Both of them laughed at this comment. Aajivak Babu took the lunch box, warmed it, and shared it without further discussion over the issue.

Aajivak Babu remarked over lunch, "You've come all prepared with food. I thought you were in a hurry and we might have to go out somewhere."

"Nowadays, when I leave home, I carry my food without fail. Otherwise it screws up my sugar levels. That's why I was a little late today."

"Why were you making the wretched old age a sacrificial goat while reaching here, *Miyan*? I still have to get many of my assignments done with your help. I won't let you off under the garb of old age."

"When do I refuse? As long as my body supports, keep this old man holding the way you can."

"Singh *Sahab*, again the same worthless intervention of old age... Can't you do or say without mentioning old age? It is wrong and unacceptable."

They had finished their lunch and the clock had struck two. After chatting for some time, Dr Tarun picked up his bag. Like on other occasions, Aajivak Babu walked him to the bus stop.

Dr Tarun said calmly, "Aajivak Babu, your concern is genuine, but I have certainly more vexing questions other than yours. For instance, how did the explosives reach the site of the incident? Despite such a huge security arrangement, the terrorists managed to carry out a suicidal attack, but how? Is it an intelligence failure? Is it an act of a traitor in the army? Maybe, an officer or any of its acquaintances, who carried out the conspiracy?"

He paused a bit and continued, "My concern is why these questions are not being emphasised at all? It cannot be an individual or a group; why isn't it ruled out? I think we first need to clean our house from spies. If required, then the score must be settled with the outside enemy. If the public attention gets diverted from the outsider, the problem will never have a solution. The public has to come forward to ask for the truth, whatever it is. Only then will the party in power can be made accountable, and the prospects of peace and tranquillity are ensured, else..."

"The negligence of an army officer or any involvement of others in the conspiracy cannot be completely ruled out; I fully agree with you."

Before Aajivak Babu could continue, Dr Tarun's bus arrived. He left saying bye-bye, and Aajivak Babu returned home with the conspiracy ghost.

❑

FIVE

Aajivak Babu was strongly against corruption. He was of the belief that sin was not limited to money transactions alone. It involved all kinds of deceit and lies where there was dishonesty and vicious manoeuvres of words. All these form a masked structure of the eyes, nose, ears, hands, feet and ultimately a body of corruption. The behaviour of various organs builds a character and the person's personality and labels him accordingly. According to Aajivak Babu, considering only the monetary aspect of corruption was itself a sin. Aajivak Babu disliked such corruption and injustice that ruined the country and humanity. Hence, he was very much bothered by the immediate environment.

While Aajivak Babu was struggling with the ghost of corruption in the light of the Pulwama terrorist attack, he had some sketches of crime in his memory. He recalled how the corrupt in different offices ignored those who needed their help . But when their demand for a bribe was accepted, whether open or concealed, the same person fawned over them and was eager to please. And he ensured that the job was done, breaking even all the procedural requirements. He had even seen noble professions like doctors and teachers deep in the conspiracy of corruption. He was annoyed with the religious institutions that were parenting compounded corruption faithfully. He had witnessed the presence and echo of fraud against CBI in the court of law. Whether genuine or fabricated, Aajivak Babu had even heard the arguments of dishonesty against the judiciary, rumbling in the atmosphere many times. And he had seen the media conference of several judges questioning the functioning of the Supreme Court.

The bribery and compounded harassment of the police had become a common feature in day-to-day life. The significance of political corruption never died down, and he could not explore any possibilities of being free of it in the time to come. There was a strange link between the police and the politicians covering all prevailing frauds. It appeared to be a symbol of authentication rather than the universalisation of India's culture of corruption in India. A dreadful picture of corruption forced Aajivak Babu to contemplate what was left in the country to fight against the shameful culture of corruption?

The question in deliberation wasn't letting Aajivak Babu heave a sigh of relief. He had heard of bribery in relation to purchase of ammunition and other military goods. He had even seen the stories of such frauds being headlines of newspapers. Corruption in trials in courts was no more surprising to the common masses. But the idea of corruption in relation to the life of soldiers absolutely terrified Aajivak Babu.

He had never heard of it before nor ever read of such terrible news. So his conscience did not allow him to stand by it. Still, it was gnawing at his mind constantly. If something like this had happened, then what was left in the country? The answer was terrifying in itself. The answer was a serious threat to all the positive fortifications of expectations and beliefs.

Aajivak Babu's wife Shalini had not yet returned from the market. Even if he had no human company, the ghost of corruption accompanied him and kept his mind agitated. Though, Aajivak Babu's pet dog Roby was present there physically. Roby came to him, but Aajivak Babu's mind was so occupied with the ghost that he was unable to put his hand on Roby's head and pat his body in response to his swinging tail. Roby looked into Aajivak Babu's eyes time and again. Finding no response, he stretched his neck, lying on the ground. Aajivak Babu was not to be blamed for this negligence. Though his eyes were wide open, he was mentally and physically in the grip of the ghost since Dr Tarun had left.

Roby was upset not because of any corruption but because of neglect by his owner. He pretended to be sleeping. Occasionally, he would look at Aajivak Babu and, seeing no response, pretend to sleep. Roby was a very calm and contented dog. He never complained if he was not fed on time or even when he was in pain. He did not demand love and attention from them. A faithful dog is miles away from corruption.

There was still no one in the house to divert Aajivak Babu's attention. So the ghost of corruption had undisputed rule over Aajivak Babu's mind. As a result, he was going through a strange dilemma. Being a responsible citizen, he had questions to ask no one else than himself and vice versa; the same was the case with answers. Roby was in no way a hurdle in the existing regular monologue as an advocate against corruption's prevailing atmosphere.

He was agitated now. This monologue in his mind was about the availability of explosives at the spot of the explosion. It was about its weight. It was an explosive that was not available in the market like vegetables, and anybody could buy any quantity comfortably.

Aajivak Babu's thoughts were not just confined to buying and selling the explosives. Some other questions took shape and often agitated Aajivak Babu's mind. "How did someone sell...How did someone buy? How did this explosive reach the spot of the terrorist attack, and what did the terrorist attack lead to? After all, who were these perpetrators of terror? What were their plans?"

Aajivak Babu jumped to hypothetical conclusions that this was perpetrated by an organisation with tremendous resources. It was still unclear as to who was behind it; everything had happened to make this operation successful, but how? This operation was not possible without any significant transactions of money involved.

Whether it was money-laundering, misuse of position or power by a person or both—Aajivak Babu found it difficult to contemplate. It was really a horrendous form of corruption. Why were these angles of crime and its investigation not being talked about? Who was accountable for this negligence? Why did the public not question a significant nexus challenging the country's security?

Still, the terrorists had succeeded without any challenge from the Indian forces. Then, it was of course, a matter of grave concern. It did not reflect well on the country's claims on security and the entire security process. So, the question arose: What does Indian security stand for? How was it even feasible for the terrorists to reach that place with such a considerable quantity of explosives?

There was no denying that without intelligence, acts such as these would have happened every day. The terrorists would have made it child's play. Thank God for that, but still, the question stood unanswered as to how and why this catastrophe came into existence.

There was a terrorist attack, and the lives of 40–50 soldiers of the country were lost. They had no chance to display their valour or defend themselves. But the question of more considerable significance was why the brutal killing of innocent soldiers had been made a slogan of martyrdom.

Why was there no mention of any concrete initiatives to expose this treasonous conspiracy...No traces of the terrorists hiding in our own houses? What was the necessity to pat yourself on the back for the heroic deeds performed by the Indian Army? And why was there a festive mood though the victims of the terrorist attack and the nation were sorrow-stricken?' He was shocked to see this new model of corruption. A new model of corruption, indeed, wasn't it so?

Aajivak Babu was struggling with 'what...why, why not,' when the doorbell rang. Roby was at the gate before Aajivak Babu to welcome the visitor. As he wasn't barking, it must be someone familiar. Aajivak Babu headed towards the door. If Roby could open the door, he would have done it himself. Aajivak Babu smiled at this and asked Roby to move from the door so that he could open it.

It was Shalini carrying some bags. He immediately took the bags from her hands, placed it on the drawing room table, and went to the kitchen to get water.

"Why have you kept these two cups of tea on the table? Did you drink two cups of tea on your own or did someone...?" Shalini left her sentence incomplete and took the empty cups from the table to the kitchen.

"Hey, how could I... I only had one cup. You know that I don't like tea much."

"So, who had the other cup? Who came?"

"Singh *Sahib*, who else will come? What approach can a Mullah have if not refused to a mosque? You know very well that no one else visit us except Dr Tarun."

"Well, so it was Singh *Sahab*... and you made the tea?" They both came to the drawing room holding their glasses of water.

" Oh! Yes! It was I, and who should have done so if I won't? I am quite good at it. Don't I make tea for you, Madamji, as and when you ask me to?" Aajivak Babu looked into Shalini's eyes and asked, smiling, "What's it that surprises you?"

"It is true, dear, but you don't do it every day. Truly, it is to be admitted that you make delicious ginger tea with a perfect combination of sugar, milk, etc. Can't you make one more cup for me? I'm a bit tired today after all my shopping."

Aajivak Babu did not know whether Shalini was complimenting him just so that he would make the tea for her. Shalini continued, "By the way, what were you doing all this while?"

Before Shalini could finish, Aajivak Babu interrupted, "I had just mentioned that Singh *Sahab* had come. Do you know that the Indian forces have conducted surgical strikes on Pakistan?"

"What!" She was shocked on hearing the word surgical strike. One more surgical strike! Her eyes were wide open while making this statement. "But I haven't heard of it, and there was nothing like that in the newspaper in the morning."

"You are right! How could the newspapers publish the news? This strike happened early in the morning, at around three, after the newspaper had been printed. I, too, didn't even know of it. I only came to know of it just before Singh *Sahab's* arrival when I had turned on the TV to pass the time."

Shalini started talking about the goods she had bought in the market, their relative merits. She did not forget to mention her skills of bargaining. But Aajivak Babu did not pay much attention as he couldn't stop thinking about the corruption. The only difference was that the needle of crime had now turned to the sale and purchase of household articles.

The faces of the bargaining shopkeepers were visible before his eyes; how they kept increasing the rates step by step and justifying the price at each level. Most of the time, even the final rates where one couldn't bargain further were also nowhere near the cost; maybe just half the cost. Profit figured at all levels of the chain. This was another form of corruption.

He also suspected massive corruption because of the difference in the prices of goods sold at small and big stores. There shouldn't be such an enormous difference in the pricing of the same brands if there was honesty. There should not be any question of bargain to reduce the prices. Aajivak Babu always preferred to buy goods from a shop with fixed prices to avoid any bargaining. On the contrary, Shalini preferred to bargain. She would not buy products from any shop without any negotiation.

As a result, Aajivak Babu and Shalini often did not shop together. Even today, Aajivak Babu was not impressed by Shalini's shopping and bargaining skills. This seemed to add another dimension to corruption in his accepted wisdom. And the rest of the day passed in analysing the puzzle of dishonesty.

Though Aajivak Babu went to sleep on time, he could not relax. In the dark of the night, he seemed to see corruption all around. The fog of sin was so dense that everything went out of comprehension. Sleep evaded him. He restlessly tossed and turned, but in vain. The ghost of corruption haunted Aajivak Babu, who tried to suppress it in vain. It seemed that neither was ready to surrender to let the other win. But Aajivak Babu was not willing to accept it as destiny.

Despite all this, Aajivak Babu was determined to sleep well. Though all the tossing and turning didn't help. Finally, he picked up the phone from the side table to confirm the time. This woke up Shalini who was in deep sleep.

"What happened… is everything okay? Not getting sleep?" Shalini asked sleepily without opening her eyes.

"Nothing like that, I'll sleep later." He made his statement calmly to assure her not to disturb her slumber.

Shalini fell asleep, but Roby was still a witness to his master's nervousness. He was lying on the floor next to his bed. He would open his eyes after a periodic interval and, finding his master in the same state of nervousness, closed his eyes. Perhaps he was could sense his master's agitation. Apart from the ghost of corruption, Shalini's snoring was becoming a villain too.

He opened his eyes and gently shook Shalini a bit to make her stop snoring. When the snoring stopped again, the struggle to sleep began afresh. Roby was next to him, alert, like a vigilant guard. He was probably protecting his master as he sensed his distress.

At this point, while Shalini was snoring and Roby was on his vigilant watch, a silly thought flashed in Aajivak Babu's mind as to whether Roby was more concerned about him than Shalini. However, the thought was frightening: Aajivak Babu did not want to create any problem for himself by pursuing such a comparison. He reassured himself that there could never be any resemblance between Roby and Shalini at all. They were both unique individuals, and could not be compared. Such a comparison may be of interest importance theoretically but not to be contemplated practically.

Seeing Roby's concern for his family, an idea floated in his imagination. Roby and other dogs might not live for themselves at all. Whatever they did or feel, was for their masters. Aajivak Babu frequently used the term 'doggie' for the canine pets but never used the popular Hindi word. Whenever others used the word kutta for canines, he would feel hurt. It sounded like gross abuse. So, he was not in favour of using any abusive words for these loyal faithfuls. It was worth defining their loyalty to humans.

The concern for these pets has so absorbed Aajivak Babu's mind when suddenly another comparison took hold of him. If every citizen of the country had the same concern for his nation like Roby had for Aajivak Babu, there would be absolutely no trace of corruption.

The culture of lies would automatically vanish; riots in the name of Hindu-Muslim rivalry, levelling castes and wasting energy on the issues of superiority and inferiority would naturally lead to extinction. Each action of the citizens would go on in the nation's interest and nothing else. Under these circumstances, what could be possible if not the peace, progress and prosperity in society? And ultimately in the country, and nothing to battle against.

This thought was comforting to Aajivak Babu. The very idea of getting rid of the country's problems brought him relief. It was just like a mirage in the boiling desert of the agony of corruption which led to his restlessness and lack of sleep. His lips framed in a smile at this comforting thought when another thought shattered the castle of his dreamland.

Though Roby and his fellow canines were devoted and loyal to their masters, they hated each other. There seemed to be nothing but enmity between them. Perhaps it is because of this that *kutta* in Hindi was used in a derogatory sense. Finally, Aajivak Babu found a close affinity in the man-to-man relationship of today with the connection among dogs, the swans in Hindi. As far as loyalty was concerned, the swan never betrayed another even at the cost of its life.

But it was difficult to make such a claim. Even so, to place so much confidence in man. His loyalty was not beyond doubt in the case of his master and his parents. He hd not been always loyal to his relationships with human values. In the current political era, as far as loyalty to the nation is concerned, it had lagged far behind social priorities. The country had an extensive range of facilities and rights automatically available to citizens. As a privileged citizen, he never even bothered to think of it seriously.

Aajivak Babu sees the similarity between the relationship between parents and children and that between the nation and its citizens. Parents do everything they can to fulfil their children's wishes, whether small or big. Every parent understands this as their sole priority and feels proud to be committed. Contrary to this, the child considers it his natural right and enjoys it. The child does not feel obligated to repay his parents.

Aajivak Babu felt the country's citizens exploit its resources like children as their birth right and a privilege. This sense of entitlement made the citizens insensitive and came in the way of their duty and commitment to their country. The question arose in his mind: Are the slogans like *Bharat Mata ki jai*, and *Vande Mataram*, enough to enjoy the country's citizenship? In the current political era, sloganeering had become synonymous with patriotism. It agitated Aajivak Babu, did not give him any no rest and didn't let him sleep at night.

The present ruling pattern had legitimised the thanklessness and selfishness of the nation. Satisfying one's interests under the umbrella of the existing regime seemed to be the ultimate goal. It had become paramount these days. It was an act of hostility to humanity. An individual's interests have turned to be his masters, means everything, and the man has become a devoted pet, a swan to the 'personal interests'.

To be loyal to the master, the man had no character or ethics. He only served his personal interests. As a result of these corrupt practices, religious and caste conflicts were at their peak. Communal riots and terrorist attacks were multiplying to be politicised.

The slavery of the master, the 'personal interest' of human beings, had made man the bearer of the Shwan culture. Today the personal interests of different small and large groups had become magnified. These groups happened to be rivals and enemies. They had become violent and India-Pakistan hostility seemed to be a bi-product of the never-ending process of the Shwan culture. This Shwan culture badly hurt Aajivak Babu. He felt disgusted at the individuals and the inimical groups; expressing their hostility openly and violently. He considered such people opportunistic and concluded that they were enemies of society and the state.

Aajivak Babu observed that insecurity and selfishness may have brought about a sense of fear among the individuals that attracted them to the Shwan culture. He saw that the business of religion and politics was in the grip of this insecurity and fear. Aajivak Babu correlated this fall in character with inherited corruption in nature. His mind struggled to find the root cause. His eyes were closed, but his brain was wide awake. It travelled to the puzzling world of history. What could have been a better option if there was no sleep?

❑

SIX

Aajivak Babu suffered from restlessness, constant discomfort and the pain of Indian masses turning into a Shwan, the dog. It was a big challenge to the concept of co-existence of human beings; it was not the first time that Aajivak Babu meandered in the maze of history. Sometimes he strolled in search of identity, looking for the causes of social and religious malpractices. Today, the challenge of fall in character and corruption lead him to the Indus Valley civilisation, also known as the Saindhav civilisation.

Here, the extreme distortion of the facts by historians agonised him. The suffering was the neglect of the contribution of today's oppressed and tribal society. The pain was in how the aboriginals had been sidelined to make Hindus inheritors of Indus valley civilisation. And to erase even the remnants from history. The historians claimed that in the Persian language, the letter 'S' is pronounced as 'H' and argue that the Indus valley civilisation is of the Hindus.

Aajivak Babu tossed and turned in the bed. He was under pressure and felt a strange panic and nervousness. He could not get consolation from anything. To get relief from this panic, he went to the kitchen and breathed a sigh of relief after drinking cold water from the pitcher.

John Marshall, the former chairperson of the department of archaeology, was visible in his memories. He saluted him for his unmatched contribution. He admired him for revealing the most shocking facts before the world: there was no shield, arrow, and war-like material in this civilisation. It exposed the conspiracy of history and liberated it from the claim of being a Hindu civilisation.

Today's Dalits and tribal communities, the oppressed ones, were the natural heirs of this glorious civilisation in which even ordinary citizens had every comfort and luxury. We cannot compare it to any other part of the culture of that time. This civilisation with peace and prosperity did not require any weapons. Neither war nor any chaotic elements created a war-like situation, and it soothed him that this civilisation was full of moral values, peace and comfort.

This comfort was not enough for Aajivak Babu to give him relief from present-day crises that had deprived him of his slumber. The struggle now reached a turning point that betrayed this splendid Saindhav civilisation. Where and when did the chaotic elements come from? How did an atmosphere of anarchy and fall in character set in? And finally, how did the corruption transform into Shwan, the dog culture? The most prominent among all these great questions was 'how'.

In search of the answer 'how', he flipped through the pages of his memory. His wanderings in the maze of history was not new. He repeatedly encountered historians like Dinanath, Kashyap and Ramsharan Sharma. They were there to show the mirror of the destruction of the Saindhav civilisation. Aajivak Babu found that the Aryans, the heirs of cowboy culture, infiltrated this rich culture like an enemy adopted all the conspiracies and cruelty of villainy, to dismantle Saindhavas and their culture.

The archaeological department revealed that the layers of the ashes were the evidence of the repeated setting of a fire. The historian Ramsharan Sharma identified Aryans as being culprits and setting fire to the cities, several times. These historians testified the Aryans' dominance strongly over the Saindhavas to force them to the forests to be tribes and the rest to be enslaved as Daas and Dasyu and what not.

The images leading to the downfall of the glorious identity of the Saindhavas into enslaved people with no dignified integrity caused Aajivak Babu's wounds to bleed. It forced him to shout, "Oh! Inheritors of Shwan, the dog culture, look at us. We are not Dalits, the oppressed ones; we are a superior race, the Saindhavas, the Aajivakas who earn their livelihood by working hard and not living parasites like you. You're a looter, intruder, terrorist, and it is you who lit our fortresses and settlements, conspired to enslave us. Look! We have broken the chain of your captivity and slavery. Watch our evidence of being tribal. Watch our trails to forests and the mountains and look at the DNA of your Shwan culture of invasion full of corruption and conspiracies. Contrary to yours, see our DNA as Saindhavas, the aboriginals of the land, thoroughly civilised, peace lovers and believers of fairness, equality and fraternity. And you, Shwan, no better than an heir of Shwan culture. Come! Come! Let me tell you what you are and what your lifestyle has been and still is."

Aajivak Babu screamed at his highest pitch. He did not know from where the pistol in his hands came from. And where did the piece-loving Saindhavas get bullets and the provocation to press the trigger? Suddenly, Aajivak Babu sat up, stared at everything around him and found himself bathed in sweat. He found Shalini undisturbed and lost in deep slumber. It didn't take long for Aajivak Babu to realise that it was just a frightening dream. Not a reality, and his screaming was just a dream. But he was terrified to think over this whole episode as he too had become a Shwan, in his dreams.

On the one hand, he was embarrassed to find that his suppressed emotions were vented through the outburst of a scream. The boil that had been festering under his skull had burst to let the whole mess go out. But the words, pistols and bullets used in the sleep were shocking and troublesome to Aajivak Babu. Anyway, now one could do nothing. After all, dreams had their domain of fascination and can't be reined in. Aajivak Babu wasn't an exception to control it. Aajivak Babu wiped off his sweat, drank water from the bedside table and lay down to have mercy from the goddess of sleep.

However, Aajivak Babu was still traumatised by the terrorist attack in Pulwama and the whirlpool of Shwan culture. The devilish acts of Aryans' atrocity, corruption and meanness of their character didn't give him relief. This led him to find links between the casteist mindset's wicked traits of Aryans with Saindhav civilisation. He saw the expansion of roots from Aryan's terrorist adventures to impose over the messengers of morality and peace, those who are known as Anarya (inferior), Asura (demon), Asprasya (untouchables) these days. And whatnot that the Aryans did to tarnish, rather ruin the glorious identity of the aboriginals, the so-called Dalits and tribals of today.

The same way as the Aryan invasion came into existence, the Hoons, Mongols, Yavans, Pathans, Mughals and the English followed the same pattern more or less. Opportunism, selfishness, isolation and a sense of insecurity ruled over the society and the nation. The same sense of danger, betrayal of trust and lack of knowledge of mutual co-existence was the root cause of Shwan culture.

Aajivak Babu found it was impossible to develop a genuinely national character despite being one nation and having a singular national identity. Hence, he saw these infiltrators entering India at different intervals pouncing upon the natural and human resources as Shwans the street dogs did with no dignity.

In this brainstorming process, Aajivak Babu recalled Usha Chopra, an unbiased historian. It was to reach the root cause of social inequality in society. And the role of

Shwan culture in putting the country in such a sorry state. He was impressed by the findings that intruders in the country defeated local kings or married into dynasties from time to time. The lowest-ranking tribal castes of the varna system established their states which were accepted as Kshatriya classes in the name of Rajputs as the continuous wars led to looting of goods by. the priests and kings. As a result, they became higher in the caste hierarchy and thus established disparity in society.

The night was dark, there was a trouble of wakefulness, but Aajivak Babu could perceive the picture of the rise of the Shwan culture from the churning of history. For this, he did not feel the need to open his eyes or to switch the light on as everything was crystal clear with no aid. The post-mortem of the Shwan culture report illustrated that the fathers of the Shwan culture must have been Aryans.

Pakistan inherited the Shwan culture from India, so it did not seem unnatural to Aajivak Babu as Pakistan had been an equal partner of the Shwan culture. Because of Shwan, the country had got repeatedly enslaved, and the same culture was responsible for all the existing internal and external, violent acts. 'External' here meant Pakistan and its sponsored terrorism from abroad and within the country.

Aajivak Babu did not get these pieces of evidence so quickly. It resulted from years of hard work that he had invested in the quest for his identity during his study. Based on these reliable confirmations, Aajivak Babu considered himself and his society as people outside the world of *varnashrama*. Aajivak Babu felt no such caste hierarchy and discrimination based on varna to be as exploitative as in India.

Superiority and inferiority in religions like Sikhism, Christianity and Islam in India are among the nasty by-products of Aryans culture, the followers of which are afraid to call them Aryans. Aajivak Babu used these remarkable facts to discourage caste mentality in his dialogues and writings.

While dealing with the issues of caste prejudice, his aim was not to insult a particular person, group or community. Neither to take revenge from anyone, instead unveil caste and religion's prejudiced, cunning and conspiratorial foundations. The purpose of exposing this inhuman mentality was only to stop the society steeped in the arrogance of ethnic and religious fundamentalism and hollow superiority.

It was to eradicate all kinds of harassment and destruction of the Shwan tendencies from the face of humanity. And to restore equality, fairness and fraternity in society, the path of brotherhood and brotherhood should be well-received. But despite all this, today, all these divisive elements had become the foundation stone of the monopolist pattern of today. Because of this, the Shwan culture was flourishing. The flow of Shwan culture in India was the most significant corruption of character.

Osho's views on caste and how it corrupts society consoled Aajivak Babu, a lot. He cautions the society: "If the Shudras know their old history, either they will become Buddhists or become Sikhs; the Hindu religion rests on the folly of the Shudras." For such purposes, Aajivak Babu, in his writings, risked making not only the Shudras familiar with the historical facts but also the radical Hindus.

He believed that the conversions had happened in Buddhists and Sikhs and Christianity and Islam. It resulted from the exploitative conspiracy of Hinduism and social, economic, political and intellectual corruption. Hence, the conversions continue even today as a symbol of opposition to the attributive corruption of Aryan culture.

Aajivak Babu got up from his bed. Aajivak Babu had no way but to visit his study to seek refuge in his books. Here, Aajivak Babu had collected a lot of material pertaining to his need and interest. In this quest for character corruption, Aajivak Babu explored the episode of Saindhava civilisation and examined Buddhist history. He had already been introduced to it during the study of the Aajivak culture. Availability of these documents was a comfort for Aajivak.

Aajivak Babu's craving to explore the current corruption in character in the light of history was a constant urge. Aajivak Babu felt the need for some tea. He entered the kitchen. Despite all his caution, he dropped a vessel. It made Shalini wake up abruptly.

Finding Aajivak Babu missing from the bed and finding the light in his study on, she reached Aajivak Babu's chamber. Secretly and stealthily, she came making no noise of her movements. Seeing Shalini, Aajivak Babu was startled but impulsively said, "Hey Madam, your sleep got disturbed. I thought the sound of the lid wouldn't have woken you, but it seems..."

"Was I sleeping...? I was trying to sleep, but can your presence in the kitchen be hidden, anyway? Don't you know you whenever you go to the kitchen, you will certainly do something awkward?"

"Oh, dear, I am so sorry to have disturbed your sleep... it is all because of me... Both things are right. But the allegations that you are making about me in the kitchen are not correct. It is not a good thing to do with a decent guy like me," Aajivak Babu said, using his pet words of a decent guy.

"Would you like to take a little tea...? Green Tea... let's make it half a cup each?"

"When you get involved in such things day and night, where will sleep come from? My sleep also disappeared when I saw your writing. Now I understand why you didn't show any interest in my shopping today. You must have been engrossed in something as usual."

Shalini's response was not due to resentment; She was not complaining but was concerned for Aajivak Babu. Aajivak Babu realised this. So, without waiting for her response for tea, he poured some tea from his mug into another.

"I was looking for the roots of corruption in the wake of this terror attack. It has taken away my sleep..."

Aajivak Babu wanted to say something further when Shalini asked, "Is this true as you have put here on this paper?"

"Madamji, I have not written anything in the list of historical adventures you have taken in your hands. I have just quoted it from different texts and popular books. Why will anybody risk his life by making such remarks about any religion? Has a mad dog bitten me to make remarks like this? Making such a remark is just like inviting 'a bull to gore me'.

"Anyway, in the present era of mob-lynching, why invite unnecessary dangers? The chaotic elements need to have simply a rope to make it a live snake to show their traits of turmoil. There is a fear that even a decent man can leave his decency to join these chaotic elements when there is such support from the existing regime. It is getting difficult for innocent people to survive where the mindless people are up to anything."

"Do you have any such intention to be part of this nexus?" Shalini remarked smiling. There had been a massive influx of defectors these days. Perhaps she wanted to make a practical joke to counter Aajivak Babu's pet words 'innocent guy'.

"If I were a part of mob-lynching, why should I wake up like an owl overnight? When I have always raised my voice against this mob-lynching. and other such acts of lawlessness, where does the question of joining them arise?"

"Hey... Hey, my dear Babu, stop. You are beating the drum of your being 'an innocent guy' every day... So I also felt why shouldn't I take the slightest advantage of it today? There is no need to give such an explanation in defence, my dear. Who knows you better if I don't?" Shalini smiled and covered Aajivak Babu's face with both hands. Shalini had her style of expressing her love. In love, Shalini calls him *Sahabji*.

This light-hearted chat didn't last long, and the very next moment, she was a little surprised and confused. The list of historical events was in her hands. She was intermittently looking at it and was sipping her tea.

"Hey, Madamji," Aajivak Babu waved hands in front of her eyes a couple of times to bring her out of the world of contemplation.

"I have heard and read stories of kings hunting in the jungle... Seen Yudhishthira betting on Draupadi in TV serials and getting defeated too." She continued further, "In the TV serial Mahabharata, I have seen gambling and the shamelessness of patriarchy in Draupadi's episode in the court of King Dhritrashtra. I have also seen causes of war, but what is this about Brahma?" Shalini commented, putting the papers forward to Aajivak Bubu.

Before Shalini raised another query, Aajivak Babu repeated whatever he had studied about Brahma–"In the scriptures, Brahma has been repeatedly described as the creator of the world. But we do not say that Brahma had three sons and a daughter. One of his sons, Daksha, married his sister . Some daughters born from this marriage married Kashyap, son of Marichi, and some married Brahma's third son Dharma. Not only that, the father could marry his daughter. Vashishta had married his daughter Shatrupa when she became an adult. Manu married his daughter Ila. All these exist as facts in our religious literature."

Waiting for a little, Aajivak Babu tried to read Shalini's facial expressions. A natural pallor covered Shalini's face, hit with strange lines of concern and anxiety. She did not show any reaction but seemed to be straining her mind. Aajivak Babu continued to narrate the dark side of history against women.

"It wasn't restricted to that; Aryans have been polygamous, many people from the same family used to have cohabitation with the same woman. Dhahaprachetani and his son Som had sexuall intimacy with Som's daughter Marisha. The history of a grandfather's marriage with his granddaughter is enough to quote. Daksha had given his daughter to his father Brahma in marriage. And because of this marriage, the famous saint Narada was born. Dauhitra had given his 27 daughters to his father, Som, for cohabitation and breeding. Aryans had no objection to openly cohabiting with women before the eyes of the people. The well-known saint Parashar had similar cohabitation with Satyawati. Sita and Draupadi were both unplanned and were born like that."

Shalini had not yet recovered from the first shock when the second setback was more than ever. Shalini's facial expression suggested that she may not be willing to listen to anything more than that. So Aajivak Babu told Shalini, "Madam, it is better to go to bed and sleep... Otherwise, you may also have to sit in my place as it is a solid need to stand by women's issues and feminism. If you too jump into this battle I am fighting for, the peace in this house will be ruined. Then neither of us will remain capable of fighting for it."

Whether Shalini agreed with this consultation, or not, was uncertain. But she quietly slipped away from the study.

Shalini went away but left a question in Aajivak Babu's mind. If she had read more! Aryans had the practice of giving their women on hire for a certain period. King Yayati gifted his daughter Madhavi to his guru Galav. Galav had given Madhavi to three other kings on hire for different periods. Then he gave her to Vishwamitra in marriage. After that, Galva took the girl back and returned her to her father, Yayati. There was no rule of virginity. A girl could have sex with a man without marrying and could give birth to children. Kunti and Matsyagandha are well-known examples of Aryan culture. Kunti had sex with several men before marrying Pandu and giving birth to children. Matsyagandha had sex with Saint Parashar before marrying Bhishma's father, Shantanu.

If Shalini had read all this, she would have been passed through great mental agony.

The most significant comfort for Aajivak Babu was sending Shalini to sleep. He didn't let her read the history of sexual assault by Aryans against animals. He had saved her from coming across the story of the sexual assault of Sage Kindam of a female dear and Sage Sun's sexual assault of a mare. The serious most was sex of a horse with a woman as an adventurous ritual of *Ashwamedh Yagya*. Knowing any of such instances by a woman of the day could have been deadly shocking.

These exploits were no less shocking to Aajivak Babu. He was grief-stricken while passing through the detestable mindset towards the woman of 600 BC. Five persons to be imposed as husbands of Draupadi, the *ras leelas*, the love affairs of Lord Krishna and their glorification filled Aajivak Babu with disapproval as these acts are a precise paradigm of woman-exploitation, including rape. The presence of malpractices against women in the twenty-first century, the alarming rise in the number of rape cases and horrifying episodes like Nirbhaya gang rape in the heart of Delhi and the glorification of such exploits by the so-called elite society link the descendants of Aryans to the present.

In states like Bihar, *Bahu Jhuthaiye* means sending the bride of the oppressed to spend the first night at the house of the dominant caste for their sexual pleasure. The nude pictures of tribal women, and the rape of a child in a place of worship are the monstrous acts that Aajivak Babu found to be products of the Aryan mindset. He found a similar persona in the subsequent intruders. The past paradigm of multiple corruption into the present by Aryans and successive intruders was a severe threat that didn't let Aajivak Babu calm down.

The time was now five o'clock in the morning. There was no point in going back to sleep now. Aajivak Babu prepared to go for his morning walk.

❑

SEVEN

Aajivak Babu had not even recovered from the trauma of the historic exploitation of women when K C Shukla added fuel to the fire by sending a video to Aajivak Babu on WhatsApp. It was the same K C Shukla, whom Aajivak Babu had blocked on WhatsApp since a long time. This video showed K C Shukla's wicked past. Aajivak Babu could sense his prejudice in the video. Shukla never failed to pass prejudiced remarks so that the wounds of Dalits and tribals bled. It seemed as though Shukla experienced a strange comfort by adding fuel to fire regarding caste issues.

He always kept an eagle eye on the weaknesses of any person, employee, officer or politician belonging to the lower community to pass his malicious judgement. He also had a bad opinion of Muslims. He was adept at twisting anything to make it worth criticising. Shukla was a specimen for whom vulgarity turned out to be a standard feature.

K C Shukla was with Aajivak Babu for more than two years. But at that time, he didn't have the opportunity to execute his evil plans. Or maybe Aajivak Babu did not give him any chance for him to do the same.

Aajivak Babu was still well-received when Shukla joined him. His Brahmin brethren, too, had showed sincere concern to Aajivak Babu. They had warned him to be vigilant in dealing with him. At the same time, they gave a character feedback of Shukla which was quite shocking.

In a nutshell, one could say that K C Shukla, a communal and casteist person had all the qualities of a practised villain. Despite this, Aajivak Babu was willing to give him the benefit of doubt.

He believed that a reasonable person may some nasty things at times, and also there may be some good quality in an evil man. Aajivak Babu always tried to see the good side of people. He followed the same policy in his personal and family life and always had fruitful results.

In the case of Shukla, Aajivak Babu adopted the same strategy, and it was a pleasant experience. Mr Shukla spent more than two years with Aajivak Babu with no controversies. And he was transferred, after completing his term successfully without showing any new villainous side to his personality. Though Aajivak Babu had never been interested in nurturing a relationship with K C Shukla, he was connected with him through Facebook and WhatsApp. If he founds anything valid in his posts on social sites, he read it thoroughly. Occasionally, he would make light remarks so as not to let this dry relationship die down.

He was not entirely comfortable with the relationship. At times, he had even deleted his messages. Aajivak Babu could not make out the video he received today. He did not know whether Shukla had concern for him or if he was satisfying his ego.

Aajivak Babu viewed the video without any prejudice or bias. Though there remained a suspicion that the current video may be related to caste prejudice. He could not comprehend whether Shukla's intention was fair or foul. But Aajivak Babu found it necessary to understand the current political scenario and its natural character of corruption.

The video was of Ms Madhulika Pandey. In the video, she addressed a gathering of the National Secular Party (NSP) at Parashuram Seva Sansthan grounds. She made a rude comment, saying, "Those who are ruling under cover of Indian Constitution, sitting on your heads. Remember, they used to clean your shoes. Today, you are a loser because we are divided; we are split. You are sitting here; I am sorry to say, my younger brother Satish Gautam may be seeing India forty years ahead from today so that your children may not turn to beggars. They may begin by saying 'Yes sir' to whom you don't even like to sit with you. Wake up, wake up and fight on the lines of Praveen Gautam until you take over, keep on fighting and fighting alone."

This lack of remorse did not end at her remarks. When a TV reporter asked Ms Pandey the reason as to why she made such an offensive comment, she brazenly replied, "I didn't say anything wrong. I do the politics of *Sarva Dharm Sambhav* which means all the religions have the same potential. My feeling was not to hurt any particular class or community. I am sorry if anybody's feelings are hurt. I meant the Constitution should give equal rights to all. Be with everybody, and everyone should grow. The sentiment is the same. The same benefit which is given to the person sitting in the last row has to be given to the person sitting in the first row."

According to Aajivak Babu, this video was a blot on the face of Indian democracy, a challenge to the Constitution of India, and it was a disaster to the Election Commission and the spirit of the Code of Conduct. Aajivak Babu sent this video to Dr Tarun.

He recalled that not a single day passed without the saffron-clad political representatives of the NSP making irresponsible remarks to spread religious disdain in political rhetoric. Some public representatives of the state and national assembly openly engaged in 'shoe and slipper war' in their public meetings. Someone talked about producing more and more children. Another woman hermit described those who matched their ideology as *Ramjade,* Rama's children and addressed others as *Haramjade*, the bastards.

Ms Pandey taught the formula of racial arrogance and provided the ammunition of casteism to start a battle among different sections of society. She didn't even bother to hide her malicious intentions but stood by it shamelessly.

Aajivak Babu felt a strange restlessness at the cheap mentality of the public representatives. He encountered an array of questions. For instance: Do our public representatives have nothing but this melancholy reflection of the past? Is this a selfish and divisive vision of our federal representatives? If our public representatives have this wisdom, what type of society and nation will they build?

When these foolish remarks became part of the everyday debates on TV, are our follies not being propagated all over the world? Could such follies show the right image of India to the world community? Would the breeders of the Shwan culture, who keep on trumpeting day and night to be the 'Vishva Guru', the teacher of the world, achieve this target based on their existing follies?

Aajivak Babu was annoyed at the stupidity and ignorance of the people. Out of frustration, he realised that the Britishers were right while making the statement: 'India needs British rule until they are civilised.' Even after seventy years of independence, had the voters and the public representatives of the country become civilised? Were they responsible? Not. Had they been accountable and educated? Would the voters choose such representatives of the government to rule? Would they have been so irresponsible and mentally bankrupt to behave like this? How could the country's dignity and sovereignty be protected when the defender of the democracy whom the public had elected were so mentally disabled? The ones who had nothing more to do other than waging war over caste and religion, how could they take the country to any progress? They could, but to further slavery.

While the storm of turmoil trapped Aajivak Babu, the mobile buzzed on and broke his chain of thoughts.

“Hello, sir... Namaskar!” The name Dr Tarun lashed on the screen.

“Hello, brother, how are you? Is all going well?” Dr Tarun said.

“I wouldn’t say all is very well, sir, but of course, I can say that things are going on.”

“Why do you talk in such a pessimistic tone, bro? Don’t be so upset. If you are pessimistic for long, you will get into extreme depression. Then troubles set in and you will be entrapped forever.”

“Dr Sahab, I feel very isolated. I feel like we are misfits in this society and system. Other people seem to be comfortable in it, and we have turned out to be mere specimens of depression.” Aajivak Babu shared his sorry state of mind. Anyway, there was no one other than Dr Tarun with whom he could share this thought.

“What to say, Aajivak Babu, the National Secular Party has crossed all limits of decency. How can their advocates and spokespersons be held accountable when the party’s top brass stands with some criminal institutions? There is no such hope for an ordinary and responsible citizen. What option is left for us besides tolerating them? We just have to bear it." Dr Tarun's remarks indicated that he had seen the video sent by Aajivak Babu.

"Dr Sahab, I don't understand how important it is to adopt Chanakya's practices in the twenty-first-century. At that time there was monarchy and not a democracy as we have today. Then what does this comparison mean except for the propaganda of political hounding?"

"I can't understand your intention, but what do you want to say about Chanakya?"

Aajivak Babu elaborated, "In a case of toppling over any state government, instances of horse-trading of MLAs are prevalent. Some saffron-clad men and women are well versed in threatening the courts these days. A man, the master, or the surveyor of National Secular Party (NSP), is more than enough to tackle all such cases single-handedly. You know that this is the ability of this man to win the title of Chanakya in the media world. It is a typical fashion to glorify every good or bad action of this gentleman. It is praised by the name of 'Chanakya Niti', the philosophy of Chanakya. You never forget his malicious mentality in your articles and debates. Do I have to tell you anymore?"

"It's okay, I do understand it. But in this twenty-first century, what is the reference of the Chanakya of the past with today's Chanakya. I still don't understand. What do you have to say about this puzzle?"

Aajivak Babu smiled and said, "Okay, okay, dear sir. The needle of your thinking is still stuck here at this point.

Well, just let me know whether you have an unlimited call facility or...?"

Dr Tarun's assurance of unlimited calls on mobile encouraged Aajivak Babu to proceed.

Aajivak Babu went on to say, "It's a strange coincidence, a deliberate plot and a well-calculated strategy. It is gross ignorance or the legacy of mental slavery that glorifies the past without fail. Consequently, the past is justified, promoted, and clad in absolute truth under cover of logistics. The same formula is in practice to glorify the epics Ramayana and Mahabharata and their characters and storylines. Staging of Ramayana every year at the political and religious level is another case to praise and encourage the irrational past to impose over the present."

Aajivak Babu found a conspiracy in this. What impact did it have on society, the country or current generation, whether good or bad? That is why our contribution was negligible in research, science and technology, because of the lack of scientific temperament and slavery to religious traditions and religious institutions.

Aajivak Babu continued, "You know Vishnugupta, Chanakya and Kautilya are all the same person. I want to share some instances about Chanakya Niti to know his real character. I read it out to you to clear the doubts about Chanakya to solve the puzzle of the present and the past of Chanakya."

There is jealousy, hatred and internal struggles and differences; they should be further enhanced. In the garb of the Acharya, quarrels should be created among the mass heroes over trivial matters.

Promote Raja Yoga within the sangh by becoming an astrologer. And motivate the sangh heroes to accept the subjectiveness of the prince and offer livestock, attendants and other things.

Use prostitutes, actresses and dancers to stimulate the work lust of union heroes. Provoke fight between the sangh heroes, motivate each other to kill and cheat one hero and go to another hero.

The detectives reach out to the persons in the garb of a sannyasin getting aroused at night. Use the aphrodisiac ointment to subdue the woman and, in turn, give the poison-dissolved cream to the enemy.

Take the form of widows and sannyasins and quarrel with each other and provoke the sangh heroes. Prostitutes or dancers should call their lovers to meet her at someplace and kill him or imprison him.

Encourage the sangh nayak, the hero describing the beauty of a poor farmer's wife, to make her his queen. When he takes her up to make his queen, he humiliates him in the sangh sabha as a sannyasi and leads him to punishment, torture, and imprisonment.

Change the dress and accuse the heroes that this man has killed a Brahmin and raped a Brahmin woman.

Wear the garb of an astrologer and predict that a married woman —the daughter of this person will become queen, and his son will become king and hence get it in any way. If this sangh nayak succeeds, provoke the opposing hero.

"Singh Sahib, this is the Chanakya alias Kautilya doctrine." Through these illustrations, Aajivak Babu threw the ball in Dr Tarun's court and waited for his reaction.

" Aajivak Babu, what you have read out to me, Chanakya's doctrine, has no morals or ethics. The current political climate is a modern version of the old Chanakya doctrine. Or one can say that today's Chanakyas are more despicable than the Chanakya of old. I am afraid that such people will become more detestable by grabbing power, and will in no way will diminish. Everywhere, there are *vivaads* or disputes but no *samvad* or dialogue anywhere. The biggest concern is that the positive dialogue that does not exist at all." He took a long breath and continued further, "If someone talks about 'dialogue', he falls prey to the trolls, becomes a traitor, and in a stroke, he is to be sent to Pakistan. His family faces a variety of threats. And what more should I say about the current situation? I think it is the biggest surgical strike on today's intellectuals and on those who love their country unconditionally. How much impact does this surgical strike have on Pakistan is a question of disputed controversy. The political masters and their trolls have left no stone unturned to silence the country's responsible citizens and intellectuals and to keep them deaf and dumb like the majority."

When Dr Tarun paused, Aajivak Babu felt that he had finished, was not willing to say anything more on this issue. So Aajivak Babu proceeded further to reveal what was buried inside, "Just tell me, Singh *Sahab*, now, what other option do we have except to be miserable? Still, you say, 'if you remain such pessimistic, you will get in trouble'."

Dr Tarun concluded by saying, "Generally, it is said that we must be positive, isn't it? If someone has a negative view, we never tell them to 'be negative'. So, stay balanced as much as possible. It is called being practical in life and the need of today; understood? Okay, see you soon." The dialogue came to an end.

Aajivak Babu watched the video again. Madhulika Pandey was openly advocating jealousy and hatred from the political platform. She was frustrated at the upliftment of Dalits and the weaker sections of society. Because of that, she held the Constitution of India to be the guilty party and made ugly remarks. She described her formula as togetherness of all, development for all. Aajivak Babu was taken aback at her bold mind.

The sole aim of a wicked person is to keep on speaking without considering what is fair or foul or if it has any logic behind it. He knows their strategy is to fill the air with mindless noise so that genuine voices may remain unheard, and their stupidity prevails as the only truth. As a result, all the ways of communication are closed here. Aajivak Babu was severely disturbed by The National Secular Party (NSP) and saw no hope of any healthy communication.

He admitted to himself that if it had only been a question of political vandalism, it could be tackled somehow. But the National Secular Party (NSP) shamelessly defended its singular agenda. If sponsoring Hindu-Muslim debates on TV, setting a pattern of mob-lynchings, and protecting chaotic elements were not a detestable extension of the corrupt Chanakya doctrine of the past, then what else could be?

The video forced Aajivak Babu to think about the blame games played during the election campaign. The opponents crossed all the political parties' limits of decency and morality. In politics and especially to win elections, there was nothing in using the army to achieve their ends, and people were provoked in the name of Mandir-Masjid. Instead of revealing achievements and plans to get a vote, the opponents were accused bluntly, and all the promises made in previous elections were all put on silent mode. What was it, if not the revised edition of Chanakya's corrupt and aggressive policy? Saffron-clad jackals in the skin of the lion meant nothing else but a new version of Chanakya Niti to ruin the true spirit of Indian democracy.

The current pattern of the political regime had left no spirit of democracy. And almost all the constitutional institutions had been made victims of the ruling party's monopoly. It was to satisfy their interests. He was not so worried about who would be in power or not. He was more concerned about what type of society we were building without moral values and ethics. He was worried about what sort of citizens and country we were becoming.

Aajivak Babu knew his worth. He also knew that when the public became a crowd and mindlessness controlled the system, hundreds and thousands of people like Aajivak Babu couldn't change the policy. But he was habitually forced to move on, however forceful the winds he had to encounter on the way. In this atmosphere of despair, he was often inspired and encouraged by the story of a bird sparrow. The story is as follows: A forest was on fire, and a small sparrow bird would bring water in her beak and pour it on the fire. This water was insufficient to douse the fire. But the bird was committed to fulfilling her responsibility with all her might.

This scene was observed by a crow. It said, "Putting water is not going to extinguish the fire. Don't be so stupid. Come and sit next to me and simply watch the scene."

The bird's reply to the crow was appreciable. It said, "Brother, I know well that spraying of water by me is not going to extinguish this fire. But that does not mean that I should shirk my responsibility."

The bird further said, "I'm abiding by my responsibilities. Whenever the history of the fire is written, my name will not be among the idle viewers of the spectacle but under the category of duty-bound and responsible persons."

There were 'crows' who considered Aajivak Babu stupid and advised him to sit far away. They accuse him of not understanding worldliness and patted themselves on their backs for being intelligence. The threat of the trolls, or the mob-lynching brigade was less scary to Aajivak Babu.

He, too, was scared. He didn't dare to watch the video of any mob-lynching. Yet, the little bird's lesson motivated him. It didn't let him silence his voice; instead energises his voice spontaneously. As a result, the flight of Aajivak Babu's struggles never died down. Had there been no good creatures like this innocent sparrow bird and Roby the dog around Aajivak Babu and no unconditional love, he would have surrendered. And if the support of a handful of human beings and books were not there, Aajivak Babu too would have become sheep; and a part of the 'pet crowd,' shouting slogans.

There was so much in favour of Aajivak Babu today. Perhaps that was why he neither became a sheep nor part of the mobs. But he has had a strange panic since his childhood. Whenever it flashed in his memory, Aajivak Babu was unable to sleep. There lay cheap politics behind this fear and his insomnia. A flood of conspiracies, the cheapness of politics, hooliganism of feudal lords, was still alive in Aajivak Babu's memory. It periodically registered its presence and threatened him time and again.

❑

EIGHT

The 'fear' that Aajivak Babu referred to was the first by-product of the village Hamirpur. The community still exists on the UP border even after 40 years. There was no threat to communal harmony like there was nowadays, sponsored by the National Secular Party (NSP). A party like the NSP may not have been born at that time. So, there was no question of any protection of hooliganism. However, many crimes were committed on the basis of caste and religion. Their crime pattern was miraculous. The control over the gun and target has always been in the grip of the unjust. But the weaker sections' shoulder to fire the weapon means the bonded ethnic strata. There was a forced pattern to kill two birds with a single stone.

Aman Singh Ahlawat, a lawyer from a neighbouring town and a friend of Narendra Chandra, Aajivak Babu's father, contested the assembly election. Narendra Chandra had a significant role in planning and managing his election. On the contrary, Hari Singh, son-in-law of the head of the same village, Hamirpur village, was a professional lawyer and fought from the same Assembly constituency. They both lost the elections, and a third candidate was elected as an MLA.

Someone had to be held responsible for the defeat of the son-in-law of the village head. In this case, there could be no other easy target than Narendra Chandra. Hence, Narendra Chandra was openly accused of the defeat of Hari Singh, the son-in-law of the village head. The election ended, but Narendra Chandra came under the grip of the post-election influence. The aftermath of the assembly elections were no way less than that of the atom bombs dropped over the two cities of Japan, Hiroshima and Nagasaki. Narendra Chandra and his family had to pass through the agony of the same.

It was not the first time that Narendra Chandra had directly crossed the way of the feudal lords of the village. Narendra Chandra had worked and retired as a teacher in the UP government. So, he was well versed in the vicious cycle of borrowing loans from landlords and money lenders. He knew the exploitation mechanism very well. Along with the hefty interest on the loan, there was a different kind of additional benefit to the feudal lords. The borrowers had to take care of animals in their courtyards. The oppressors forced them to work on their farms with no benefits, so that they ended up paying more than the accounted interest and the principal amount.

It was a common practice in the village. Narendra Chandra was a revolutionary by nature; that is why he called a meeting of the victims to form a cooperative society. It was decided to collect twenty rupees per member per month. Twenty rupees was of great importance at that time. Thus, the amount raised was given to the neediest applicant. Collectively, they identified the most disadvantaged and appropriate applicant and credit was granted. This amount was sufficient to meet the poor applicants' essential needs like marriage, building a house, etc.

It freed the poor from the payment of loans, within a few months. Now, all their needs were met by this cooperative society. The people were liberated from exorbitant interests as bonded labourers in caring for the landowner's cattle and fields. Now, these people were almost free from the debt of bondage. It was a challenge to the unquestioned imperative dominance of the so-called upper castes. It was like a bone stuck in the throat of the bullies, neither to swallow nor to spit out. The role of Narendra Chandra in the Assembly elections and the defeat of the village head's son-in-law added fuel to the fire and multiplied the light of the vendetta.

The guns were out and the target was perfect; it was Narendra Chandra. But they were not getting any bonded shoulders. Suddenly, a 12-year-old boy, son of Makhan Lal went missing in Narendra Chandra's neighbourhood. Since the village head was the ancestral landlord of Makhan Lal, he used his sympathy as a bait to trap the wounded, and Makhan Lal had no option left but to wag his tail at the zamindar's door. He saw his landlord as the only hope. Makhan Lal knew the landlord's influence in the police department and courts. He knew that no one else could help him in his son's case. Narendra Chandra was of no use in this case. So, he set up a meeting with the zamindar.

Hari Singh, the son-in-law of the zamindar who suffered a defeat in the election, was no less than an injured serpent ready to strike back. He also joined the battle to ensure justice and wipe out the tears of the victim. Things took a dangerous turn. And two days later, instead of Makhan Lal's son returning alive, his body was recovered from Nurpur village in Delhi across the border. Makhan Lal's family created havoc in the whole settlement. In this hour of grief, Narendra Chandra and his family were at the forefront to help and support the family of Makhan Lal.

The police arrived in the village, investigated the case and finally returned, taking Narendra Chandra and his two sons Rajendra and Satyendra and three more people from the town to the police post for questioning. All the men were speechless at this sudden development. But nobody could do anything. And nobody dared to ask the police to show an arrest warrant or ask who they were arresting. It could have been a significant threat.

There was no awareness of rights and no means of communication like today. For the poor, the police had been autocratic in the past. And more or less, it is autocratic today as well. Nothing has changed for the unfortunate, and present circumstances indicate no remarkable change in the future. Yet Narendra Chandra hoped that Makhan Lal would speak to the police to stop this arrest. But nothing like that happened; instead of stopping the police or making an effort, Makhan Lal turned his eyes to another side.

It didn't take long for Narendra Chandra to understand what was happening. Police took all six people to the police post, saying they would be released in a day after questioning. Aajivak Babu was then Deepak Kumar, a student. He was at home and had no option other than to trust the police. The entire settlement was forced to have hope against hope. Aajivak Babu's mother asked him, "Son, why did they arrest our family members? Why did Makhan Lal not say anything to support your *Babuji*? What didn't we do for Makhan Lal and his family?"

"I feel there is nothing to worry about, *Maa*. The police said that they would release them tomorrow after interrogation. Why are you so worried?" Not a single neighbour came to their house to console the family that evening. But Deepak's mother, was worried about the consequences. She then became vocal about her fear.

"You don't know; the cops are rascals. Why did they take away your brother Raju and Sattu along with your *Babuji*? My children, students of class ninth and tenth, are innocent. Your Babuji did nothing but teach the students. He is always helping the poor and the deprived. How can he be a witness to any kidnap or a murder? How would he have any idea as to how Makhan Lal's innocent child Kapil landed in the well?"

His mother's questions Deepak uneasy. Neither mother nor Deepak could sleep a wink that night. He was up the whole night to console his mother. Finally, the mother and the son passed the night hoping that tomorrow would not be as ruthless as today. But their suspicions overruled any hope they had.

The next day the circumstances worsened. The police released three of the accused, but Narendra Chandra and his two sons were imprisoned in the same police post.

When Bhanwari got to know of the return of the three others and none of her family, her fears grew. She visited their houses with Deepak and asked, "Why didn't they release Deepak's *Babuji* and my sons Raju and Sattu?"

The three gave the same reply, "We have given five hundred rupees to the policemen. The zamindar deposited our share of the money. That's it."

"What was the landlord there for?"

"The zamindar and his son-in-law, lawyer *Babu*, came there in a car. They rescued all of us."

"Didn't he talk about the release of Deepak's *Babuji*?"

'We don't know anything about it. The zamindar and his son-in-law had left by the time we were released. We did not get a chance to see them."

Having heard them, she came to know who was behind the whole conspiracy. It was a severe shock to Bhanwari, and she felt as if the ground had been pulled out from under her feet. She pleaded with two or three men in the neighbourhood to accompany her to the Nurpur police post, but no one was willing to go along. The fear of the police was so terrifying that no one was ready to muster their courage.

Birmo, Makhan Lal's wife was dreaded by all. No one dared to come in her way. Even her husband, Makhan Lal, was not an exception in this case. In any case, everyone realised that Makhan Lal and his wife Birmo were behind the arrest of Narendra Chandra and his two sons. Everyone feared Birmo so much that they had forgotten Narendra Babu and the service he had rendered to others.

There was no time for Deepak and his mother to inform their relatives and seek their help; anyway no one would come. Bhanwari and Deepak had no option but to go to the police post alone. Deepak was ignorant of the functioning of the police and the courts. It was worse in Bhanwari's case, as she was an uneducated woman unaware of the outside world. The circumstances had put them in a do or die situation. The two rushed to the police post.

As soon as she saw a policeman, Bhanwari began to cry.

"*Darogaji*," Bhanwari begged with folded hands. "My husband is innocent, and so are my children. He has spent his whole life been teaching the students. He can't commit such an ugly crime." Bhanwari did not know who she was repeatedly addressing as *Daroga* was a head constable, and not a *Daroga*, a police inspector. Deepak could not explain the hierarchy of the police to his mother at that point. So, he remained silent, thinking that his mother's pain could help soften the attitude of the police.

"O lady, don't make a row here. We are sure that you are aware of the murderer. We also know that your husband is innocent, but he knows who is behind the scandal and the murder? Until he tells, we are not going to leave. Your children will be freed if your man tells us the name of the murderer." The head constable gave his verdict in a single line.

But Bhanwari was not that kind of lady to surrender so quickly. She further begged, "*Darogaji*, somebody has misguided the police, lied about this. If my husband knew of it, he would have told you. He is a gentleman."

"Don't make a fuss here. Get lost." The head constable rejected her plea ruthlessly.

Bhanwari took out some money and gave it to the constable. "Take the money and leave my husband and children."

The constable took five hundred rupees, not too small at that time. It is more substantial, even ten thousand today. But the pain of parting with such a significant amount in such a crisis didn't matter to Bhanwari. However, it was several months' ration for the family of Narendra Chandra to survive. Narendra Chandra's family saved the money in pennies, which the heartless constable did not care about. He only had to loot the cash not to analyse the family's hardship on how hard they had to work to earn this money. So he pocketed it comfortably and spoke more politely.

"Well, we will leave all of them within a day or two after the investigation is over."

"But *Daroga*..."

Without hearing Bhanwari, the man said threateningly, "I did say they would be released within a day or two. No more argument now, or I will put both of you inside. Get lost from here."

Both had no other option but to leave. The money had gone, and nothing was achieved. Both were upset. Deepak was shocked that he could not speak even a single word as the money went away, and nothing was accomplished. What would have happened if his mother had not been there? Would he be able to offer cash to the police? What would happen if these policemen took the money and still did not release *Babuji*?

He had an idea that Karma Singh, a distant relative, was a sub-inspector; could he do something to support them? He wasn't sure whether he would help them or not. Deepak was entangled in these issues and forgot that his mother was beside him. His mother was in a similar situation. Both were together but in their respective worlds. His mother acted as if she was deaf. Whatever was taking shape in her mind was flowing out of her eyes, which she seemed unaware of.

Deepak wiped away her tears and said, "Tomorrow, I will go to Karma Singh. Let's see if he will help us." Bhanwari didn't respond. She knew that he was of no use.

The police was no better than the wild beast who had tasted human blood, got addicted and was always ready to quenching its thirst. During these two or three days, the police visited the village twice or thrice to arrest several people at Birmo's behest. Birmo's attitude made the arrests seem like a balm to the pain of her son's death. So, the arrests went on. And the bribe of rupees five hundred was a by-product in case of these arrests. They all had to pay the amount to the police except four or five families in the Dalit settlement.

No one even came to Narendra Chandra's house for fear lest Makhan Lal's wife Birmo may drag them into the jaws of the autocratic police. It was highly profitable for the police for every reason, and Birmo's revengeful approach was known to all. But it was not known as to why? The question was a puzzle for everyone. It seemed as if the family of Narendra Chandra was at the centre of controversy and whatever she was doing was to compensate for the death of her son. She was no less dangerous than a sadist in this case.

Under this terror-prone atmosphere, Bhanwari with her two daughters and Deepak were literally imprisoned at home. They would cry together and wipe away each other's tears and were lost in the world of contemplation. They didn't make proper meals but ate just enough to survive. None of them knew how Narendra Chandra and his two sons were in custody.

How were they being treated? Whether they were given proper food or not? How were the police treating them? All these serious questions were not giving any comfort to them. They felt miserable. They were like birds whose wings were cut off; just a flurry of helplessness was left, and nothing but disorder and captivity.

Finally on the fifth day, Narendra Chandra came home with his two sons, Raju and Sattu, but with a bandage on his head. The dressing on Narendra Chandra's head deprived them of the little joy at their return from police custody. Narendra Chandra himself took control of the situation to calm everyone down. But Bhanwari was not ready to listen to anything. Her impatience was beyond control, and the array of questions had no bound.

"Just tell me as to how you got hit on the head? Who did it? When did this happen?"

All the family members sat on the cots under the neem tree. Deepak's sisters brought all of them glasses of water. Bhanwari asked again, "How did you get hurt?"

The tears were still flowing from Bhanwari's eyes while she repeated the question nonstop.

Narendra Chandra put his hand on her shoulder to soothe her and spoke, "No one hurt anyone. I hit my head on the wall, and hurt my head. In fact, the police then took me to the dispensary and bandaged my head." Narendra Chandra could not say anything beyond that or didn't want to. But it was not enough to comfort Bhanwari and his family.

He knew well that he could not hide anything from Bhanwari. The children's faces were flat, but their eyes were fixed on the faces of both parents. Sattu and Raju's pain was unnoticed before Narendra Chandra's agony.

"Why did you hit your head? There must be something serious behind it. How bad was the wound and how many stitches were needed?"

It was not easy for Narendra Chandra to answer so many questions simultaneously. If Narendra Chandra didn't stop Bhanwari, her questions would have continued. But Narendra Chandra was relieved to be back with his family.

No one from the neighbourhood dared visit them to know the family's state of affairs as of now. Perhaps the terror of Makhan Lal's wife, Birmo, had still not faded. Finally, Narendra Chandra had to explain the whole painful episode. "The cops beat me up. Somehow I bore it, but I could not bear it when I heard the beating and crying of my children in the adjacent cell. I felt helpless that I couldn't help my children. I felt that my life was worthless and I tried to kill myself by banging my head against the wall. Then I don't know what happened. When I regained consciousness, I was in the dispensary, and two or three policemen surrounded me."

Straining his mind as if trying to recall, he proceeded further, "A policeman addressed me and said, "*Babuji*, we understand, you are innocent. Now we will cause no suffering to you and your children. *Sahab*, the SHO is willing to release you all immediately, but you have got hurt now, and it will not be appropriate to release you in such a condition. We will release you as soon as you recover."

Another policeman reassured me by saying, "Give us only two or three days; all will be fine."

Narendra Chandra tried to reassure Bhanwari by saying this.

"And you agreed?" Bhanwari counterquestioned, frowning.

"And what could I do? After all, you too know well that to err is human. I do know that the police are brutal. What would I do if I didn't forgive the police officers when they admitted whatever they did was wrong and condemnable?"

Despite being willing to say something different, he could simply say that he couldn't do anything else. If it were so easy, he would have resisted his illegal arrest with his two kids. Narendra Chandra was shrewd enough to understand that it was not an ordinary case but that of the murder of an innocent child. He was meticulous in calculating the power of the upper caste lords of the village.

Bhanwari, too knew the powerful dominance of the village lords. Narendra knew well how spineless the Dalits were to stand up against the feudal lords who were all-powerful in the village irrespective of the provisions of democracy and the rule of law. And the dangerous fact he was well aware of was that he didn't have any godfather at all who could stand by him to ensure justice. But she had forgotten this all in the flow of emotions.

In the heat of Bhanwari's array of questions, the children felt neglected by their father. That is why Narendra Chandra had a mixed sense of victory and anguish on his face as he covered his helplessness under the cover of forgiveness. To compensate for the overlook of the children, he showered his love individually on each one.

Finally, to normalise the situation, he said that he was hungry. The activities in the kitchen resumed for the first time after five days. Even after eating their food, they couldn't talk normally. The suffering remained buried in each mind, not letting anything replace this space. They didn't even want to enhance their woes by talking about them anymore. So, at bedtime, all went to their respective beds with relief.

Though Narendra Chandra did act as a hero to restore normalcy, he didn't allow even a bit of his sorrow and suffering to spill out from his chest, where he had buried it deep. But he couldn't hide anything from himself; the solitary cell, with no facilities, the filthy smell, sleeping on the floor, the inhuman treatment of the police—with no respect for his age and noble profession.

He had lived his life as an ideal teacher, a role model for many students and teachers. Now everything seemed worthless. He had been treated like a criminal by the police, the worst criminals on the earth. They had no intention to seek the truth or know the innocence of a person in custody. Everything seemed to be sneering at him in the dark of the night while he tried to sleep. He was haunted by how he had lost control and tried to commit suicide in the police post.

For hours, everything continued to play like a movie about how he saved the villagers from debt. He was deeply hurt by the indifference of the villagers, the cowardly people. As a result of his selfless service, Narendra Chandra faced police brutality and physical and mental agony. He concluded that a horse can be forcibly taken to the riverbank, but it cannot be forced to drink water. He had taken the villagers to the river to drink water to be the true heir of the gift of nature to live with dignity, not to be enslaved but to be a free man. The slave mentality remained, so the villagers let evil win to defeat virtue.

Narendra Chandra did not hold the villagers alone guilty for the dreadful episode in this hour of contemplation of his sufferings. It had shaken his revolutionary vision; which he had dreamt of for the villagers' quality of life. He was caught in the row of negative thoughts and helplessly floated like a straw in the strong current of the hooliganism of feudal lords. He was not even getting a foothold. He concluded that the villagers weren't to be blamed because they were slaves to the circumstances, too helpless. The system enabled some anarchists to abuse the constitutional provisions under cover of provincial law enforcing agencies.

Narendra Chandra kept on analysing the current situation in more detail to reach an appropriate conclusion. He realised that the domineering landowners of the village had become autocratic rulers. The police were their tools as most of them were of their caste. The feudal lords must be celebrating as they had succeeded in teaching Narendra Chandra a lesson of going against the social and village hierarchy.

On the contrary, Narendra Chandra's family had lost all hopes of any comfort and justice. The words democracy and constitution seemed to his family no better than ghosts, the natural bouncers of the mighty. There was nothing left for Narendra Chandra's family to comfort them, not even a beam of any hope. They were alone, just alone, but the feet on the land and the sky above as sole companions of their survival.

Narendra Chandra thought, "Is standing with the contesting candidate of one's choice to participate in representative proceedings, a crime? Is not acting as a puppet of the village feudal lords a violation of representative proceedings? Is it mandatory to be deaf and dumb for the poor and oppressed for the rapist of democracy to glorify its hypocrisy? Is it such a big crime that a family has to live as corpses to keep democracy alive? Isn't it such a sacrifice to be made by the have-nots to keep the democracy alive to ensure autocratic powers to the haves?"

"No, no, absolutely not," he said to himself. "Can it never be a healthy sign of democracy and justice?" How far did the caravan of Narendra Chandra's thoughts go? But Aajivak Babu remembered that Narendra Chandra had sold everything from this village within three months, never to return to this village and the settlement of oppressed castes. Finally, he bade everyone goodbye, even to the Makhan Lal family. He did not care for the requests to stay behind in the village and the tears that were shed at their time of departure.

Aajivak Babu today found himself standing at the same crossroads where his Babuji, Narendra Chandra stood forty years ago. He still saw that the sparrow of democracy was imprisoned in the cage of ill-famed autocratic political heads. Almost all the constitutional institutions had been crippled, and their existence had been a significant threat. The Supreme Court's decorum itself was under suspicion, and ethics and human values were almost on the verge of extinction. The poison of communalism was showing its colour everywhere. The spirit of brotherhood and harmony was taking its last breath,. Above all, the existence of the Constitution, the watchdog of democracy, was not beyond threat.

History was repeating itself. In the face of the current turmoil and chaos, Aajivak Babu felt that migration was not an option to be considered. Which world was safe and sound for all, these days? The whole country was more or less the same. Aajivak Babu's thoughts took a contradictory turn from his father's. He recollected that any evil, crime, anarchy, chaos, and whatever would continue to increase until one stood up against injustice.

He knew many journalists who loved the country and were trolled because of the opposition to this anarchy. How their mothers and sisters were publicly abused in forums. To cope up with a variety of issues, controversies had become a daily routine. The one who keeps democracy, the nation's sovereignty and judiciary, above all, have to lose their lives.

Bhagat Singh was right on the top of the list of martyrs who made the supreme sacrifice and kept the nation's pride supreme. He considered it an authentic tribute and honour to the great soul. There was a need to honour his soul and ensure his martyrdom was not in vain.

He wondered why we wish Sardar Bhagat Singh should be born in a neighbour's house, to sacrifice his life. Why not in our homes, and why not every apartment and courtyard have the distinction of rearing a Bhagat Singh? And finally, Aajivak Babu's emphasis on why Bhagat Singh must reside, yes, in every human being to stand against anything evil.

In the hour of need, why not, for the sake of sovereignty, responsible citizens of the country should get ready to kiss the death trap like Bhagat Singh. It is a hard fact that today's opportunistic era is full of wicked merchants who are in the business of buying and selling of conscience. Some people of the upper stratum can be seen with the tag 'for sale'. And they have already sold their own souls.

He was of the firm opinion that to be a Bhagat Singh, there must be no place for bargaining of human being and humanity. Perhaps, this was the recent call of the present. It should be fulfilled in the interest of upholding democracy, democratic values, and the nation's sovereignty. What ought to be and whatnot, this series of questions had become an essential aspect of the life of Aajivak Babu. It seemed that Aajivak Babu had no existence without being a practical specimen of what he was advocating in the journey of his firm beliefs.

❑

NINE

The sky was full of political rhetoric, and the heated atmosphere seemed to constrict the breath. It was a big challenge for the people and their peace and harmony. The vision of hope was so bad that the present was crippled, and there was no positive feeling for the future. There seemed to be no light at the end of the tunnel. The political surgical strike on the layers of democracy had led to a feeling of gloom. Aajivak Babu went on a morning walk to clear his thoughts.

All the plants in the park were attractive. Nature remained calm and blissful. The pavement seemed to welcome the pedestrians with outstretched arms. The birds chirped merrily, unaware of any political hypocrisy. Seeing this entire natural environment, Aajivak Babu felt comforted. Taking a deep breath, he muttered, "Thankfully, nature is untouched by this dirty game of politics. The political masters have no control on nature. If nature was under the domain of political regime, then...?"

Aajivak Babu suddenly halted in his tracks like a horse stops when faced with danger. Not knowing why, Aajivak Babu just smiled and proceeded. He had only moved further a little when Shaheed-e-Azam Bhagat Singh came alive in his memory with a fresh gust of wind. Bhagat Singh's unique philosophical point became actively related to the 'relationship of shoulders and living life'. He explained it as 'the life is lived on his shoulders; on the shoulders of others, it is a funeral bier'.

Bhagat Singh's philosophies brought Aajivak Babu back to the garb of political rhetoric and the deteriorating conditions of the country. It brought him into a world of citizens who had turned out to be a crowd and herd of sheep. He was back in the world of human beings behaving like the Shwans, the dogs. It meant that Aajivak Babu returned to the world of human beings to get alienated. Nowadays, the festival of democracy, the general election, was being propagated all over its peak. So, the rhetoric around was the same, and nothing was there but rhetoric. He whispered , "Election means rhetoric, and the rhetoric has become a fierce competition. If not, what else?" The answer to this question was not beyond the comprehension of Aajivak Babu. The bigger the rhetoric, the more it would be at the centre of discussion. The more it would be at the centre of the discussion rather than in controversy, the more established the person would be and more prominent a leader. With this rhetoric, if the leader used mimicry to mislead the people, the more he would be entitled to the biggest throne of democratic India.

He continued whispering, "Democratic values are nowhere. The scale of false propagandists' popularity will become equally attractive, and success will undoubtedly kiss his footsteps. That's why today's trend has crossed all limits. Whether true or false, a leader who covers his evil and frightening misdeeds against his opponent is a merit today. He'll be a capable and successful leader of today. These days, the stars of such leaders are elevated. And others are lagging in the race of a new political paradigm that their political future is getting at the stake in the absence of winnable merits of today's politics."

Aajivak Babu went on to measure the graph of oratory with the stature of today's leaders. The leaders who intentionally dragged the mothers, sisters, and others in the family lineage to the election campaign to defame and character assassinate them, were the heroes of today's new type of politics. The more effective acting and *jumlebazi*, the rhetoric with loud shouting and screaming, the more guaranteed the victory. These people mirrored our democracy. This was the criteria for political and non-political issues. It was the standard model of political success these days.

At the present gamut of thoughts, a question flashed in Aajivak Bubu's mind. "Is there no way out of this kind of politics?"

Aajivak Babu walked around the park. But the flight of his thoughts was very high. The uneasiness and search for his questions were getting intense. But Aajivak Babu understood neither the beginning nor the end of their journey. Suddenly, Aajivak Babu couldn't handle both his mental as well as physical exertion. So he sat on a bench in the park. Wiping the sweat from the forehead, he sighed in relief. He took in deep breaths of air to relax his body and mind. Now the physical strain was not there. But the thoughts and the uneasiness of the arising questions continued. The mental journey was more tiring than the physical one, yet it was unrelenting.

Perhaps Aajivak Babu had no control over these mental voyages, just as there was no control over the gang rape of democracy on the pretext of electoral passion. The warriors caught up in the gang rape had no control over themselves. The victims of the gang rape, bleeding, with helpless tears, groaned in pain. However, the people's representatives did not realise the pain of the poor, nor did they have the time or inclination to know of it. They had no choice but to fulfil their political lust.

Aajivak Babu was also suffering like a rape victim, sitting on the bench to caress his wounds. Seeing Aajivak Babu sitting on the bench, D C Gupta came to him.

"How did the moon of Eid come out in the park today without Eid?"

"I think you've become very busy after retirement. I neither see you in the park, nor on the streets." Guptaji tossed the second question without waiting for the first to be answered.

"Hey Guptaji, I walk in the park daily from 5 a.m. to 6 a.m. When do you care about senior citizens like me? Yes, I do go out if there is a need for me to do so."

Deepak Kumar reacted with a smile. Guptaji did not know about Deepak Kumar's other name as Aajivak Babu, for he had nothing to do with the world of authors. Others in the colony also addressed him as Deepak Kumar, not Aajivak Babu. If someone on the phone called him Aajivak Babu, it merely meant that the person belongs to the world of literature. The person who addressed Deepak Kumar by his real name either a relative or known to him in other ways.

"Still, what keeps you in the house all day long? I mean, how do you spend your day at home?" Gupta asked.

Deepak Kumar also smiled and said, "Brother, don't say I stay idle. I keep on engaging myself in one thing or the other in my library of books. If I sit down to read or write on the computer, there is no count of the hours or time of the day or night. I don't know bother about lunch or dinner. You know that, right?"

Guptaji interrupted and said, "Okay, okay, I know that. You have enough work to occupy you at home. But what're you doing here, sitting all alone here, silently? No yoga, no pranayama or any physical exercise?'

"I have already completed my quota of morning walks. I was lost in thought when you came and now, I am talking to you."

"Thoughts of politics, I guess?" Gupta asked, smiling and keeping an eye to eye contact with Deepak Kumar.

"And what other issue is there to think about these days, if not today's political chaos?" Aajivak Babu responded.

"Tells us something as what is going on in your mind regarding today's politics. Whom are you supporting to win? Which party is going to form the government in the centre? Just let me know about your assessment." Guptaji showered a volley of questions light-heartedly.

"Guptaji, which party is going to form a government or not, is not the issue of my contemplation. I'm not at all interested in this business. The issue of my concern is the declining standard of politics. It seems as if there is no decency left in the political arena. When a politician narrates a true or false story of his intimidation over our neighbouring country to befool the voters, the crowd cheers. It starts clapping, whistling, shouting and raising slogans to greet the wicked politicians mindlessly; this pains me a lot. It forces me to consider such acts as mental bankruptcy at both public and political levels."

He continued breathlessly, "The same picture is seen at all the political gatherings today. When a politician makes fun of his opponent, attacks below the belt and talks rubbish to defame his rival for no reason but to gain the favour of the public to win. And obscenities are mouthed liberally against other old ruling parties to cover up the failures and foolishness of the existing ruling parties instead of publicising their achievements. The cheap behaviour of the political leadership is cheered in the same way by clapping, whistling, shouting slogans, etc. This hurts me a lot and that's why I don't bother a least who wins or loses."

Finding Guptaji listening to him intently, Aajivak Babu availed himself of the opportunity. He said, "Guptaji, I find this crowd of people no better than a flock of sheep. They have no thinking, and their reasoning is far-fetched. They neither question any leader about his ongoing promises nor evaluate the claims of his achievements. The crowd does not think of the realisation of new populist promises or how they will be achieved. Perhaps they have no comprehensible words like what, where, when, how, etc., in their dictionary. Then there is no question of asking questions associated with these words. Consequently, there is further no question of accountability to the promises made to the crowd by irresponsible politicians."

Without waiting for Guptaji's response, he went on to say, "Guptaji, a question constantly echoes on the media, especially on social media, that politicians pay for mobilisation of the crowd. Hence the crowd don't become voters or the country's responsible citizens; their sole purpose is to make money. How can these people who have rented their souls for some coins ask questions to their masters? All their questions succumb to the money they are given. As a result, what other role can they have other than to clap, whistle, shout slogans?

"Just tell me, Guptaji, what is left with this mindless crowd. I think they are merely puppets moving on the strings held by their masters' fingers, isn't it so?"

Gupta's face was inexpressive. Perhaps he did not have the logic to counter it. Deepak Kumar knew that Guptaji, a man who was money-minded, would not be able to digest this. Finally, he articulated out of courtesy, "Deepakji, you are right. I do see something like that. But what can be done? Let's leave this topic; I don't find any change to take place in the pattern of the ruling class."

Finally, he made a statement, "I have to complete my morning walk; I am already late." Saying this, Guptaji left for his walk and left Deepak Kumar in his world of deliberations.

Aajivak Babu didn't have much expectations from Guptaji. These issues were beyond the level of Guptaji's calibre. He had tested Guptaji Socrates influenced Aajivak Babu greatly. He realised that Guptaji was a weak-minded man. In any case, his priority was to make money. He even worked late at night to give private tuitions. He also dedicated his vote to those who ensured his economic and financial interests. And had no concern as to whether the rulers were moral or not.

Socrates always talked of the mindset of people. As Aajivak Babu considered himself to be one of the 'first-class' people, he always talked about 'thoughts'. He was engrossed day and night in the world of thoughts As a result, he was a misfit, isolated in the world of easy-going people like Guptaji. Aajivak Babu's books and computers had become his only source of comfort.

Aajivak Babu returned home with images of speeches from politicians which did not give him any mental comfort.

And he returned home hearing the clapping and the upheaval of the crowd. Aajivak Babu felt the sacrifice made by martyrs like Bhagat Singh were wasted. He found that the people were shouldering the politicians' burdens. And the leaders were thrusting their responsibility on the people. But in the present political era, neither the people nor the leaders shared the onus on their shoulders.

Consequently, the nation and democracy were bound to bear this burden, the *janazah*. It was *janazah* of human values and humanity as well. Aajivak Babu feared that if the nation and the democracy continued to carry the *janazah* of the people and the politicians the same way, then the day is not far away when the nation and its democracy would turn into a *janazah*, with no life.

"If democracy turns to be a bier, the *janazah*, who would be blamed, then?" The question agitated Aajivak Babu's mind. No matter how adverse the circumstances were, Aajivak Babu favoured shouldering his responsibilities. He doesn't want to shoulder others'. Aajivak Babu was confident that if others shouldered his responsibilities, it would be Aajivak Babu's bier, the *janazah*. Thus it could not be called a life. It wasn't a healthy sign for the nation and the democracy to be a bier.

Aajivak Babu considered the possible reason for this severe threat to be the failure of the Constitution and democratic provisions. The lack of human values and humanity put the Constitution and democracy in such a drastic situation. Aajivak Babu kept on analysing the situation.

"It is not the failure of the Constitution but the failure of the implementing authorities. The success or failure of the Constitution depends on the will of the implementers. No matter how good the Constitution, it can still fail because of the 'weak will power' and however weak the Constitution, it can still succeed because of 'strong will power." He recalled Dr Ambedkar's views on the success and failure of the Constitution.

Aajivak Babu did not understand whether the 'willing power' safeguarded the Constitution or broke the law. If the political will had been used to protect the structure, how could some wicked people have the courage to burn the copies of the Constitution?

Surprisingly, they had the audacity to publicly burn copies of the Indian Constitution. The Dalits people and the intelligent class were agitated, but the ruling people responsible for saving the Constitution looked indifferent; why?

The intention of the ruling government to protect the law became suspect in the eyes of Aajivak Babu. When the law was in danger, what meaning did democracy have? Going through this ideological conflict, a tricky question popped in Aajivak Babu's mind. If what he feared happened, only some autocratic political masters and their pet crowd, the herd of sheep and some chaotic elements would survive.

The answer to the questions was scary for Aajivak Babu. He saw that less than a quarter of the country's conscious population were being called villains for their different thinking. These people who disagreed with the government had already been listed as traitors. Would they be sent to Pakistan? Would they be sent to gas chambers, like the Jews in Nazi Germany? Would thousands of people be killed like in the genocides of 1984 or 2002?

Aajivak Babu still clung to hope. "Is there any possibility that the politicians may abstain from destroying the Constitution and start respecting it? Of the election process to be freed from the grip of the money mafia so that any responsible citizen could have a dream of contesting elections? Could the country's constitutional institutions stand with a healthy spine to strengthen the Constitution? Could there be any possibility to ensure the sanctity of the law, and should there be public awareness against narrow-mindedness and conservative beliefs? Everyone may understand his responsibilities to be loyal to them. And never be a bier, the *janazah* of anyone, whether it's a politician, a muscleman or maybe the Almighty God itself.

❑

TEN

The stupidity of the language and actions of star campaigners in the election had overtaken that of the street born *tapories*, the ruffians. On the one hand, the mercury was rising day by day, and on the other, the election campaign was breaking its old records but setting new records in indecency. As a result, Aajivak Babu did not have the courage to even watch TV. He also did not give in to the fascination of looking at the headlines of the newspaper.

Aajivak Babu found it meaningless to discuss such topics in his neighbourhood. Each person was either a blind follower of a party or a supporter of a dead leader. The issues of Hindu-Muslim fundamentalism and caste groups had become so substantial that pride in the country had vanished from day-to-day life. The famine of human values had spoiled the blissfulness of the weather.

In this dangerous weather of political turmoil, Dr Tarun's phone provided relief like a pleasant gust of wind. Aajivak Babu felt each word of the phone call, a soothing effect in his state of nervousness.

"Satish Gautam is coming to see me. If you can spare some time, accompany him. It would be nice if all three of us could meet."

Aajivak Babu jumped at this opportunity as he was bored. Happily, he agreed to meet them.

"I'll let you know after I speak to Gautam." Aajivak Babu told Dr Tarun. He then dialled Gautam's number. Finding his phone constantly engaged, Aajivak Babu had to dial his mobile number several times and finally succeeded in talking to him.

Though the meeting was scheduled at two o'clock, out of sheer habit, Gautam reached fifteen minutes late. Aajivak Babu had to stand in the sweltering heat at the bus stop for a quarter of an hour. Aajivak Babu found corruption and tardiness the common characteristics of everyday life, as if both of them were an integral part of Indian culture. Raising questions over these two issues was hazardous, like throwing a big pebble in the smooth running of clear waters of the river. He was often mentally prepared to face such challenges anyway.

Since Aajivak Babu had understood the compulsion of the Indian culture well, he avoided questioning anyone if they were not on time. He thought of two reasons for this lack of punctuality. One was the lack of quality management of time, and the other was the ignorance of the importance of time. He observed that liberation from corruption and tardiness, was not the priority of the present generation.

Aajivak Babu did not compromise in both these situations because of his inbuilt sense of punctuality. Hence, paying for the price of the tardiness of others had become his destiny. In weddings, Aajivak Babu often returned home without enjoying the banquet as there would be a delay. So, he didn't react to Gautam's lack of punctuality even though it disturbed him a lot. He knew that any such a reaction would spoil the fun of their meeting, which Aajivak Babu couldn't afford at any cost. Gautam purchased bottles of cold drinks from a grocery shop on the road. Dr Tarun was waiting for them at his house. He welcomed Aajivak Babu and Gautam heartily.

All the three bottles were opened together, cheers was said and gulps of the drink enjoyed. Gautam made a naughty remark, "See how much fun it is to have a drinks party. I don't know why people enjoy drinking alcohol. It tastes so bitter."

"It's a matter of the choice of an individual. Don't people eat bitter gourd? Bitter gourd is bitter. But in the case of alcohol, the first couple of pegs taste bitter, and then it becomes sweet as it becomes intoxicating; in that case, it does not matter whether it is sweet or bitter." Dr Tarun said, even though he never drank to the point where he was addicted to it. “But that does not mean that I support drinking. I am just responding to what you said.”

Gautam never surrendered so quickly; hence mockingly, he played his trump card. To justify his point, he said, “Who eats bitter gourd daily; but there is no harm in eating bitter gourd occasionally.”

“The same rule applies to *daroo* or alcohol. Daroo is not drunk daily, and the one who drinks every day wonders if he is a normal human being or a sick person. It is a matter of choice; some like sweet things, and others bitter. What difference does it make?”

Gautam nodded his head and said, “I don’t believe this argument. This logic makes no sense anyway.”

Aajivak Babu chimed in in support of Dr Tarun. “Chilly has a burning taste, and it is hot, then why do people eat it every day? And not just once in a day, people eat it several times a day.”

Gautam laughed out aloud and said “I won't agree with you. Both of you are in support of daroo. You are both fake Ambedkarites. I am real, an Ambedkarite; neither do I drink nor support it. You are fakes.” The trio laughed at this. Gautam changed the subject.

“Now, you both keep quiet. I have heard enough in support of daroo. Now listen to what I have to say. There is trouble in my office.” On seeing the dubious looks on their faces, Gautam continued, “There is a new director in our office. She calls me several times a day in her cabin and candidly discusses making India a Hindu nation. She talks of Hindu Rashtra Nirman Mahasabha (Hiranim). She wants to build India a Muslim free nation and a nation free from Christians as well."

"What does that mean? Dr Tarun's eyes wide opened with surprise. But Aajivak Babu remained silent, staring at Gautam's face.

"Yes, sir, I am right. All this has been going on openly in our office since the new boss joined the office."

Before Gautam could conclude his point, Dr Tarun gave his unsolicited opinion. "Restrict yourself to the office, and don't give any response. There is a popular saying, 'Boss is always right'. I have seen their world of dominance. Whether the case is official or unofficial, keep out of it. The same is the case with policemen; neither their friendship nor their enmity is worth accepting. Stay away or you'll get entangled in one issue or the other, one day. These officers have hundreds of handcuffs to rein in your ego. So, keep a distance, and there is no need to become an Ambedkarite; to be over enthusiastic. Keep the office away from your Ambedkarism. Never let your office and personal world meet."

Dr Tarun spoke aggressively. It seemed as if Gautam had touched a sore spot. After fiery eloquence, Dr Tarun was a little embarrassed.

Gautam's addressing Dr Tarun as '*Sahabji*' was an indicator of the general situation. Gautam usually addressed

Dr Tarun as '*Sahabji*', but when he was caught in a debate, he forgot '*Sahabji*'. Gautam went on to say, "*Sahabji*, you are late in giving your opinion. Now, this consultation is worthless."

'Why? What do you mean?"

"The thing is, I am already involved in this discussion with my boss. For ten or fifteen minutes, I listened to her avoiding any participation. I was silent, but at some point, I could not remain silent. Whatever is to happen will be seen." While Gautam was making his point, a strange void was visible in his eyes. There was a shadow of helplessness visible on his face.

The next moment, the atmosphere filled with silence, and the trio looked into each other's faces.

Now, Aajivak Babu got to know the purpose of today's meeting. Gautam wanted some words of consolation and guidance from Dr Tarun and Aajivak Babu. He perhaps wanted to take advantage of their experiences related to such situations. Dr Tarun and Aajivak Babu were well aware of Gautam's short temper. He couldn't resist from giving his views on Ambedkarism and Buddhism and was caught up in new controversies every day.

Aajivak Babu recalled Gautam's visit to his house the previous Saturday. Then the issue was Facebook, and there was excellent communication between the two. Though the problem was severe, the atmosphere was humorous. There was no dispute, and the matter was not as problematic as today's. The whole episode of last Saturday's conversation was alive in front of his eyes. Another episode of Hindu Rashtra Nirman Mahasabha (Hiranim) related to Facebook and its troll team. Aajivak Babu had warned him to be cautious about the activities of Hiranim.

"In the world of democracy, Facebook has a remarkable existence. Why ensnare Facebook, time and again? Learn to judge the direction of the wind's current, dear. If you flutter your wings like the name of democracy in the regime of a new mood, you will become traitors and be exported to Pakistan without a passport. Hey brother, whether the trolls have no faces to show or hearts to feel, don't shrink from showering 'likes' on Facebook. Even if the post is on mob-lynching, murder, accident, illness or any hospitalisation, they don't bother to distinguish but touch 'like' button liberally." Finding no reaction from Gautam, Aajivak Babu had continued, jokingly, "You reprimand those who tag you on their posts and warn to unfriend them. Dear, just look at the generosity of the gang, yet never forget to suffix 'like' whatever happens. Whether you get it or not, they impulsively use a bait to trap you. Whether you accept their hospitality or not; it is your choice. They keep on following their tradition of 'the guest is a form of a god'. Does anyone ever object to such a thing? Whether you like it or not, it is your choice to take it seriously or quit. They don't need to read your lengthy posts, but they don't bother to hand you over lollipops of 'like'. Have they ever forgotten to do so?"

Suddenly, Aajivak Babu had asked Satish Gautam, "Tell me... just tell me?" His face was bland, free from emotions but a little agitated. It was strange to know when the ideological river in Aajivak Babu flooded to overflow the shores. It seemed as if Aajivak Babu's drawing room had been converted into a classroom, and Satish Gautam alone represented a class of students.

His eyes were fixed on Satish Gautam's face. And it seemed as if he wanted to transmit the knowledge he had about Hiranim directly from his eyes into Satish Gautam's brain as a committed teacher.

They were lost in their own world, with no connections to anyone else. The furniture in the drawing room, curtains, windows, fan and lights all had lost their presence in the heat of conversation. There was nothing left between the two but words.

Satish was just as spellbound and did not utter a single word. His face indicated no expressions as the ECG showed the health of the heart of a person. This eternal silence on Gautam's part reminded one of the straight line that the cardiologists and doctors called by medical terms like 'dead' or 'no more'. And one could not say whether it was the pressure of the questions or the heat of Aajivak Babu's words, but Satish Gautam remained silent. Aajivak Babu then proceeded to re-establish his lifeline.

"No. It is not an appropriate solution to unfriend Facebook friends, the trolls or entangle them through Facebook dialogues. It is wrong to expect anything more from these mythical monkeys coving their eyes, ears and mouths. It would be an injustice to expect anything more from these trolls. The minister of animal rights can also land in the fray if it happens. It wouldn't be a healthy practice." Aajivak Babu further intervened, smiling, "Well, it is better, dear, just to keep out of these communal flames."

Aajivak Babu made his point as follows. "It is because of these lovers of 'like' on Facebook that the governments are throned or dethroned these days. They are the protectors of the cow mother. Turning into mobs, they make the dreams of political masers come true, isn't it something like that?"

After such a long dialogue, Aajivak Babu recalled that Satish Gautam had finally gained a foothold on the ideological river bank. Now his lifeline was no longer a straight line; it moved up and down in the graph. The expressions on his face could be easily read. He had left the Facebook world in the ideological river. But now, his ideas were stuck on the issue of government formation. He asked, "How do the people fond of 'likes' on Facebook, throne or dethrone the government? It is beyond my comprehension. The puzzle is beyond my understanding, Aajivak Babu."

In the present-day situation, Aajivak Babu remembered what he had talked of about Hindu Rashtra Nirman Mahasabha (Hiranim) with Satish Gautam last Saturday. He continued further, "Hindu Rashtra Nirman Mahasabha (Hiranim) is an organisation that acts as a lifeline to the streets, school colleges, offices and media houses. Twitter, Facebook, WhatsApp etc., nothing in the world is left where it doesn't have its dominance and accessibility.

This organisation seems to be a modern version of Hitler's propaganda minister, Paul Joseph Goebbels and works on the pattern to transform lies into truths. It probably works faster than that."

He recalled that the discussion was not over as Satish Gautam had received a phone call and he had to get back home. Aajivak Babu returned to the present from the journey of the past. He looked at Satish Gautam and Dr Singh to know the focus of their discussion. Aajivak Babu had realised that he had missed nothing substantial out of this conversation. He soon figured whatever was going on between Dr Tarun and Satish Gautam. Now again, he was an active participant in the trio.

The issue of Satish Gautam's office couldn't be ignored. Anyway, it wasn't an appropriate option. Whatever damage it could cause had already happened, but it was the sole responsibility of the trio to stop further harm, if any. Sitting idle was no solution, and no responsible person could afford to anyway. That's why Dr Tarun questioned, "Gautamji, just share the whole episode in detail in the same sequence of the happenings. What did your director say? And how did you respond?" While Dr Tarun was raising queries, he was somewhat bothered. He was bothered perhaps because Gautam was paying no heed to whatever he was told time and again to avoid such problems.

Gautam strained a little to recall the conversation sequence and then began repeating the director madam's episode very sincerely. "It was what she said in that particular meeting, 'Gautamji, you should vote in favour of the present government. The head of this government is the one who wants to make Hindustan free from Muslims and Christians. It is imperative to save the ancient Indian culture. These Muslims and Christians can anyway, never be true patriots.' She gave an instance of a Muslim saying that she asked question to that Muslim that if had to choose between the Constitution of India or the Quran, what would be his first choice? Then in a dramatic style, she asked me if I could you guess what the answer was? Without waiting for my response, she told me that he preferred the Quran with a scornful face. 'Just see the mentality, the country that feeds these traitors, those who have no respect for its Constitution. Just think, Gautam, to make India free from Muslims, who should you vote for if not the ruling party?'"

Gautam went on to say in pain of disagreement, "I could hear the pinching words no more and had no option left but to react. After all, there is a limit to everything; just let me know what you could have done in such a situation?" Gautam looked into Dr Tarun's eyes, hoping for some sympathy.

"I can understand your position, but just let me know as to how you responded. Without knowing your exact response, it is impossible to understand the intensity of the issue." Dr Tarun was impatient to know Gautam's answer. But it was strange on the part of Aajivak Babu to be silent and mysterious.

"I said nothing offensive if you are keen to know the whole truth." He took a long breath and repeated his exact words, "I said, 'Sorry, Madam, I am of a different opinion on this issue. I beg pardon if you permit me to ask the same question in a little different frame as to what would you prefer—the Constitution of India or the Bhagavad Gita'?"

"She had replied indiscriminately, 'Bhagavad Gita, the most sacred epic of more than eighty per cent Hindus. It is no less than the Constitution of India, the belief of the majoritarian religion'."

"At her arrogant attitude, I could have just said, 'I am too small to comment over such issues.' I dared not say, 'What is the difference between you and the Muslim whom you are calling a traitor?' I couldn't say neither book could be of greater importance than the Constitution of India. But one comment that I ought not to have made in this current political environment is that I would vote to favour Social Justice Party (SJP). In fact, I also made an unnecessary statement that it is our party and you should vote for the SJP because the chief of this party is a woman. If the women don't come forward for their empowerment, then who else will? I just said so and returned to my seat without waiting for her response."

Dr Tarun was not satisfied with what Gautam had done. He was upset but controlled his anger. He suggested to him, "I am not happy with what you have done. What was the need for you to advise her on whom she should cast her vote for? The simple answer is that vote casting is personal and confidential. Why don't you understand the people associated with Hindu Rashtra Nirman Mahasabha? I mean

'Hiranim' have an unquestionable dictatorship." He paused a little then continued further, "If it wasn't so, she couldn't have reacted in such an autocratic manner. It would be best if you had avoided such controversies. That is why they have become synonymous with the government. Anyway, one thing to keep in mind is there is no need to join any such dialogue. Keep in mind; never mix office and personal life. If you bring the office to your home, the home affairs will be in trouble, and if you take the house to the office, the office affairs will be in trouble."

When Dr Tarun finished, Aajivak Babu could not resist adding, "Gautamji, I simply want to add one more thing. The matter is not confined to your office. Nowadays, this is the situation in the entire country. The open dictatorship of the Hiranim is present in all offices. Police and administration work as if under Hiranim. The present government and the subordinate media follow its guidelines. I would even say that the goons of the streets enjoy undeclared power."

Gautam didn't question what was said to him in this present situation of chaos. Despite this episode, he put another event forward to establish that the problem in his office was not as bad as they feared. Referring to the celebration of Dr Ambedkar's birth anniversary on 14 April in his office, Gautam commented, "The two IAS officers in our office bestowed great honour on Dr Ambedkar, beyond my expectation. Both the officers emphasised reading Dr Ambedkar's philosophy to adopt their ideals in life. They also told us that they had also ordered books on Dr Ambedkar on Flipkart to know something more about him." Gautam made this statement out of excitement and enthusiasm.

He remarked further, "I'm very impressed to hear them say beautiful words in his honour. Despite the ideological differences, such a positive and inspiring gesture is worth appreciable."

Aajivak Babu puckered his brow. But still, he allowed Gautam to conclude. Whatever Gautam said was a challenge to the basic understanding of Dr Ambedkar's philosophy. Aajivak Babu tried to lean back in his chair and relax, but the emotions in him spewed out like the lava from a volcano. "Brother Gautam, you will feel awkward, but I am bound to say that you have failed even on the first step of Baba Sahab's philosophy, which is to 'be educated'. Then what does the second and third step that is 'struggle' and 'stay organised', mean for a person like you, the educated and the writer?"

Gautam wanted to say something before Aajivak Babu concluded his statement. Still, the ideological storm in Aajivak Babu was so massive that he didn't give him a chance to stand in the way. His words burst out in a storm. "It is natural for you to feel bad, but let me complete first. Then you are free to react the way you like. I won't interrupt you at all."

Gautam had no option but to wait till Aajivak Babu finished talking. Gautam's body language indicated that the harsh remarks he was facing were making him uncomfortable. It was such a severe situation that Aajivak Babu had to make harsh remarks, and Gautam was not being spared. Aajivak Babu was already infamous for his caustic comments. So he reacted with no consideration that he was one of his close friends.

"Gautamji, first of all, let's assume that there is a big gulf between the preaching and practice of the serpents sheltered by organisations like Hiranim. Secondly, according to your statement, both the IAS officers ordered books from Flipkart and advised all that Dr Ambedkar should be read. How can you assume that they had read the books themselves? Isn't it the hypocritic character of the duo? Just let me know, can Dr Ambedkar be understood with the help of a single book that a couple of officers have ordered? If they had the slightest respect for Dr Ambedkar, could your director even describe the Bhagavad Gita as being above the Constitution of India? But she still described the Bhagavad Gita as being above the Constitution."

"If your director madam had any commitment to the Constitution of India and Dr Ambedkar, she wouldn't have asked you to vote in favour of any individual or government. Would she dare talk, sitting in a government office, of liberating the country from Muslims and Christians? Then, how can anyone be trustworthy? Dr Ambedkar's fundamental principle, 'be educated', talks about opening the layers of the truth. It talks about stopping someone from becoming a fool. It speaks of the optimum use of the power of reasoning. It talks about keeping oneself in an experimental state and about contemporary decision-making and reasonable conduct. Now, tell us whether your prejudiced officers deserve to be appreciated."

Gautam now seemed to understand Aajivak Babu's point of view. In response to Aajivak Babu's words, Gautam tried to console him by saying, "I was talking about his words; I didn't pay attention to the intentions."

"Gautam Bro, words have no significance if they are hollow and are free from the guts of reality. If you eat jaggery (raw sugar) yourself and preach to others of its demerits and tell them not to eat, your preaching will remain a sermon. It can never turn into reality. The same thing applies to the serpents and their parental organisations like Hiranim." Aajivak Babu glanced at Dr Tarun to know his views on the matter.

"I fully agree with what you are talking of to prove your point of view." Dr Tarun said, quoting Aajivak Babu's pet dialogue of 'mindless mob and sheep'

"I would also like to tell Gautam that we are neither the crowd nor the sheep. We are responsible citizens of the country with all reasonable discretion. We are no way in the trade of Hindu-Muslim politics at all."

As Dr Tarun concluded, it was Gautam's turn to react. "Well, dear sirs, I have made a mistake; forgive me now." Gautam mockingly said, as usual, to sum up the meetings. "I felt attacked in such a way that I feared if there would be any hairs left on my skull at the end of the session or not."

Gautam's words made the trio laugh, and the meeting ended with the decision that they would meet regularly every week. It lightened their mind and they could have healthy discussions on current issues. On Gautam's concluding note, not only was their meeting over, but the trio took their bags and left together.

Dr Tarun was not confident of driving a vehicle on his own, but this was not the case with Gautam and Aajivak Babu. It was by chance that both of them had reached Dr Tarun's house by bus today. Soon, all three reached the bus stand on foot, making general conversation. On the arrival of the buses, Gautam and Aajivak Babu boarded their respective buses and went home. However, Aajivak Babu could not save himself from the felony storm of Hiranim and returned home with an agitated mind.

❑

ELEVEN

Though several days had passed since their meeting, the storm that had set in Aajivak Babu's mind due to Hindu Rashtra Nirman Mahasabha (Hiranim) showed no signs of abating. The master campaigners of the election had fooled the country and the public had turned into the mindless crowd.

Aajivak Babu felt very upset and listless. He somehow managed to carry on with his daily routine and other activities of worldliness. However, when night fell, Aajivak Babu felt imprisoned in the unlawful custody of Hiranim. This unshackled imprisonment had no bounds. The darkness of Hiranim's world terrified Aajivak Babu, and this dreadful situation troubled him the entire night to find the alternative and nothing else.

The array of questions didn't let him get a wink of sleep. For instance: 'Are the people of Hiranim insensitive and heartless? Don't they understand the sufferings and humiliation of others? Does it cause any harm to them if others have different views and religious beliefs from them? Are these Aryans of history terrified of the country's aboriginals who don't believe in their corrupt ideological beliefs sheltered by violent and oppressive mentality? Do they see the inheritor of Saindhav culture in them, so are the permanent enemies? Do they wish to make their hollow patriotism real by shouting and echoing slogans like *Vande Mataram and Bharat Mata ki jai* and want to be the natural heir of this country?'

The journey of his queries took him to the past. 'Do the people of Hiranim want to change history on the pretext of making the country a Hindu nation? Do the inheritors of an Aryan culture feel insecure even after living for thousands of years together? Are they afraid of being displaced from the country and being labelled intruders? Or do they fear their superiority, what they have imposed over the aboriginals over hundreds of years, would be threatened?'

He retuned back to the present to look into the mind of Hiranim and its people. 'Do they want to become different types of rulers and the owners of the country? Do they intend for the Dalits, Christians and Muslims of today who are more or less oppressed and exploited to make them a different kind of subject? Do they want to form a Hindu nation based on violence, arson, rape and exploitation? Do they want to recreate a new variety of Dalits and tribals for the new country by repeating history under the guise of the founding of the Hindu nation?'

Many real, false, fictitious or baseless questions kept taking different shapes in his mind. He suspected the hidden agenda of Hiranim; the documents of their secret plan. He undoubtedly understood that the people of Hiranim had no ability to empathise with anyone's pain. Because they were not human beings, they were inanimate machines and worked like machines. Obviously, for a machine, the country and its patriotic norms were not like that of a human being. But a computer has nothing to do with the universal perception of the country and patriotism.

Aajivak Babu got an intuition that in the schools of Hiranim, human beings were turned into machines or robots. The school of thought, under Hiranim, worked at the national level. The software programming in these robots was done so that there was no room for human emotions like compassion, empathy and affection. The first and the foremost goal of the school of thought of Hiranim was to make India a Hindu nation, whatever cost the country had to pay for this. This has been going on for decades using all popular tools, whether fair or foul, to achieve the target.

After a sleepless night, the dawn brought optimism. Aajivak Babu used Google to learn more about the world of robots. There, he got surprising information. A robot named SAM claimed to be the first leader robot in New Zealand. It was also contended that the leader robot SAM would participate in New Zealand's electoral fight at the end of 2020.

But the following information available on Google Baba about the robot was shocking for Aajivak Babu. As a result of this information, Aajivak Babu was appalled by his ignorance about India's achievement. This was an embarrassment for him. This achievement was hundreds of years old as Google said, 'Even in the ancient scriptures of India, robots are mentioned. And if we talk of the Ramayana, Sita (the queen of Rama, the king of Ayodhya), while she was in exile, went to fetch water with her son Luv one day. Sage Valmiki in whose ashram she was living thought that the wilds animal had eaten Luv; so he built a child, Kush, with grass, resembling Luv.'

It is incredible that the grass child later became a lively character in the epic Ramayana and is still known as Kush, the real brother of Luv, the second son of king Ram Chandra. The disciples of the Hiranim school of thought strongly claimed such technology was available a thousand years ago at the time of Ramayana. It was many more steps ahead of the invention of the robot. Having known of this miracle, Aajivak Babu felt a satirical beam sparkle in his mind as it may be a conspiracy against India to deny such an outstanding historical achievement.

He smiled a little while, whispering, "That's why New Zealand's achievement is being boasted of by denying India's unique achievement. It is a conspiracy to keep India from being a world leader, which is one of the most popular claims of the Hiranim school of thought. If it is not a conspiracy against India, what else can it be?"

On the same pattern, Aajivak Babu first started exploring the present to rectify his ignorance He used the spectacles of Hiranim to view the whole episode and found that New Zealand's 'Leader Robot' Sam was a part of the conspiracy to call it the world's first 'leader robot'. He felt that the New Zealanders had stolen our formula for making a 'leader robot'. Our two largest 'leader-robots' MAS work brilliantly at the national and international levels. They changed our double robots 'M' and 'A S' to SAM, the single one. Instead of the two, they will make the one 'leader robot' in 2020 that is SAM; it is not yet entirely made. But we have had the two for decades. Is the claim of the invention of SAM not purely a shallow copy of existing Indian robots?

We may have two robot leaders, 'M' and 'A S', but both are perfect. Both of them work to implement the software programme produced by Hiranim. They have nothing to do with human-like sentiments, fair or foul and ethics. That is why the business of Hindu-Muslim and mob-lynching is getting grossly profitable nowadays, even at the national level. Under this culture, public speaking continues to silence everything disagreeable to the mighty ears. The constitutional institutions are on the ventilator.

While Aajivak Babu was lost in the world of robots, Aajivak Babu's pet Roby snored nearby. The snoring was in no way different from that of human beings Roby reminded Aajivak Babu of his presence. Perhaps Roby's integrity began to make Aajivak Babu's focus shift from Hiranim and his robotic world to Roby's world.

Aajivak Babu could not ignore Roby's presence. He felt like Roby, and his relationship had a familiar resemblance with the relationship between Hindu Rashtra Nirman Mahasabha, the Hiranim and its robotic army. But Aajivak Babu observed the only difference that separated the two. Roby and the robot army of Hiranim had to live for their masters and die for their masters as well. Both had no personal life or pleasures. Roby's fraternity was his worst enemy, whereas the world of robots was united. Hiranim software was the masterpiece, and its programming of mutual nexus was marvellous and created havoc all over India.

Aajivak Babu went on to post-mortem the world of robots. He realised that the Hiranim robots stood at the forefront at all levels. They were well connected to the government's private departments in the country. May it be any small and most significant educational institution or any state or national university; the robots of Hiranim were dominating the scene. The government and the media houses had become their secure shelters. Religion and religious organisations were bunkers that provided them with security and convenient platforms to keep them agitated for the attacks and terror-prone environment against their opponents.

Aajivak Babu was in constant pain. And he felt it had become the destiny of the others who loved the country. It is not known how long Aajivak Babu kept thinking, but it was certain that such contemplations had become a regular feature which caused sleepless nights.

The following day, Aajivak Babu received a phone call from Manish Kumar Shukla, popularly known as M K

Shukla. Having learnt of Aajivak Babu's recent movements, there was a question from the other side, "Sir, aren't you busy today?"

"Why, what's it, brother? Why are you asking this? Is there anything special?" Aajivak Babu asked curiously.

"No sir, there's no such thing. Today, my brother and I are coming to come to see a flat in your area. The idea is to buy a flat for my younger brother. We decided to kill two birds with a single stone; seeing the flat and meeting you. I have not met you in a long time."

Aajivak Babu also welcomed the idea enthusiastically, saying, "Well, we shall meet on the pretext of seeing the flat, at least." The conversation was cut off with a loud laugh.

Aajivak Babu informed Shalini that they were to expect two guests that day. The arrival of guests was in direct proportion to an increase in the activities in the kitchen. This increase depended on the warmth of the relationship between the guest and the host. Shalini knew both of them very well. The two were among the peers of Aajivak Babu, whose ideological beliefs were similar to those of Aajivak Babu. The country and its interests were paramount, and the same was the case with human values for the trio. It was as though they had inherited this principle of never compromising their ideology.

The two knocked on the door at about 1 a.m. Aajivak Babu opened the door. They all shook hands and hugged each other. They felt as though they had found something precious, what had been lost for years. It was an ecstasy of the mind and heart.

Shalini was alerted by the ringing of the doorbell. Within seconds, she greeted the guests with a tray carrying glasses of water. Both the visitors greeted her with great respect, and Shalini greeted them with a familiar smile. Shalini's familiarity with both visitors was such that instead of Aajivak Babu, Shalini addressed the two and asked the first question.

"Would you prefer a cold or hot drink?"

"Something hot would be nice, Madam."

After she left the room, they started conversing. No one had prepared any questionnaire for anyone. But it was automatically decided that the conversation graph would oscillate between local and global issues. The first question came from Manish. "How is your health, sir? How are you occupying yourself, I mean after retirement?"

Through the question was raised by Manish, but Aajivak Babu saw a repetition of the same in Rajendra's eyes. However, it was very relevant to ask the question as Aajivak Babu had retired almost two years ago.

Aajivak Babu felt that phone calls, the smartphones and the digital world were no match to the happiness gained from face-to-face talk. It is said that bathing in the rain is natural, but it is not easy to take a bath in rain every day. So enjoying this mood of comfort, the smile on the face of Aajivak Babu made things evident. "I am very content. Need I say anything about my health?"

"You both know so well that I am in the habit of reading and writing. It is a kind of addiction now. Hence all my spare time is dedicated to this addiction now. Once I sit down on my computer to write, I don't know how time passes. Life is quite busy nowadays. It's my choice, so I do a lot of things. You also know that I don't write on paper these days; I write directly on the computer screen, I mean digitally. Hence, there is little chance of going back and forth. It is the books and computers that have become my new world."

Aajivak Babu asked, smiling, "Manish Babu, whose government are you supporting this time? Give us your opinion." There was no need for such a question while they were working together and had regular meetings, but now things had changed. Therefore, it had become necessary to ask this question.

Keeping an eye on Rajendra and without waiting for Manish Babu's response, Aajivak Babu said, "Manish Babu predicted the previous two governments. So, I am asking the question of whether his old stand is still intact or there is some change this time."

There was a different story behind asking this question of Manish Babu. During the last elections, Manish Babu often argued in support of the National Secular Party (NSP) at the centre and Janata Janardan Party (JJP) for the state. He always presented irrefutable arguments to support his point of view. At times, Manish Babu was also aggressive to some extent. Aajivak Babu could get such pieces of information directly or through his colleagues in a natural way.

Aajivak Babu has never been a party in such political discussions. He did not do it today as well. He just discussed issues and was never judgemental. It was not part of his vocabulary as to what to do or not and for whom one should cast his vote. On the other, Manish Babu used to be judgemental on such occasions; and made a hullabaloo in support of his favourite party.

Aajivak Babu was very fond of his honesty and fairness. But when any policy matters were messed up and or an elected candidate did something wrong, Aajivak Babu did not forget to remind Manish Babu. He didn't forget to pull his leg one way or the other. Manish Babu's sincerity did not make him hesitate to criticise the government and his stand with the right side. This sincerity and integrity continued to be an essential foundation for deepening bilateral relations. Today's question was also an excuse for Aajivak Babu to test his loyalty to his commitments.

Manish Babu had not changed his choice even today, but his arguments were reversed. Manish Babu, while defending himself, said, "Sir, I consider Mukesh Raghav to be a very dim-witted man for MP, totally ineligible. He did nothing for the public of the area. He has no vision, nor does he intend to do something for our region. But still, I will give my vote to the NSP as the NSP has a tough leader at the centre. He is a reliable alternative to the post of PM. On the contrary, the opposition does not have a strong leader for the position of PM. So, I will not vote for the opposition."

Aajivak Babu, in his response, said, "Manish Babu, I disagree with your argument. Now it's time not to vote for the party but the right candidate. If we vote for a qualified candidate, the offenders or those with irresponsible mindsets will not be in the parliament. The same way this action of the voters would rein in the candidates who reach the parliament based on the power of money."

He added further to silence any further query, "There may be some problems in the beginning. But deserving and sensible people will find an appropriate alternative to form the government collectively, and it will be in the country's interest. Another significant advantage is that even a common man, who has neither muscle power nor money, can dream of contesting elections. And can contribute to the peace and progress of the country. I think it is essential to take such steps to re-establish democracy which has become a mere spectacle today."

Rajendra Kumar, directly associated with the JJP, had direct links with the party's top office-bearers. He was an active activist and a staunch supporter of his party. The bitter reality was that JJP and NSP had a 'snake and a weasel' relationship. They never missed any chance of attacking each other for political gains. Aajivak Babu spoke in a simple, restrained manner. But Rajendra Kumar came into the fray with his ammunition and said, "Not only Mukesh Raghav, but your favourite and the loved one is one of the biggest liars and a fraud. The entire NSP has become a new example of goons' paradise in today's election. There seems to be a competition among them as to who are better liars." Rajendra Kumar's facial expressions had changed completely. He seemed to say more than that, but Manish Babu was not accustomed to hearing such criticism and jumped in the fray to make his point.

"Which party or leader does not violate the set norms and code of conduct? All of them have risen in power on the basis of bullying. Then, it is wrong to be biased about a party. Your party JJP is in no way different as it had claimed to be, to come in power. It is the most upbeat at juggling and making false accusations against others. Only because of these false allegations could they form the government. Otherwise, who cares about such people anyway? I don't know how many such crooks have come and gone the same way. If your leader is true, why does he ask for forgiveness in different cases? Therefore, it is not fair to make personal allegations."

When the boxers in the ring violate the rules, the referee's intervention is necessary. In the present situation, the role of Aajivak Babu was no more than a referee between Manish Babu and Rajendra Kumar as he had to keep the rule position intact and simultaneously by putting his job clear.

"Look, brothers, I think this blame game is not going to help anyone. It is necessary to see the root cause to begin with, and reach a proper conclusion. Wrong is never right, but if the other piles up the wrongs to compete with the other in a race, none can be right in such cases. In such a situation, both are guilty, and the only difference may just be in degrees, one person who is more guilty than the other. It requires us to review step by step and analyse in totality to conclude."

"Secondly, it is not as important as the one who let the tongue loose first; the bigger question is what is being messaged in public by the rhetoric of the leaders. What impact it is creating on society and the nation. And the most significant issue is what image of the nation it will make in the world community. We must stand with any leader or party by seriously bearing in mind such questions. Otherwise, there can be no difference between an intellectual and the devotees of the crowd, can there be?"

While making his point, the pain that the current political situation was causing him was visible on Aajivak Babu's face. In any case, Aajivak Babu didn't know the art of hiding his emotions. The reality was reflected in his body language. But it was a pleasant feeling that Aajivak Babu had managed to stop the debate going in the wrong direction. It was a relief for all three.

Meanwhile, Shalini appeared with tea, snacks and some sweets. It provided them with a break in the flow of the current subject.

Sipping tea, Aajivak Babu turned to be a little philosophical in tone. He addressed the duo as *Bandhuwar*, "Even if the road is full of thorns, the right kind of shoes can help us carry out the journey. But when the spines are inside the shoes, the idea of reaching the target turns to be a fool's paradise." He looked into the eyes of both and continued further, "Nowadays, we are going through a period where the condition of the co-partner of the political journey, I mean the commoner, is worse than that of the shoes, to reach the destination. Hence there is no progress and prosperity at all. It is mere rhetoric to carry the garbage of the past and smear it on the face of the present for political gain. A bitter reality is that those who do not have a present can have no future. I am sorry to say that we, as responsible citizens of the country, are victims of the present and have no future secured. The political situation is alarming, but I find no beam of light to pierce the extreme dark of the present."

Both Rajendra Kumar and Manish Kumar understood where the focus of Aajivak Babu's concern was. But Manish Babu, did not summon the courage to speak against the present regime. It was a matter of surprise for Aajivak Babu. He did not understand why Manish Babu, infamous for making such ugly and open remarks, was silent today. Had he got into the nexus with the advocates of building the Hindu nation? Was he beginning to feel comfortable with the Hindutva agenda to suit his caste and religion, the sole ideology of Hiranim? Had Manish Kumar become Hiranim's robot?

Aajivak Babu was entangled in the net of speculation. Rajendra interrupted by saying, "I know the horoscope of the one whom Manish Babu claims to be the most suitable watchdog of Indian democracy. If Manish Babu dares to listen, I am ready to explain."

Whether Manish Babu had become a 'Hiranim robot' or a part of the sheep was uncertain. But one thing was sure that he was still stinging on the courage of accepting any challenge. Noticeably, Manish Kumar took Rajendra Kumar's challenge and admitted that he would not interrupt until Rajendra completed. This trait of Manish Babu's personality is worth appreciable.

They had finished their tea by now. Before picking up the empty cups of tea, Shalini placed a platter of melon on the table. "Madam, the tea was delicious, and the sweets turned the meeting into a festival; I enjoyed it." Manish Kumar shared his heartfelt sentiments.

How could Rajendra Kumar be left behind in the race? He also made his best of the chance and spoke, "I was a little hungry now. I don't know how our stomach called out to you that you have fulfilled our wish without asking for it. Thanks a lot, Madam."

Shalin said, "It is our duty. You guys came after so long."

" *Sahab* has no time to spare for guys like us." remarked the guests. Aajivak Babu said, "The weather is notfavourable, and my book still has some work left. I will meet you again as soon as I am free. I do feel very eager to meet colleagues like you."

Shalini left, and the three returned to the unfinished point that Rajendra Kumar was going to make about the 'boss', the one who called himself, the humble servant of the public. The intervention caused by tea and melons didn't let them forget that Rajendra Kumar had to talk of the horoscope of the big boss. Rajendra Kumar revealed the whole propaganda of superiority. "This dictator whom you are calling the most capable person of democracy, is no more than a criminal. I just saw black lettered misdeeds on YouTube, which made all my old wounds bleed again."

"We must not be as judgemental as that. But yes, what is concerned should be said with a sense of responsibility, and it should be discussed from a positive point of view." Aajivak Babu spoke, intending to stop the boiling of the blood of Rajendra Babu's youthhood. However, Manish remained silent. Undoubtedly, he kept his word, not interrupting Rajendra until he completed.

"No, I don't intend to insult anybody, but sir, the reality is even more frightening. Let's see; the truth needs no explanation, does it? Take a look on your own." With these remarks, Rajendra Kumar played a YouTube video on his iPad.

It depicted one person, Raju Bajrangi. He had been held responsible for killing eighty-six people by the High Court. The person was talking about a mass massacre in 2002 in front of the camera. And proudly mentioned Sahib's name and the role that he played. "No one can do what he has done. Nothing could have been done without Sahib's support. Nobody else could have supported it. The police were standing in front, watching, doing nothing. They had their mouth shuts and eyes closed."

Meanwhile, a woman on camera said, "We heard voices—'Hit and kill, hit and kill, slay and kill, these Miyan brothers are not needed in India.'"

Another woman said, "My son was thrown into the blazing fire. They killed the women and humiliated and raped some of them."

Then a woman said, "Someone gagged my mouth, my clothes were torn, and some women were stripped naked. A pregnant woman who was standing with us. Her belly was cut off with a sword."

Bajrangi Bhai justified this barbaric act by saying, "We told her what it means to mess with the Hindus."

Another woman said, "My three-year-old daughter was thrown out of my lap and three people raped me. My family was killed in the presence of the crowd."

Bajrangi then boasted, "We are proud. Only one or two more chances are to come. Just one or two; the rest will be all right."

Another woman told her story, "We were coming in a tempo from Dharolan to Karolina. Anamika Society in Karol. Our tempo was halted at the Anamika Society in Karol and our men were killed. One of the man's legs was smashed, thrown into the tempo and set on fire by pouring kerosene on it. My clothes were torn. The police officers were not doing anything."

After seeing the video, everyone's face changed colour. Perhaps the agony of these tragic tragedies was on everyone's mind and heart. No one dared to even talk of it. Manish Kumar's face turned blank. There was no scope for any argument. Now the battle was in favour of Rajendra Kumar to win. He, therefore, went on to say that another so-called monk of the same National Secular Party had even spoken about the founding of the Hindu nation in public forums.

"The day when this nation will be Hindu, the country will come into the hands of Hiranim and young sages like us. Muslims will become second-class citizens. Their right to vote will be taken away. If they kill one Hindu, we will also kill a hundred Muslims. If they take a Hindu girl, we will take at least hundred Muslim girls."

"Now, you can see that the leadership of the country will be in the hands of people who are responsible for all kinds of communal riots. And the so-called sage mouths obscenities on public forums as to what the nation's future can be. If you remain silent on such terrible venom, does it simply not mean that Sahib is silent to the exploits of the Hindu nation producers? Is it not an alarming situation for Indian democracy? So, I used the term 'criminal' for the people of Sahib and his opportunists. Don't the actions point to a criminal mentality?" Rajendra had a victorious look while he made his concluding remark.

It was seven in the evening. Shalini felt that her husband and his guests might be hungry as they had been closeted together for six to seven hours. So she brought cheese and potato dumplings or *pakodas* for them. Though their drawing room was often used to welcome guests, today, it had been a venue for a debate. Aajivak Babu was delighted with Shalini's hospitality. It was a matter of pride for him too.

This third round of refreshments with tea and *pakodas* was not free from debate. Their conversation seemed like an introductory workshop of political researchers. But they were neither bored nor fatigued by it. Meanwhile, Manish Babu and Rajendra received calls from their houses.

Their meeting continued till 9:30 p.m. and ended with a note that no party was trustworthy and everyone had the same character, more or less. So, the important thing was that we shouldn't become a pawn to any political party or individual but act as a responsible citizen of the country. We should never be part of a flock of sheep, nor be insensitive robotic machines that political parties insisted that we be, to win the election. What if the voters worked precisely on the same pattern as politicians did and leave no stone unturned to evaluate their appropriate public representatives? In that case, we can end political filth to a great extent.

Finally, Aajivak Babu concluded the meeting. He did not want his companions to return home with any discord and so made a brief remark, "Whether it's appreciation or criticism, both have the advantages as both of them open the way to motivation and improvement."

❑

TWELVE

As decided by Satish Gautam in the previous meeting, this was the first Saturday for the trio of Satish, Aajivak Babu and Dr Tarun to meet. Satish Gautam had possibly chosen to discuss literature and current affairs on Saturday and held his first meeting at his home. He had already dedicated his Sunday to the Buddha Vihar of his colony. The credit went to Satish Gautam for carrying out the session. Gautam was an Ambedkarite and considered Buddhism an essential part of Ambedkarism. However, though Ambedkarism had been one of the critical priorities of Dr Tarun and Aajivak Babu, they had left their doors open for other ideologies as well.

Before going to the meeting, Aajivak Babu naturally had Hiranim's actions in his mind. He knew that the targets of Hiranim were Muslims, but this was not completely true. The truth was that Muslims and Christians, and converted Dalits were on their declared agenda. Dalits-—tribals and the other backward classes were on the second plan; the other backward classes or the OBCs were on the third undeclared agenda. In Aajivak Babu's eyes, Hiranim's one-point and secret programme was to make India free from all these aboriginal natives. This was the ultimate plan of the Aryans, the aim of Hindutva. Significantly, the three announced and undisclosed lists would be completed in three phases as part of their planned strategy. These three agendas were not a matter of concern for Aajivak Babu. His particular interest was the lack of awareness of these legends of the natives.

Aajivak Babu was convinced that the present government was working to take the agenda of Hiranim to make it a success. Today's media had taken the role of the private army of the regime. In support of Hiranim and the rule, the media was involved in secret guerrilla wars. The sting operation of Cobra Post in the eyes of Aajivak Babu is a living example of his actions. The sting operation scrapped the mask of hypocrisy from the face of the media and exposed it. As they were ready to run any story to widen the gulf between Hindus and Muslims.

Several newspapers and TV channels across the country agreed to run the news of the mutual confrontation of the Hindus and Muslim. The media was prepared to manipulate stories to defame the previous regimes and publicise their policies as anti-Hindu, rather anti-national. Forgetting the fundamental role of the media, it decided to repeat the old stories of the debate and make fun of the opposition parties. It agreed to accept a large sum of money as a bribe in cash and other forms convenient to it only to avoid tax, GST, etc.

The nexus between Hiranim and the existing ruling regime, Aajivak Babu felt, was the worst enemy to the peace of his mind. He was well aware that the upper brass of bureaucracy is from the stratum of the so-called upper caste, and the same was the picture of the party in rule. They were united to make one plus one eleven and nothing else. This situation was like killing two birds with a single stone. Consequently, the bureaucrats categorically stood by the regime through fair and foul. It gave them job security and on the other hand, satisfied their ego and established the supremacy of their caste. The same was the picture with the media houses. Aajivak Babu had no doubt that this nexus would work under the cover of caste and religion. And he didn't have much hope of applying balm on the wounds of the victims, the Dalits and the religious minorities, especially the Muslims, as the first target for establishing Hindu Rashtra.

It is not beyond Aajivak Babu's understanding as to how corporate houses were the fourth strong allies of this nexus. His analysis of how the communication, aviation and banking sectors were going bankrupt and the favourite corporate houses establishing their dominance pained him. Corporate houses were the moneylenders on hand and the debtors on the other. The economic interests of the regime and the media were under the table.

Ultimately, these were the trouble-shooters, and financial gods. This vicious cycle was crystal clear to Aajivak Babu, that works on the philosophy as 'you scratch my back and I yours'. With the grace of Ramji, the god, the government did not hesitate to take ride on the back of the army to grab power. The mere recitation of *Bharat Mata*, *Gau Mata* and *Ganga Maiya* with each breath was enough to prove their loyalty to the nation. The rest of the fellow citizens who were not part of this idiot's paradise, became traitors. He asked himself shockingly, "Is there anything left to corrupt democracy in the country now?"

Aajivak Babu knew very well who was behind Hiranim running the agenda of the Hindu Rashtra. He knew the silent forces keeping the constitutional bodies, the backbone of the Constitution, on a ventilator. On the contrary, Aajivak Babu knew who would be orphaned without constitutional institutions.

Aajivak Babu was frustrated with the behaviour of the victims who mindlessly browsed the social platforms like Facebook and WhatsApp and didn't raise their voice. But kept on blaming others for not having their representation in mainstream media. 'Media is *Manuvadi*' is another slogan frequently raised by these victims. Aajivak Babu raises a question over this blame game and asks a bitter question as to why we are becoming sacrificial goats for their sacrificial ceremonies. 'Why are we the ones digging our graves? And why are we waiting for our burial? Why?'

Aajivak Babu was entangled in the search for the answers storming his mind. In the meantime, the long-awaited mobile call came. The voice sounded from the other end, "I'm arriving within ten minutes." Aajivak Babu's guess was perfect. It was a phone call from Dr Tarun with a white beard as an identity of his impressive personality. Despite being over seventy, he was not willing to compromise on his charm.

"Okay, sir, please do come. Let's meet at the bus stand."

"Okay." Hearing the words from Dr Tarun, Aajivak Babu left for the bus stand. Aajivak Babu and Dr Tarun had to reach Gautam's house on foot from the bus stand. On reaching the destination, the duo settled themselves comfortably on the sofa in Satish Gautam's drawing room. Gossip was one of the healthiest parts of the refreshments. Finally, the trio came directly to the fundamental point of worldliness.

Satish was more excited this time than before. On Dr Ambedkar's birth anniversary, Satish was very enthusiastic about representing his colony at Parliament Street. Dr Tarun was not there because of his poor health, though Gautam and Aajivak Babu were all together at Parliament Street but did not share each other's experiences. Satish raised the issue again, proud of what he had done to mobilise the people of his neighbourhood for social awareness.

He said, "Now the people are happier to be part of Baba Saheb's birth anniversary at Parliament Street. Seeing the crowd there, I noted the change in their enthusiasm. The possibility of change cannot be ruled out. I think there is awakening. Now let's see how this seed of awareness grows." Gautam had a look of joy at the end of his remarks, and his eyes were particularly fixed on the face of Aajivak Babu. He was also looking to take stock of his body language before reacting.

Aajivak Babu smiled but could not conceal what was going on in his mind. He spoke, "I don't think the way you do, on this current development of activity. I know many people who are just confined to chanting Baba Saheb's speeches and writings. They quote whatever Dr Ambedkar has said and nothing else. Such people are missing the real spirit of the content, and they make his quotes mere slogans to shout on different occasions."

Breathing a little longer, he proceeded further, "You may disagree. But I believe that the person engaged in just shouting slogans doesn't have anything tangible of his own. Hollow slogans are not effective anymore. The person, who has done something in his credit, needn't raise any slogans; His shall sound louder than any hollow slogan. The episode you are talking of is no more than a crowd of people shouting slogans with nothing significant in their credit. I don't have much hopes from them. I am sorry to say that Dalit writers are simply literates and far better than this mindless crowd. Both are content with turning any serious event into a ritual with no strategic achievement."

Aajivak Babu was so upset about this activity that he didn't bother to wait for their response and continued analysing the way of celebrating the birth anniversary. "Every year, I observe that people just pounce upon food, and I feel that the real purpose of the event dies down under the garbage of different foodstuff. Nowadays, there is no shortage of other vendors. It is becoming a mini-*kumbh* of the *Dalits*, and the similar rituals have a bigger question on

Dalit intellect and philosophy of Buddhism. This crowd is directionless, free from leadership and remains a gathering with no big agenda. Nor is there any movement to shape it into a constructive achievement. I find it all a total waste of workforce, energy and time. Our sole concern must be to contemplate and not get mesmerised. It is my personal belief, and others needn't agree with it."

It turned into a monologue, but Aajivak Babu seemed not bothered by it in the least. Instead of knowing Satish's view and looking into Dr Tarun's eyes, he said, "Dr *Sahab*, tell me. On 14 April, there are food and drinks already scheduled, and if they are withdrawn, I don't feel the crowd will be there. However, I don't think that the slogans shouted by the group is more than an expression of momentary excitement. I wish to know your reaction to the issue. What do you say about this crowd and its enthusiasm in the absence of stalls of foodstuffs and drink?"

"I do agree with you to a more significant extent, but what are the options? But I believe there would be no moment if the so-called rituals were stopped. Anyway, I have no solid arguments in this matter because I have never thought of it before. Still, I agree with Gautamji that something is better than nothing. At least such actions are likely to pave the way ahead." Dr Tarun gave his opinion. Contrary to it, his response was a great relief to Gautam as it seemed to support him.

Aajivak Babu recalled Swamiji, a character in the movie 'PK', in the reaction extended by Dr Tarun. Swami advocated the people who refused God in the hour of need or in any disaster they were caught in. He justified it by saying that hopeful people are no harm because of God. If a man is saved from suicide, what harm is going to God's refuge? On the other hand, there is much courage to cope with the troubles. Aajivak Babu said, "If God's refuse is so fruitful , and then there is no scope of atheism and scientific temperament that leads to invention, Satish Babu, your arguments take us to the fantasy of falsehood. It is against Buddhism and Ambedkarism that you claim is your mission, isn't it?"

Aajivak Babu's rigid remarks ruined Gautam's castle of hope and achievement. It was enough to agitate Gautam to pour out whatever was boiling inside. "Aajivak Babu, I think you don't understand anybody. Perhaps you don't want to understand anything else. You always dismiss the other point of view. You just know to criticise. Maybe it is your pleasure. By the way, I would like to know what the way out of such a situation is. Just tell us what Aajivak Babu's philosophy is to deal with such an issue."

Aajivak Babu smiled a little on hearing Gautam's words. It was not the first time Gautam talked that way. Such a hot exchange of words was prevalent in almost every meeting. Both were well aware of it. But for more than twenty years, the two remained friendly and did not let such disagreements ruin their friendship.

So he made his point with tremendous ease. "You have a right to be angry, dear brother. But when a person takes refuge in a particular ritual; or shelters in a particular person and a book; or surrenders to a particular 'ism', then the life, the individuality, and identity of the person concerned, I mean the real self of the person loses his individuality and its sparkle. And the person turns to be merely a puppet of too many masters to serve. In such cases, there is no future of Ambedkarism, Buddhism, Lokayat and Charvak, which you are fighting for."

"As far as the question of the philosophy of Aajivak Babu is concerned, dear bro, I must confess that an ordinary man like me can have no philosophy. And, of course, I don't have any such philosophy at all. But I consider that a person must be the centre of activity of every individual. I believe that a 'healthy environment' is mandatory for a person, and it should be the first and foremost priority for all. A person should get abundant opportunity to be 'appo deepo bhava' meaning 'be an island unto yourself'. But in our case, it seems we are a true example of the saying 'we had gone to get our namaz forgiven, but roza, the fasts came to be a compulsion'."

He continued, "In terms of the canvas of vision, I view the person as a global citizen and not confined to the shackles of any streets, region or nation. I expect the same in the matter of discharge of duties of the individuals. Sorry, I find the condition of Ambedkarism and Buddhism no far better than 'the camel going to seek horns but lost his ears'. I must say that Ambedkarism and Buddhism are far from the individual's lifestyle. They have merely become a hardcore religion to observe the same pattern as the Hindus' fundamentalists in India."

Dr Tarun became vocal. "You are raising questions on the future of Ambedkarism and Buddhism. Away! Begone! Let's assume that your point is okay. The gathering at Parliament Street in the name of Ambedkar is more than that in the meetings of the Social Justice Party (SJP). Based on this gathering and votes, SJP got the status of a national party. It is one of the outstanding achievements of SJP. At times it occupied the power of the state. How successfully the party ruled over the state is worth appreciable, and it is unquestionable as well. My question is simpler than you, Aajivak Babu, as to how these people can be irresponsible and immature?"

Dr Tarun's reaction was like oxygen, fairly a catalyst to Satish Gautam's nervousness. He didn't let Aajivak Babu respond to Dr Tarun's query and put his energy in top gear to react correspondingly, "I had even told my boss in the last meeting that I would give my vote to my SJP. 'You should also give your vote to this party. If one woman does not vote for another, then who will? How can there be women empowerment?' I believe that our party will perform better than earlier this time. And *Geeta Behanji* will come up with a prime ministerial candidate. Aajivak Babu, wait and watch, and a self-evident fact requires no proof. And I will let you know whatever wrong will be proved to be wrong and vice versa in the end."

Satish Gautam's enthusiasm and self-confidence were terrific. Even if Dr Tarun did not fully agree with him, Satish Gautam said 'we' meaning Gautam and Dr Tarun. By saying 'we', he alienated Aajivak Babu from this trio. Though this isolation was momentary, Aajivak Babu was permanently isolated and forsaken among friends and relatives because of his different thinking. He was disturbed but had no way out to change himself accordingly. Such a change was like suicide for him. He was neither fragile nor a coward. Hence, he stood by his principles and never compromised.

It was Aajivak Babu's turn to defend himself. "Just listen to me, brothers. My focus was on the genuineness of an individual and the intellectuality. I was talking of a better lifestyle, and still, I am firm on my stand. Secondly, you have linked the person's upliftment to politics, which is not logical. Even a criminal mindset in politics can go to the pinnacle of democracy. He can be a party president, minister of any calibre and maybe an absolute sovereign."

He revealed the side of the coin, "In present-day democracy, the herd of sheep plays the part well. In the case of the SJP, Dr Ambedkarism has no role to play; his credentials are being encashed. Just politics in the name of Dr Ambedkar, and nobody has to do anything with his ideological commitments. If it so happened, the picture of the society and the country would have been fantastic. Nothing is permanent here. I am not a pessimist, but I still see the possibility of it being negligible because of the vices of modern politics."

However, Aajivak Babu couldn't dare share his mind with them. He thought the SJP's chief was not qualified for prime ministerial candidature. He knew another aspect of the coin. If any political compulsion led the head of SJP to a prime ministerial candidate, the racist dragon would swallow all morals and the laws of the legislation. History would repeat itself, and all the norms of secularism would be dumped under the filthy state of the present politics.

It did not mean that Aajivak Babu believed that no person from the Dalit society was eligible for the post of PM. There may be so many; from the other social strata as well. But the past had burning examples to illustrate that caste superiority was such an essential qualification for a prime ministerial candidate that a downtrodden perhaps could never aspire to it. Whatever may be preached and secularism or democratic rights glorified, reality was different.

Aajivak Babu was sure that the SJP supreme would not be the next PM, whatever be the political compulsions. By saying this, Aajivak Babu did not want to shock both of his friends. But he was very clear about the fact. If a person from the Dalit community can do justice to the post of president of India, then why couldn't he be the PM of the nation?

Meanwhile, Mrs Gautam appeared with some snacks and drinks. Mrs Gautam greeted the guests with the exchange of 'Jai Bheem'. Meanwhile, a thought flashed in Aajivak Babu's mind. "It's the pastime, rather a passion of men like the three of us arguing over one issue or the other, but the poor women are unnecessarily trapped in this. These women have to live on high alert to host the guests like the first aid team stay in the second line during a war or war-like situation to treat the injured soldiers."

It was not known whether they were interested in the discussions of their husbands or not. And how much suffering they had to undergo because of the literary intercourse of their husbands. He feels that a survey must be conducted to reveal the fact; it may be an interesting one. But Aajivak Babu did not make his heartfelt curiosity public. He left it as another future agenda for discussion.

After replying to Dr Tarun and Satish Gautam's questions, it was Aajivak Babu's turn to ask questions. he focused on a different issue of a political character. "When a Dalit leader, MP, MLA or maybe a party president is caught in bribery, misappropriation of funds or any scandal he stands alone without any support; this is worth appreciable." Both of them consented unanimously as nobody's wrongdoing or criminal acts should indeed be defused.

Contrary to this situation, he remarked, "Vice versa, if a non-Dalit is involved even in larger crimes, maybe genocide, the picture is different. Take the case of mob-lynching or the cases of burning of people alive publicly, or if the casteist is guilty of challenging the Constitution and the Supreme Court. Or in the cases of vandalism, communal felony or if someone is accused of anti-national and terrorist activities, the party stands with the person or the gangs with limitless ugly arguments to justify it at any cost. Why?"

He paused for a moment. "They get all possible assistance needed for their defence. The offenders are even honoured in public functions and provided opportunities to fight elections. They even enjoy higher ministerial perks, awarded for their misdeeds. I know very well that all the crimes are covered under the umbrella of caste and religion. Still, my question to both of you is, 'Why do the people, politicians, or political parties associated with Dalit society adopt the criminal tactics while it is the monopoly of upper strata of the caste and religion and their political parties? If they are dedicated solely to the Constitution; and the father of the Constitution, why do they commit a crime, whatsoever it may be? Why?'"

Aajivak Babu's remarks somewhat faded the sense of confidence and victories from the faces of the two, but there was a mixed reaction. First, Dr Tarun made his point. "I fully agree that all of the acts of unethical and criminal nature, like any bribe, should be avoided. And left out to non-Dalits who are comfortable as the police do support them directly; they have no money and acquaintance even in the judiciary based on their caste and religious hierarchy. On the other hand, I must say that downtrodden and weaker sections must stay away from these vices. The Dalits, because of their lack of support and precisely from a moral point of view, must avoid any rhetoric. Only then they will be able to fight for the weaker sections of the society."

He further made his point of view clear by saying, "I am dead sure. No non-Dalit organisation or political party will fight for Dalits as strongly as they ought to be. Even thinking that way would be a blunder. If that were the case, there wouldn't have been any problem with Dalits, and they wouldn't have been forced to call themselves Dalits in society. Nowadays, Dalit politicians working for non-Dalit political parties mean nothing. They are merely to satisfy their wasted personal interests at the cost of society and provisions ensured by the Constitution of India. If they desire to work according to the spirit of the Constitution, they can't. The condition of Dalit representatives is not better than the poor under feudal lords in the traditional villages. So, I too find no scope for the questions of the oppressed class addressed to an amicable solution."

It wasn't sure whether Dr Tarun had something to say, but Gautam looked too excited to give others a chance. He took full advantage of his turn and made his point with great concern. "One thing is beyond my comprehension. In this political collapse, why is it expected that entire moral responsibility rests on the shoulders of Dalits and the Dalit party and no one else? Why shouldn't be it the sole concern of the others who enjoy everything with no commitment?"

He paused for a while, looking into Aajivak Babu's eyes in the hope of finding an answer but in vain. He went ahead in the same flow, "If Dalits remain stuck in this cycle of morality, they will never come to power. If they aren't in power, how can their interests remain protected? I think the market for atrocities and exploitation will be hotter then. The spread of a little bit of education among the Dalits or the little economic situation that has improved is because of the constitutional provisions of reservation. It will be wasted if the vandalism goes unchecked in terms of politics and counter politics. We would be back to square zero where we stood before the reservation policy came into force, isn't it?"

Dr Tarun wanted to specify the issue. Hence he took command of the re-discussion as Gautam finished. "It is the job of all the intellectuals and responsible citizens of the country. Non-Dalit intellectuals can also play an important role in the mission. The true intellectual, who rises above narrow-mindedness of caste, religion and superiority or inferiority, can be a great help. But even in the current political era, a handful of journalists think of the nation. They are putting their jobs, mental peace, and even lives at stake. They are standing together against political conspiracies. They are standing in the pool to protest against Hindutva. Despite that, I would say that in this campaign, Dalit intellectuals and writers must be passionate, otherwise..."

Reaching the word 'otherwise,' Dr Tarun left his sentence incomplete and leaned back on the sofa to rest. He curiously looked at Aajivak Babu as Gautam had already made his point. Now, the ball was in Aajivak Babu's court to make his point.

Aajivak Babu was a little upset and, out of habit, didn't bother to put his words bluntly. "My response to your word 'otherwise' may look awkward to both of you. But it is the reality of life–'less the complaints, the happier the one'. On the contrary, most of our writers have complaints, no redressal. As a result, the world of solutions has seemed barren since the beginning. I also know writers who have been writing for twenty-five years, still passing worn-out remarks on Brahmanism and nothing else. They are stripping it apart, and there is no outcome of the exercise at all but create bitterness in mutual relations."

The state of affairs has made Aajivak Babu a bit harsh in dealing with these guys. He added further, "I feel they have invested their energies in aggression. All the frills of their writings and beliefs lead them to an accusation that has become stereotyped. It does not mean that there should be no complaints, but the way out must be the focus. It should not be confined to the propaganda of the status quo. Where will the solution come from if we remain entangled in such a cycle? At times, it seems that the majority have accepted this hostility against Brahmanism as a solution. Consequently, the aggression is multiplying instead of resolution."

He further added, "It is not the monopoly of the writers but the readers. The words Wow! Bravo! Perfect! Amazing! It is the spontaneous rather faithful output of this hostility from the readership. As an exaggerated reaction, it seems that the readership doesn't even know of any other way to react. It pains me a lot when I see Dalits have created a new culture through their writers' associations. There are writers' associations without writers. There are meetings, politics, factionalism, distribution of shawls, and certificates but no literary workshop, no face-to-face interaction on contemporary issues and strategy to cope with. Perhaps the ideological vacuum is the most accurate definition of writer's associations today. I see this as a total waste of human resources and energy."

Aajivak Babu continued, "I have to talk to you more on the subject. Because I strongly believe that our focus should be on our critical assessment rather than finding fault with others. Emphasis should be on introspection as it provides all the raw materials for future dreams to come true. It is sad; that's not happening. A new trend of award distribution by Dalits is taking place. It has nothing to do with any creative work. The awards are to set new standards of groupism. It is pure politics, setting up a new activity record on Facebook. This is nothing more than event management. However, event management skill is also a demand of the day. On the issue of event management, the government has a new era of politics. There is no denying the possibility that the skill of event management will lead to a new achievement in the politics of Dalits."

While reacting, Aajivak Babu constantly looked at Dr Tarun and Gautam looked to take stock of their gestures. However, there was no reaction. But he was sure of the vital response over such a severe remark from him. Since nothing was happening, Aajivak Babu didn't want to let the opportunity pass. "Nowadays, a separate set of awardees has been created, which has become a gimmick to win only the award. In this reference, I would like Dr Tarun to explain the pattern of getting an award. I expect him to share a personal experience with Prof. L K Nigam. I was happy when Prof. Nigam advocated the logic of getting the award. I also got an opportunity to understand the logic of the award in the presence of Dr Tarun."

Dr Tarun de-coded the award formula that Prof. L K Nigam had shared. "There is a committee to decide the award. Somebody may be enrolled in the list of awardees even without any biodata, based on personal relationships. Prof. L K Nigam has also been an honorary member in the department, where the lists of various awarding committees were finalised. Awards are based on personal relationships as one of the popular criteria. The names of the favourites have already been submitted. He knows the story of awarding child-literature awards even without submission of the manuscript."

He coughed a little, sipped some water and then proceeded further, "Communal forces play a decisive role in the nomination of awardees where the caste, religion and flattery are the major tools to fetch awards. It is more in practice today. The politics of the award is despicable. No matter how many fathers the award seeker adopts or disowns. But the poor mother remains the same who has to face the defamation of repeated illegal acts of self-indulging children for the award. But the mother is a symbol of stamina. Even after such a child has been repeatedly called illegitimate, she does not disown the child; maybe never."

The award politics that Dr Tarun was talking of was not applicable just in the context of Dalits. It must be said that this business was equally applicable to non-Dalits as well.

Aajivak Babu said, "You both will be amazed, but it is my personal experience that there is a sense of insecurity among the senior Dalit writers. They are always afraid of their seniors and junior writers. These so-called monastics are so frightened that they are found involved in conspiracies against their juniors. Where there is such a lack of security, can any space is left for mutual cooperation? They leave no opportunity to blame the Brahmins for ignoring co-existence and mutual cooperation. But in many such cases. Dalits are no less than a fundamentalist Brahmin in this race to root out their co-writers. I see it as a lack of dignity. The personal interest of the individual is paramount, and the interests of the movement are nothing. It is a matter of concern for any movement."

Aajivak Babu asked Dr Tarun and Gautam to break the silence, "If you have to add, you can make your point. I don't want Gautam to reproach me later that you did not have the opportunity to speak."

But both wanted Aajivak Babu to continue, so said in unison, "You may complete what you have to say. Wherever necessary, we will automatically butt in."

Aajivak Babu took a sip of water and said, " Can't I even drink water in the middle of the conversation?" Hearing Aajivak Babu, Gautam went to get some water to drink too.

Aajivak Babu quenched his thirst and expressed concern about the famine to appear. "I see a sense of insecurity in Hiranim, and so all its activities remain critical. It will cause serious damage to society and the nation As a result, the country's social, political, and economic fabric is on the verge of ruin due to similar insecurity and fear. The world of Dalit intellectuals has become different. The struggle of the writers' community is limited to becoming a part of the curriculum. To get published in one journal or the other, getting awards and being part of the curriculum is one of the rigorous struggles of today. There is so much rigging of getting part of the syllabus though the book wasn't published properly. Nobody knows what it says; however, there is a demand of the book to be the part of the syllabus." The pain of the face of Aajivak Babu found expression in his words.

"It is a popular image of sycophants known as 'birds of the same feather flock together'. Nowadays, a professor with weak intellectuality gets the writings of a writer popularised in the news. Opportunistic relations play key roles for a writer to be part of a curriculum. In the contemporary era of materialism, everything reaches the target with a calculated profit; nothing succeeds without reference and bribery; where genuineness matters nothing. Standing with genuineness has become like standing with the truth. It means the person and his genuineness, rather than truth, come under suspicion. It has become worthless in day-to-day life, and evil practices are ruling the mind of today's so-called practical guys. Does such a vicious nexus leave any scope for the justice-like concept?"

It encouraged Dr Tarun to speak a little on this subject. "When a writer writes, he usually takes an ideal stand and sets a standard for society and humanity. Without taking such an ultimate position, nothing good can be said. But the writer, the politician, the guru, the religious leader etc., have a big gulf between preaching and practice, and then the matter is of grave concern. The victims are Dalit writers. The same situation applies to the media, but, regrettably, all these values have become a refuge for political corruption. The fathers of corruption and immorality are surprised and the self-acclaimed symbol of patriotism and social service. They, too, have the most significant fan following in the country that falls under the record-breaking category. The circumstances force us to comment that there is little hope to protect the interest of society and the nation."

With such a lengthy discussion, it seems all were exhausted of the ammunition they had for the day. But Satish Gautam had lagged in today's conversation. Perhaps because he was the host. His aggression also appeared once or twice. If he was not hospitable, how many sixes he would have hit was unpredictable. Gautam commented in the same spirit, "Nothing else, it all goes on. Even if you are not afraid, you may be frightened during the discussion."

While walking, he quotes two lines of an unknown poet to drive away the fear. It said:

"I can't get too weak to take the sword on my chest.

But the blows are not from behind but from the front."

Gautam had a smile on his face before he pronounced the line of the poetry. This smile was the triumphant finale of the first meeting at his residence or maybe of something else. The lines, however, had put a smile on all their faces, which was completely absent during the entire conversation.

❑

THIRTEEN

As soon as the meeting concluded, Satish Gautam walked with Dr Tarun and Aajivak Babu to the bus stand. They all enjoyed the 10–15-minute walk in a relaxed frame of mind. Though they were all comfortable in Satish Gautam's house, and his family members well-known to Aajivak Babu and Dr Tarun, they felt relieved to be out in the open. Aajivak Babu felt as if he was returning from the examination hall after the exam was over. Such conversations were no less than a kind of examination for the trio.

The examination that the trio was returning from was unique, contrary to the traditional examination. There was no pre-determined syllabus. Every activity of the society, religion, politics, and philosophy could constitute the syllabus. Unlike the political boundaries of a nation, there were no such restricted areas of the curriculum.

There was no set pattern of questions like essay type, multiple-choice, matching type, nor tick-mark nature of questions. Aajivak Babu felt like an examiner and examinee at the same time. He was well aware that these exams would not end, and no outcome was expected.

The relief that Aajivak Babu was enjoying returning from Gautam's house did not even last as he reached his house. He was uncomfortable after reaching home. He had observed some uneasiness on the faces of Satish Gautam and Dr Tarun during the conversation. Because of Aajivak Babu's different way of thinking and interpretation. He knew that every individual had his mindset to derive his conclusions accordingly. But the passion of the post-mortem of specific issues was frightening to Aajivak Babu.

Suddenly, an old familiar question struck his mind. 'Will my way of thinking affect our relations? Would the trio break apart, leaving me out of it? Would today's episode have grave consequences?' This series of questions was getting unbearable. Abruptly, there a voice whispered in his mind, "No, no, I can't let that happen. If so, it would be a different kind of surgical strike."

Aajivak Babu was looking for a solution to kill the snake and save the stick. He was obsessed with a dialogue between his conscious and subconscious selves. It was the fragmentation of his sweet ties in the past. "When I felt, I was an infant in the world of literature. I was still crawling on my knees. But Prof. Lalit was the pinnacle of the world of his literature. It was the time of the publication of my first book, but Prof. Lalit mentioned strange conspiracies."

"My stand against the word 'Dalit' has caused the ultimate damage to all my relationships. I have become a villain in their arena. How do I meet, embrace what my conscience doesn't allow me to swallow? How to let them shear the wings of my flight? And how do I leave the Indus civilisation flights to the heights of my heritage? How to disown me from the legacy of being an aboriginal of the land? And how do I accept to be a 'Dalit', have a 'Dalit' identity forever? How do I accept that 'Dalit' is my present, 'Dalit' is my future and 'Dalit', my world of ethical and ideological asylum? How can 'Dalit' the disgusting legacy be the pride of the future generations to come?"

The interrogation of oneself proceeded further. "No! I can't go hand in hand with such guys who don't have any logistics of a word, language and its impact on the present and future. I can't be part of the crowd who comment on posts on Facebook—'Wow!' 'Awesome!' 'Perfect!' So it's acceptable for me to be evicted from the world of Facebook. I don't have any grudge if this crowd boycotts me. It's better to gather the sun and shadow on my own, take the water and air of my share essential for the flight of my dreams and then live with my dream and make them a reality. I feel it is my comfort zone to enjoy my life in a positive open environment, and there can be no other way to get rid of the collective imprisonment of 'Dalit' and 'Dalit-hood'."

Despite having lost a lot in terms of personal relations, Aajivak Babu was in the comfort zone, but could not understand the current political scenario. The veins of his brain were strained like electric wires while the picture of the contemporary corruption moved like a movie in his memory. The head of Hiranim (Hindu Rashtra Nirman Mahasabha) had been hurling sticks. He was striking the existing political robot like a herd of animals. He claimed the robots were his army, that was patriotic and destined to follow his directions. Because the controlling software was his and the programming controls perfect in all respects. While the chief of Hiranim made these claims, Aajivak Babu's helplessness was trying to break the entire previous records of his pulse rate. It was lucky for Aajivak Babu when suddenly an interval like scenario appeared and the movie vanished from the screen.

After the interval, caste, religion, media, army as well as cows, buffalo and human beings, both dead and alive, were seen screaming, like sacrificial goats. This herd of beings was sorted and taken to different political forums, slaughtered, and segregated. The crowd applauded this celebratory event and put a stamp on the legitimacy of this sacrificial practice amidst a lot of noise. Finally, Mogambo, the boss, was extremely pleased. The movie continued playing, engrossing Aajivak Babu's mind.

Again and again, the new crowds, the unique sacrificial ceremony, the new kind of killings, the latest celebrity, and the new ways to keep Mogambo happy. In the name of Bharat Mata, the mother of India, the *tamasha* or the cruel show was enacted. It was at a rapid pace, the genuine exploits by Hiranim software. No part of Mother India's cloak of vanity and humanity was left unstained by the blood stains from these sacrificial ceremonies. Aajivak Babu realised that Hiranim's robotic mission would not stop until the entire sacred cloak of Mother India was shaded with the devilish cruelty.

The film abruptly came to an end as though the ribbon of the moving film has broken. At the same time, Aajivak Babu sat up. It was not a movie but a mirror of reality. Aajivak Babu understood that all the efforts made from nooks and corners to stop this sacrificial practice had proved to be inadequate. A query stirred him. He murmured, "What is left to do now, except to see a complete loss, the little peace and comfort of the day and night." Awkwardness, the everlasting companion of Aajivak Babu's daily routine for months, had brought him on his knees, made him surrender, today.

Aajivak Babu was in no state of mind to bear further restlessness and to pass through mental agony anymore. At this point, he remembered M K Shukla again for these two lines he had spoken to Aajivak Babu when he was a little disturbed by an official impractical practice of the superior bosses. He whispered the same beautiful lines in a light mood that suits the situation:

"Jab bhi milen uljhane, yon kijie,

Whenever one encounters confusion, do one thing,

Ho aaeene se roobroo har ganth kholie

Face the mirror and open every knot."

Aajivak Babu told his inner self, "My complications are not of a day; it's going to be a lifetime. I don't have the options to get rid of them. The world of writing that I have stepped into is now an addiction. The emotional fool I have been can't rest now without embracing them anyway. No accountable citizens of the world community can stay away unaffected if he has a little concern to humanity."

His caravan of judgement made him introspect. "In a way, I am doing nothing special but a little different in contemporary situations where stress is naturally a common feature and nothing else. I am trying to open up the knots of confusion in the current electoral climate. My fingers are fumbling to untie the knots; hence, complications are there now, an offshoot to the diverse way of accepted wisdom must be little threat to the peace of mind."

The existing unruly political monkey business arguably breaks Aajivak Babu, and he cannot see anything except for darkness all around. He is not finding any way out of the nervousness. In the meantime, other lines from the same M.K. Shukla gave a knock to his mind to undertone:

"Bahte hue pani ko na ashkon se toliye

Do not weigh the flowing water with tears,

Jab bhi pavan ruken, chalne ko bolie.

Whenever you stop, speak to the steps to go on."

Today, M K Shukla's words proved to be a suitable balm for Aajivak Babu's headache. He was amazed that he had such a nice friend. Though he was not with him right now, he felt his absence; his words made up for his absence. He smiled and muttered to himself, "The current political climate is also flowing water. It will be swept away after some time in a gutter. What is the need to shed tears on this? What is the use of crying? There is no break from the current political anarchy. Let it be; if it is incurable through existing means available, then why tears?"

He interpreted the other side of the coin that was the public. He talked to his inner self. A common saying is, 'such as king and subjects'; today's political scenario was the same. The king's character was like that of an ordinary individual. There was no change after his incarnation as a king, the representative of the public from an average person. The fair or foul traits of his masters and his character as an individual have been crystal clear. The people, rather the slave mentality of colossal past, forgot that they were the citizens of a democratic country. Consequently, the dense crowd blindly followed the king and his team as the unquestionable monarchs.

Hence the saying, 'such as the king and the subjects', has become a standard of democracy in the state. Nowadays, the issues have become the same as the king. There is no priority to the genuine and deserving candidates in the existing corrupt politics. The situation was similar to the pipe piper who took the mice to the river. The same seemed to be happening today, and Aajivak Babu felt that devastation would soon follow.

Now, he remembered the following lines of the poem as if it was written for him and written to resolve the present situation. So the idea of 'keep on walking' was not a mirage but a reality of life to deal with the current situation. This thought significantly boosted Aajivak Babu's enthusiasm, since he had lost his foothold in the upheaval of political corruption which resulted in his long journey of agony. He told himself, "It is time to apply balm on the wounds burning due to the distress caused by the month." He thanked M K Shukla for the beautiful lines that proved to be the key to his restlessness.

Early in the morning, Aajivak Babu performed a surgical strike in his own house, giving the good news that they were to go to Mussoorie. Shalini was delighted to hear the good news. She, was fed up with Aajivak Babu's lifestyle in the house. Though he was at home, he was always in his own world. The news for Shalini was like, 'a blind person wishes for nothing else but two eyes'.

Shalini wanted a break from the dull atmosphere at home, but she did not insist on anything. Moreover, Roby had to be looked after. He could not be left alone at home. There was no shelter nearby. Hence, a close relative living in the neighbourhood agreed to take responsibility for Roby.

It seemed as if the circumstances were waiting to support Aajivak Babu to come out of his sufferings. Aajivak Babu smiled at the thought that all living and non-living objects around him were to help in the pessimistic environment. Now nothing was left for Aajivak Babu but to pick up his car to head on for Mussoorie, the queen of the hills, for some comfort. Humming these lines in ecstasy, he departed early in the morning with a clear sky over his head.

"*Chal kanin aur chal, aye mere hamnasheen*

Let's go elsewhere, O, my beloved one,

Is chaman main to apna guzara nahin

This flower garden is not worth living in."

❑

RAKESH BANSAL, a post graduate in International Business Management, approached stock market in year 1998 to make livelihood from trading. He is a result driven professional with over 16 years of rich experience in the areas of Technical Analysis, Wealth Management, Investment Analysis and Portfolio Management. He is appearing regularly on financial news channels like CNBC Awaaz, Zee Business, ET NOW, DD News and CNBC TV18, etc.

He is presently working as a Vice President with R K Global. He has earlier worked with SMC Global Securities Limited, as a Head, Technical Analysis Department (Institutional Desk) and with BLB Limited, as a Head, Technical Analysis Department.

PROFITABLE SHORT TERM TRADING STRATEGIES

HOW TO MAKE MONEY USING MARKET PROVEN TRADING STRATEGIES

RAKESH BANSAL

www.visionbooksindia.com

www.visionbooksindia.com

Disclaimer

Trading involves considerable risk. Trade at your own risk to the extent you are comfortable. Neither the author, nor the publisher would be responsible for any losses incurred for acting on any trading set up explained in this book. This book is purely for educational purpose.

First Published, 2015
Reprinted, 2016, 2018, 2020, 2022, 2023, 2024

A Vision Books Original

ISBN 10: 81-7094-905-X
ISBN 13: 978-81-7094-905-3

Published by
Vision Books Pvt. Ltd.
(Incorporating Orient Paperbacks and CARING imprints)
24 Feroze Gandhi Road, Lajpat Nagar 3
New Delhi 110024, India.
Phone: (+91-11) 2984 0821 / 22
e-mail: visionbooks@gmail.com

Printed at
Ashim Print Line
38/2, 35 &36 Sahibabad Industrial Area, Ghaziabad
Uttar Pradesh 201010, India.

Dedication

SHRI S. N. BANSAL

This book is a special mark of respect to my father, late Shri S. N. Bansal.

I would like to take this opportunity to share someone very special with you. I am dedicating this book to my father, to thank him from the bottom of my heart for everything he did, and to show how much he really means to me.

A man is remembered not for the wealth he has accumulated, but for the love he inspired in his near and dear ones.

My father was a man of unlimited love and humanity. He always stood behind me in whatever I did. I have learnt the meaning of love, honesty and hard work from him. I am truly blessed to have had such a wonderful father, whom I could also call my friend.

Thank you, Dad, for everything you did for me, along with all the others you took care of through the years.

We all love and miss you so very much!

Contents

Preface

This book is all about technical trading strategies which if followed with discipline and patience can help you accumulate wealth.

Each chapter in this book presents information in a logically sequential fashion. The material in each chapter is built upon the information presented in the preceding chapters. The reader should therefore proceed chapter-wise, from the beginning to the end, in order to clearly grasp the logic of technical trading.

The book starts with the basic concepts, assuming that the reader doesn't have much prior knowledge of technical trading. Each and every topic is thereafter explained in detail with examples from the Indian markets.

Technical trading is not an easy path to walk but what I have attempted in this book is to build in the book's readers a level of competent command of profitable technical trading.

RAKESH BANSAL

1

Technical Trading – An Introduction

Technical analysis is the backbone of trading. It is basically the study of demand and supply in a financial market in an attempt to determine what direction the market may take in the future. For the purpose of forecasting future price trends, technical analysis studies market movement primarily through the use of price charts. Technical analysis is one of the best tools available which can be effectively and efficiently used for accumulating wealth.

Let me share two real market related instances from my life to highlight the potential of technical analysis.

In the beginning of April 1992, I was pursuing my Bachelor's degree in pharmaceutical sciences and had come home during the vacation. My father, a chartered accountant had bought the stock of ICICI Ltd. (this later got merged into ICICI Bank) at ₹ 3,000 level; thereafter it even went up to ₹ 3,400. Unofficially, news of the Harshad Mehta scam was rife in the market on 2 April 1992. The news became official on 23 April 1992 in *The Times of India* and India's premier exchange, the Bombay Stock Exchange (BSE), was closed that day for trading. My father called up a broker of Cochin Stock Exchange which was open. At that time, the rates in Cochin used to be 10% higher than on BSE but the catch was that payments were made after three months. The Cochin broker refused to give any guarantee for payment arising out of any sale of shares. My father was depressed as he had a large position of ICICI shares in the forward market, i.e. the futures market of today, and kept repeating that if he was losing somebody else must be gaining. He immediately bought a desktop computer, which was quite expensive in those days, and asked me to enter the data for all the leading scrips in a spreadsheet. He had a fair knowledge of technical analysis and he also had sufficient time for analysis as BSE was closed. After studying the trades, he came to the conclusion that he was on the wrong side of the market. Accordingly, when BSE opened on 28 April 1992, he first boldly booked his loss —

and then went short. The prices thereafter declined 50% from those levels.

The second incident relates to 1996-97, when I was pursuing my MBA. I picked Infosys at around ₹ 2,500 levels based on its fundamentals. I also suggested to my father to buy the share but he replied firmly that he would do so only above ₹ 2,700 as that would represent a breakout from the ascending right angle triangle, a chart pattern which is technically considered very bullish. Nothing happened for the next four months as the stock languished in a trading range. But once it broke out above ₹ 2,700, Infosys became a multibagger and went on to cross ₹ 10,000.

I have shared the above instances to illustrate the potential of technical analysis. If followed with patience and discipline, technical analysis can certainly help you accumulate wealth.

Trading is based on tools that technical analysis employs to analyse chart patterns in search of profit. The key advantage of technical trading is that nothing is left to guesswork since the risk involved, i.e. the worst possible outcome of a trade, is known in advance even before the trade is initiated.

Of course, this requires analysing graphs, chart patterns, and some mathematical and statistical analyses. It is not an easy path to walk, but this book will help you build a level of competent command over technical trading which can help you create wealth for yourself.

2

The Essentials of Charts

A chart is a graphical representation of price behaviour. More specifically, it's a working tool of the technical analyst and holds the same significance in the life of a technical trader as did a bow and arrow in Arjuna's life.

There are two axes in a graphical representation, namely Axis X and Axis Y.

- The X-axis normally displays the time period, which could be daily, weekly, monthly, or intraday - - i.e. 5 minutes, 15 minutes, 60 minutes, etc.
- The Y-axis displays price.

There are many types of price charts available but the most popular ones are:

1. Bar chart,
2. Candlestick chart, and
3. Line chart.

Bar Chart

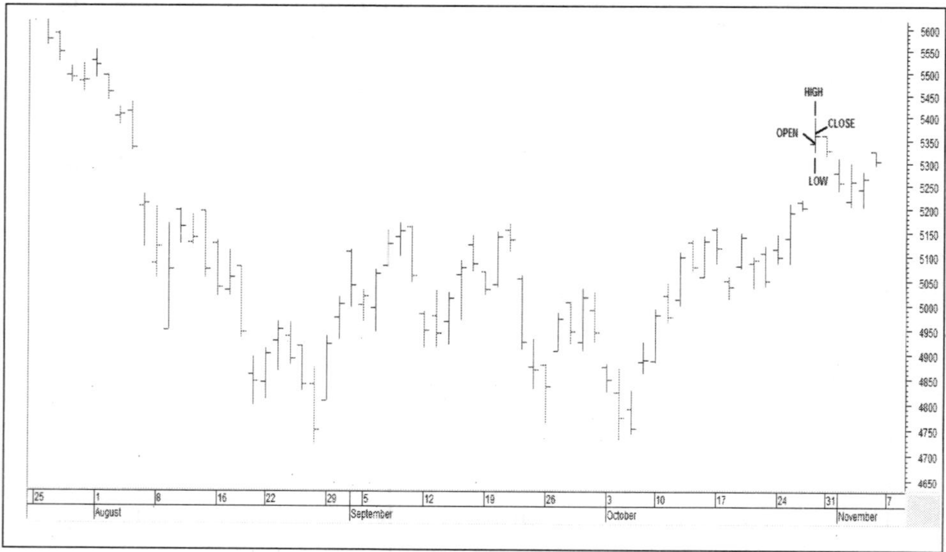

Figure 2.1: **Daily bar chart of Nifty. The bars show the highest price, the lowest price, as well the opening and closing prices**

Figure 2.1 illustrates a bar chart. The top of each vertical bar represents the highest price at which the concerned security traded during the period represented by the bar, while the bottom of each bar represents the security's lowest traded price during the same period.

The tick displayed on the right side of the bar designates the closing price while the opening price is displayed by a tick on the left side of the bar.

Candlestick Chart

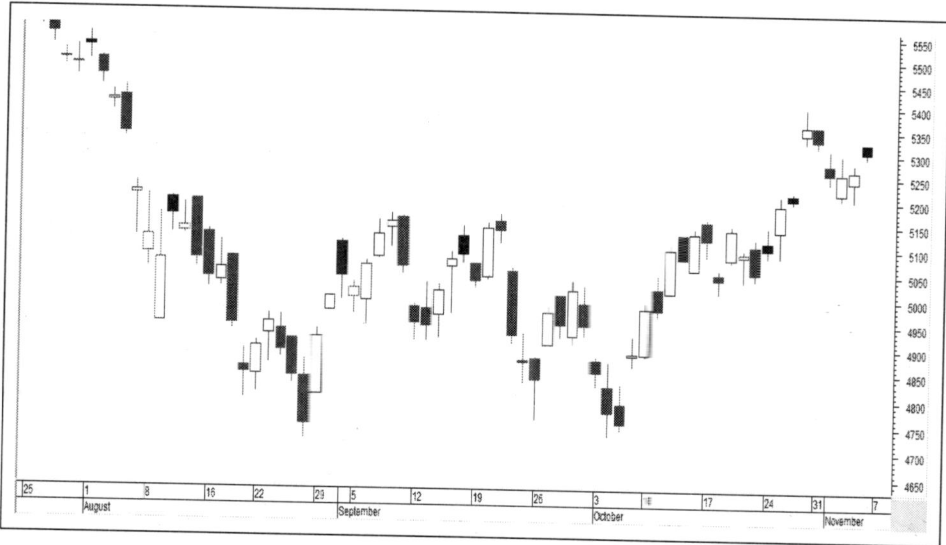

Figure 2.2: **Daily candlestick chart of Nifty**

Figure 2.2 illustrates a candlestick chart. Each bar, called a candle, is defined differently depending on the opening and closing of the security with respect to the high and low for the day. This is a self-determining analytical tool which originated in Japan and is now very popular all over the world.

Line Chart

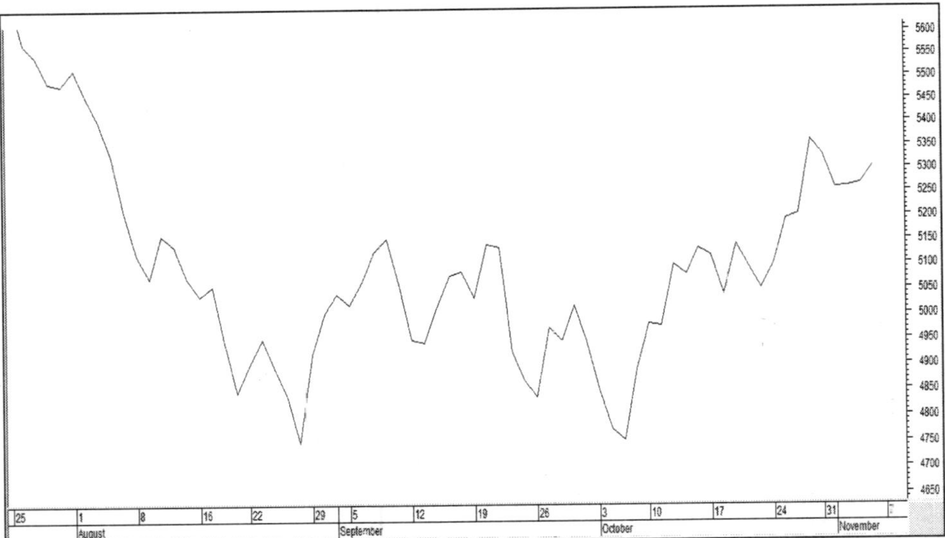

Figure 2.3: **Daily line chart of Nifty**

Figure 2.3 illustrates a line chart which is the simplest type of chart where a single point represents the security's closing price and a line is formed by joining all the points together.

Which Chart to Use

- Candlestick charts have more to do with day-to-day or, more precisely, intraday trading. They play little role in positional trading which is the real path to wealth creation and which is what we would mainly be concentrating on in this book. For positional trading, I am not in favour of using candlestick charts.

- A line chart does not reflect the highs and lows of a day, but only the day's closing price. Highs and lows are required for examining the security's internal strength. For this reason, we will not be using line charts either.

- I prefer bar charts and would recommend their use. A bar chart is simple and by its very nature doesn't pull you towards day-to-day or, more precisely, intraday trading. This is why I prefer bar charts and would suggest their use, at least to start with.

- I would also suggest that one should use daily and weekly time frames while analysing charts and intraday time frames should be avoided for trend determination.

  Basically intraday trading is done to make a quick profit by undertaking a small risk, i.e. by placing a small stop loss*. Most times these anticipated quick profits roll into losses as the stop losses placed for such quick profits get triggered. Hence, one needs to have clarity in one's mind with regard to stop loss before initiating a trade, i.e. whether to keep a distant stop loss which is rarely triggered — or to keep a tight stop loss which is triggered frequently.

  Intraday time frames are most profitably used in mechanical trading which is discussed later in the book (*see* Chapter 11).

You will succeed in technical trading only when you analyse an appropriate type of chart on the appropriate time frame. I know of a number of technical traders who lost their entire trading capital in intraday trading.

---

* For a full understanding of stop losses, please see *Stop Orders — A Practical Guide to Using Stop Orders for Traders and Investors* (Vision Books, New Delhi, www.visionbooksindia.com).

Analysing the appropriate chart type on an appropriate time frame is an indispensable foundation of technical trading, and the path to wealth creation.

3

The Essentials of Trends

The first thing you need to do as a technical trader is to determine the trend, namely determine whether it is:

1. Up, or
2. Down.

Equally, in order to forecast the future trend, one has first to identify the ongoing trend.

Trend Identification

A trend can be one of three types:

1. Primary trend.
2. Secondary trend.
3. Minor trend.

The Primary Trend

- The primary trend is the main trend and is the trader's best friend because it never disappoints so long as you trade in its direction.
- When the primary trend is up, we say that the trend is up, or that the markets are bullish.
- Conversely, when the primary trend is down, we say that the trend is down, or that the markets are bearish.

- Once the primary trend is established, it remains in force until and unless there are signals of a change in the direction of the trend — and generally these signals do not occur all at once.
- One should always trade in the direction of the primary trend.

The Secondary Trend

- Secondary trends are basically the periodic, temporary corrections in the primary trend, namely the price falls which take place in a bull market and the pullbacks — price upmoves — which occur in a bear market.
- Typically, secondary trends last for a short term and have the potential to change direction quickly. Accordingly, one should avoid taking trades in the direction of secondary trends as these can change their direction even overnight.

The Minor Trend

- This is basically the day-to-day price movement, or the intraday price movement.
- One should never even try to predict the minor trend as it is next to impossible to do so.

Figure 3.1 illustrates that A-B, C-D, E-F are moves of the primary trend, and B-C and D-E are secondary trends, in this case downward corrections in the uptrend. Here the primary trend is up, so one should buy — and preferably do so on dips, i.e. at points C and E.

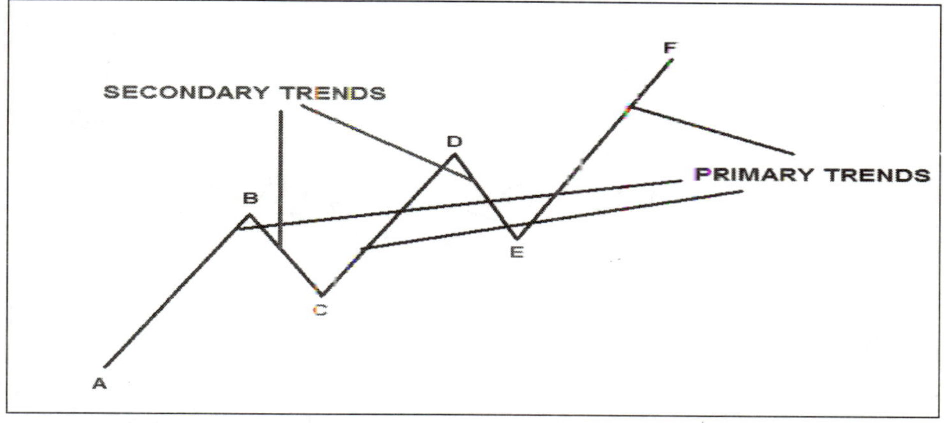

Figure 3.1: **A primary uptrend and secondary downtrends**

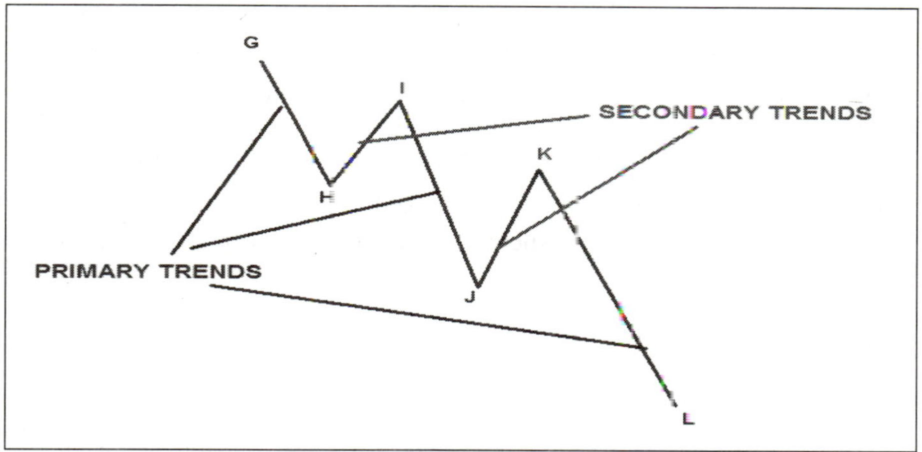

Figure 3.2: **A primary downtrend and secondary uptrends**

In Figure 3.2, G-H, I-J, K-L represent the primary trend and H-I and J-K are the secondary trends, in this case pullbacks in the primary downtrend. Since the primary trend in this case is down, one should sell, and do so preferably on rallies.

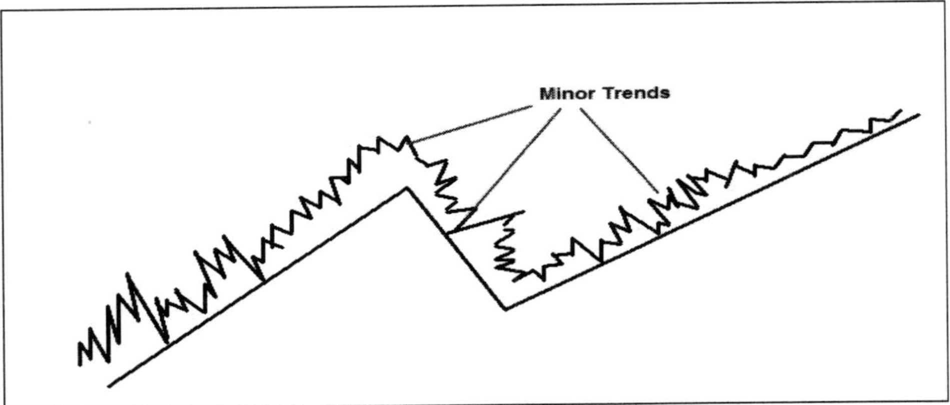

Figure 3.3; **Primary and secondary trends comprise of many minor trends**

In real life, prices don't move smoothly in a straight line as illustrated in Figure 3.1 and Figure 3.2; rather, there are day-to-day price movements, plus intraday price fluctuations. Hence, primary and secondary trends actually comprise of many minor trends as illustrated in Figure 3.3.

Thus, Figure 3.3 illustrates how primary and secondary trends consist of minor trends which are revealed by a zigzag line. As cautioned earlier, one should stay away from predicting and trading minor trends as this is more of a financial suicide.

Uptrend

So long as each successive top is higher than the previous top, and each successive bottom is higher than the previous bottom, the trend is considered to be up and we say that the markets are bullish. This is illustrated in Figure 3.4.

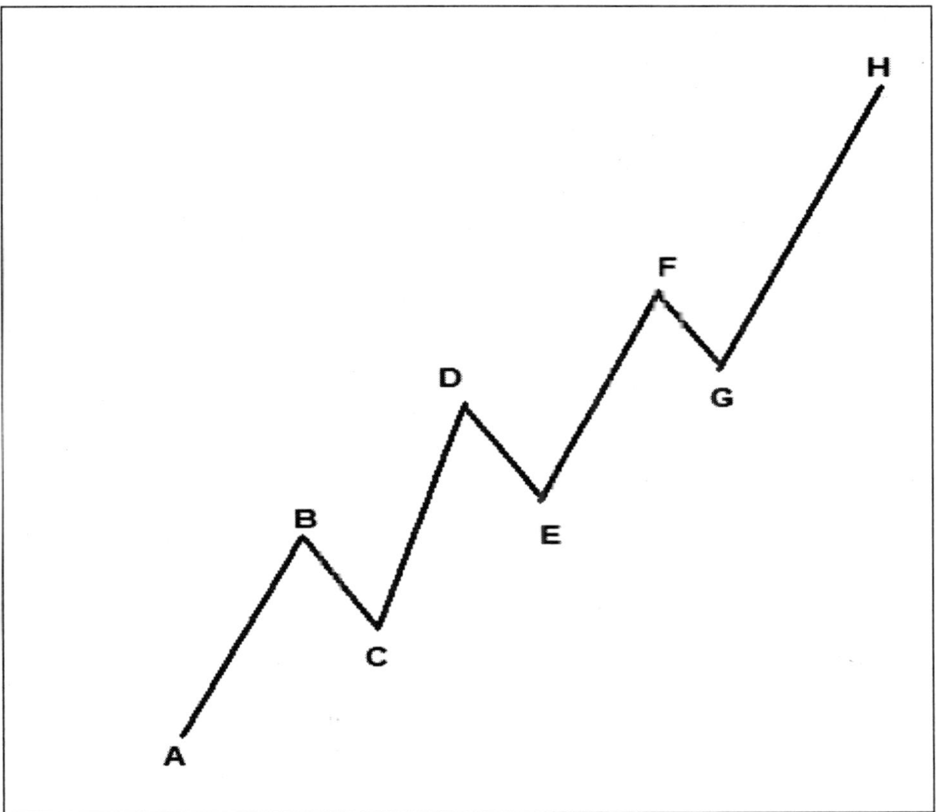

Figure 3.4: **Uptrend — successive higher tops and higher bottoms characterize an uptrend**

Figure 3.4 illustrates that each successive top, namely points D, F and H, respectively, is higher than the previous top, and each successive bottom, namely E and G, is higher than the previous bottom; hence the trend is considered up.

Downtrend

As illustrated in Figure 3.5, as long as each successive bottom is lower than the previous bottom and each successive top is lower than the previous top, the trend is considered down and we say the markets are bearish.

Figure 3.5 illustrates that each successive bottom, namely points D, F and H, is respectively lower than the previous bottom, and each successive top, namely points E and G, is respectively lower than the previous top, hence the trend is considered down.

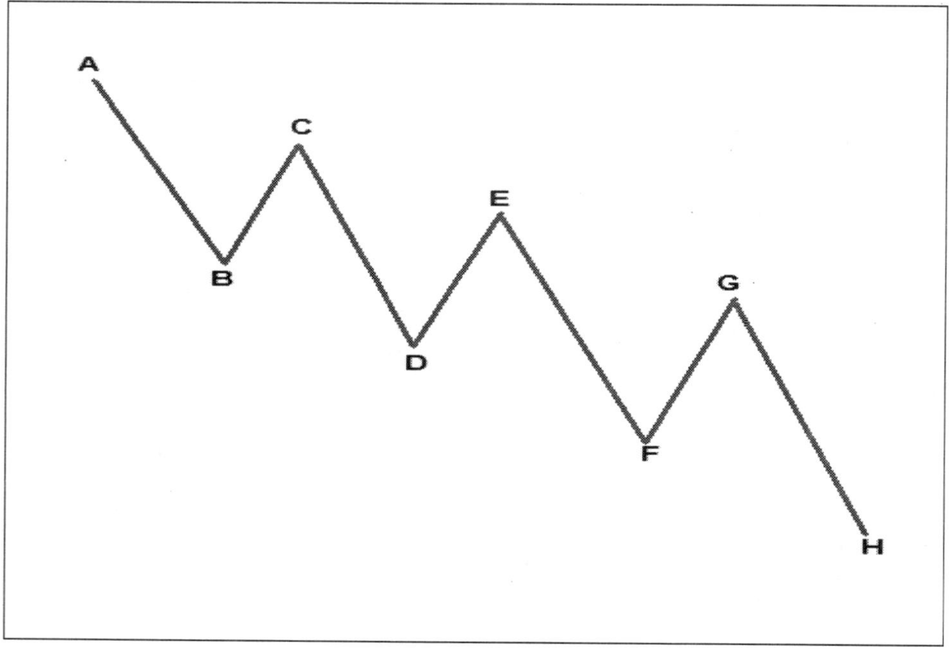

Figure 3.5: **Successive lower tops and lower bottoms characterize a downtrend**

4

Profitable Trend Trading Strategies

Trading *via* trends is the soul of technical trading. Trend trading can broadly be classified into four categories as follows:

1. Trading higher top, higher bottom formations.
2. Trading lower top, lower bottom formations.
3. Buying when only the lower top is breached.
4. Selling when only the higher bottom is breached.

Trading Higher Top, Higher Bottom Formations

A higher top, higher bottom is technically considered very bullish. In trading such a formation, one should buy when the first higher top, higher bottom formation occurs. Ideally, one should buy when the level of the first higher top is crossed during the subsequent rise after a correction, with a stop loss below the first higher bottom.

When successive higher tops and bottoms are formed, you can push up the stop loss to successive higher bottoms. You would notice that with the passage of time, the stop loss would in most cases be higher than the purchase price, thus guaranteeing trading profits.

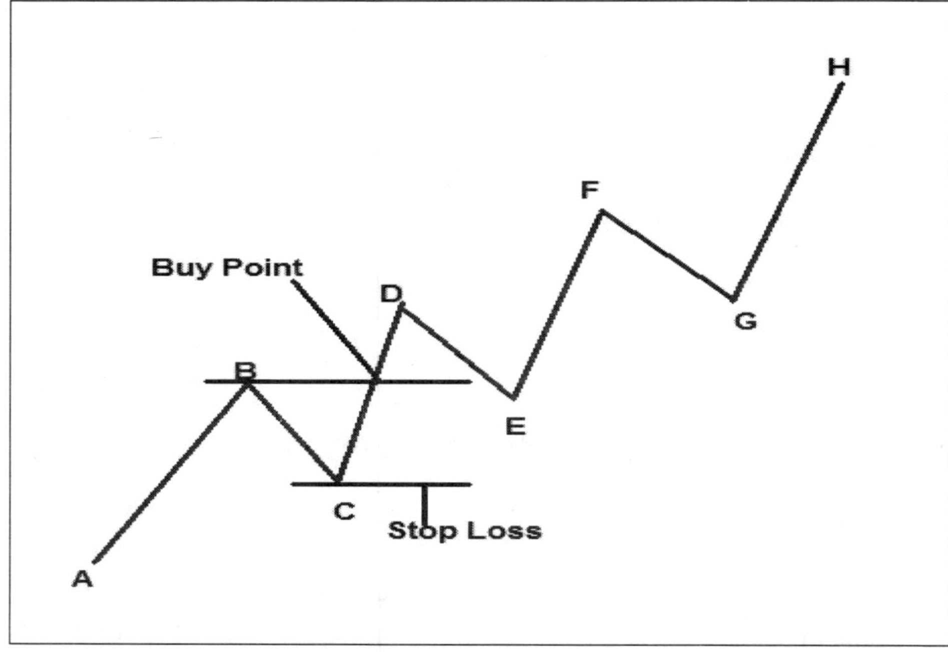

Figure 4.1: **Trading higher top, higher bottom formations**

Figure 4.1 illustrates this stragety: one should buy when the level of Point B is crossed during the next upmove from Point C, with a stop loss placed below Point C. Subsequently, when the level of Point D is crossed during the upmove from Point E, one should raise the stop loss to Point E, and similarly when the level of Point F is crossed during the upmove from Point G, the stop loss should be raised to Point G. Now, we can clearly see that Point G is above the entry Point B. Thus, once your stop loss reaches Point G, there is guaranteed profit in the trade.

Caution

Many market participants and traders initiate buy side positions when each successive higher top is crossed. Thus, for example, they would buy when Point D is crossed during the leg E-F with a stop loss below Point

E. Thereafter they buy again when Point F is crossed during the leg G-H with a stop loss below Point G, and so on in each successive up leg. Unless you are an experienced and proficient trader, I would not suggest buying at each successive higher top because by doing so one is taking only small profits which are not big enough to take care of a loss which usually comes in when stop gets triggered due to an abrupt market correction. In other words, one only makes small profits by buying at each successive higher top but when the trend reverses or an abrupt market correction takes place, one finally ends up with a loss which is often large enough in wiping out all the previous small accumulated profits. So buying at each successive higher top is not advisable.

Initially, it may seem that it's difficult to identify primary and secondary trends as minor trends tend to cause confuse at least for beginners. Those who are not able to distinguish between primary and secondary trends should avoid taking into account any move which is less than 5%, irrespective of its direction. By doing so, one can avoid getting lost in minor trends since moves which are less than 5% are mostly minor trends in reality.

This rule is basically for beginners who are not able to identify primary and secondary trends due to the puzzling minor trends. Those who are able to identify primary and secondary trends obviously need not follow this rule.

Let's now understand this strategy with the help of some real life market examples.

Example 1

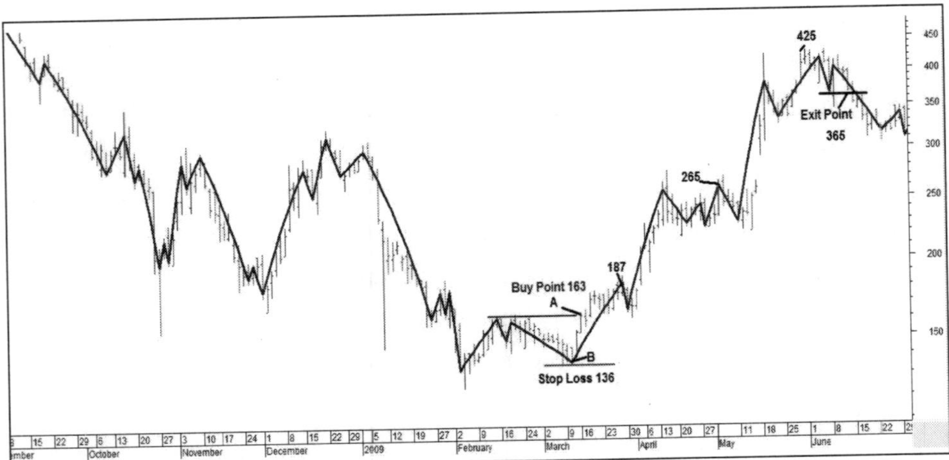

Figure 4.2: **Trading higher top, higher bottom formation in the daily chart of DLF**

Figure 4.2 illustrates that DLF made its first higher top, higher bottom formation at ₹ 163 (Point A) in March 2009. One could have bought it when the price reclaimed ₹ 163 after making the low, B, with a stop loss below ₹ 136 (Point B).

Thereafter, we saw a series of higher tops, successively at ₹ 187, ₹ 265 and ₹ 425 and, finally, the exit signal was given at ₹ 365 level. Here the exit signal is basically a sell signal which has been generated due to the formation of a lower top, lower bottom pattern. This sell signal is explained later in this chapter under the heading, "Trading Lower Top, Lower Bottom Formations" (Figures 4.4, 4.5 and 4.6).

Example 2

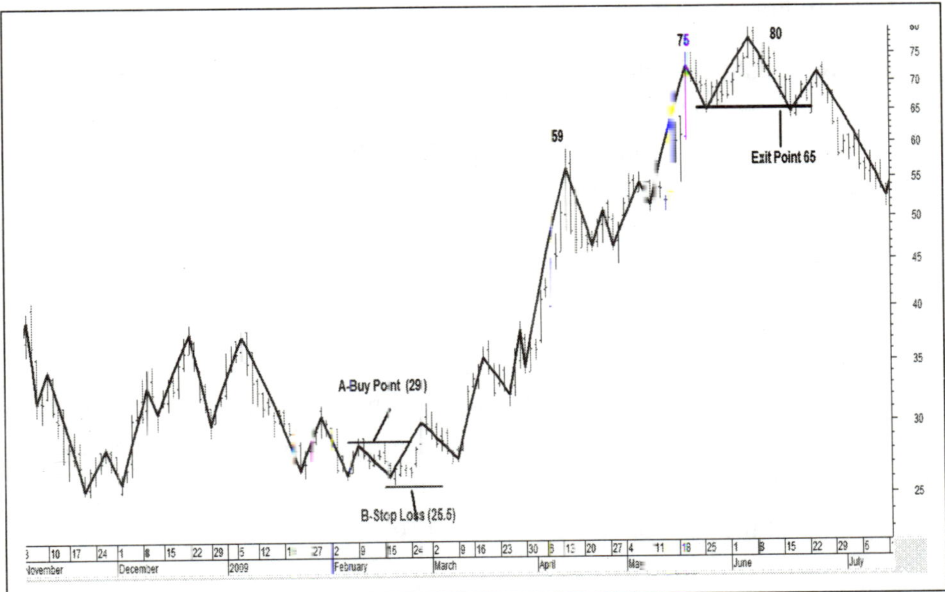

Figure 4.3: **Trading higher top, higher bottom formation in the daily chart of Tata Motors**

Figure 4.3 illustrates that Tata Motors made its first higher top, higher bottom formation at ₹ 29 (Point A) in February 2009. One could have bought it when it reclaimed the level of ₹ 29 in the next upmove with a stop loss below ₹ 25.50 (Point B). Thereafter, the price made a series of higher tops at ₹ 59, ₹ 75 and ₹ 80 and, finally, the exit signal was given at ₹ 66 level. Here, too, the exit signal is nothing but the occurrence of a lower top, lower bottom formation which, in fact, is a sell signal. This is further explained later in this chapter under the heading, "Trading Lower Top, Lower Bottom Formations" (Figures 4.4, 4.5 and 4.6).

Option Trading Strategy for Higher Top, Higher Bottom Formations

- You should consider selling at-the-money put options when the first higher top, higher bottom formation is formed. If the immediate preceding lower bottom is breached after selling at-the-money put options, then one should close the position with a loss. Subsequently you could then consider buying at-the-money put options since a pattern failure has taken place and the price might therefore crash with a downside momentum.

- On the other hand, you should avoid buying at-the-money call options when the first higher top, higher bottom formation is formed because most times price consolidates after the breakout and hence the time value of the call option might get eroded.

Trading Lower Top, Lower Bottom Formations

A lower top, lower bottom formation is technically considered bearish. Accordingly, one should sell when the first lower top, lower bottom formation occurs. Ideally, one should sell when the level of the first lower bottom is breached in the subsequent downmove after a pullback, with a stop loss above the first lower top. When successive lower tops and bottoms are formed, move the stop loss to each successive lower top. With the passage of time, the stop loss so trailed is lower than the entry level, thus guaranteeing you trading profits in most cases.

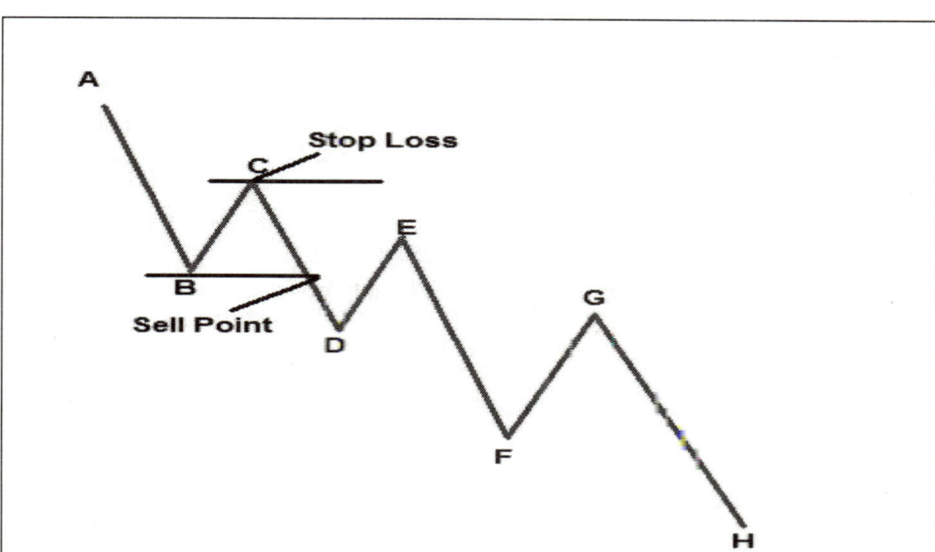

Figure 4.4: **Trading lower top, lower bottom formations**

Figure 4.4 illustrates that one should sell when the level of Point B is breached during the subsequent downmove from Point C with a stop loss above the level of Point C. Once Point D is breached during the subsequent E-F downmove, shift your stop loss to Point E. Similarly, when the level of Point F is breached during the subsequent G-H downmove, the stop loss should be moved to Point G. Now, we can clearly see that Point G is below the entry point B, thus ensuring guaranteed profits.

Caution

Many traders initiate sell side positions when each successive lower bottom is cracked. In Figure 4.4, for example, they would sell when Point D is breached with a stop loss above Point E. Then, they would again sell when Point F is breached with a stop loss above Point G. I would not suggest selling at each successive lower bottom because that is more of speculation rather than a disciplined form of trading.

Moreover, one makes only small profit by selling at each successive lower bottom but when trend reversal takes place one finally ends up with a loss which is fairly large and many wipe out the previous small accumulated profits. In practice, then, one incurs a loss by following a strategy of selling at each successive lower bottom.

Let's now understand this strategy with the help of some real life market examples.

Example 1

Figure 4.5 shows that Reliance Capital made its first lower bottom of a lower top, lower bottom formation at ₹ 1,210 (Point A) in September 2008. One could have sold once the price reclaimed this level of ₹ 1,210 when it started falling again after the pullback with a stop loss above ₹ 1,443 (Point B). Thereafter, we saw a series of lower bottoms at ₹ 975 and ₹ 580 and, finally, the exit signal was given at ₹ 700 (Point C).

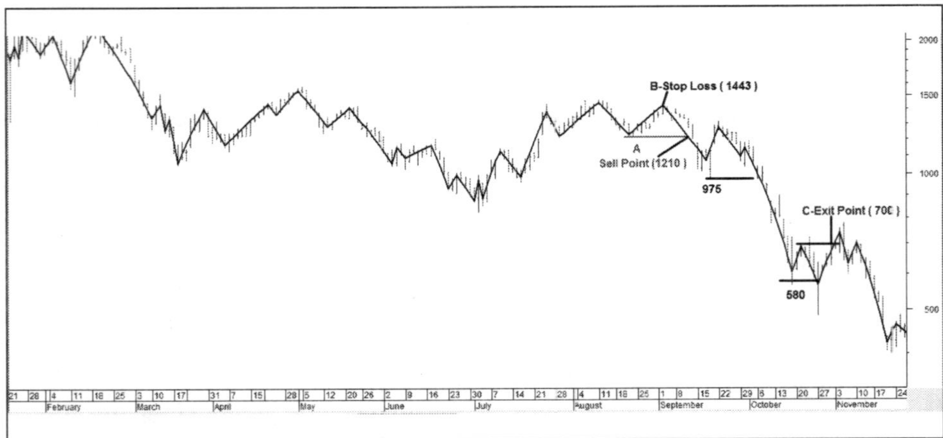

Figure 4.5: **Trading lower top, lower bottom formation in the daily chart of Reliance Capital**

Example 2

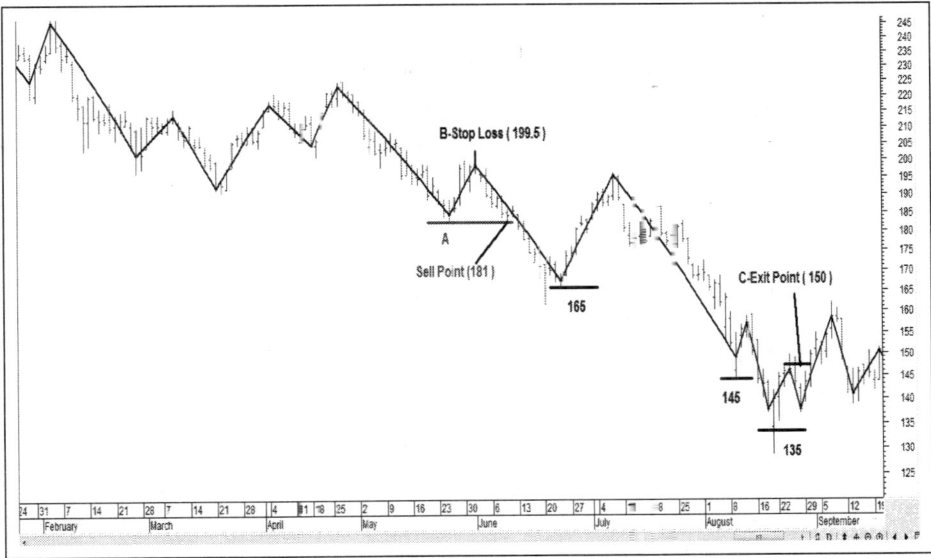

Figure 4.6: **Lower top, lower bottom formation in the daily chart of Hindalco**

Figure 4.6 shows Hindalco making first, lower bottom at ₹ 181 (Point A) in September 2011. Thereafter, the stock price rallied upward to ₹ 199.5 levels, i.e. Point B (Lower top). The stock price then again started declining and one should sell when ₹ 181 level, i.e. the level of Point A is cracked in this decline, with a stop loss above ₹ 199.5 (Point B). Thereafter, we saw a series of lower bottoms at ₹ 165, ₹ 145 and ₹ 135, and finally the exit signal was triggered when the ₹ 150 level, namely the level of Point C was cracked on the upside. Here the exit signal is basically a buy signal generated due to the formation of a higher top, higher bottom pattern. This buy signal has already been explained in this chapter under the heading, "Trading Higher Top, Higher Bottom Formations" (Figures 4.1 and 4.2).

Option Trading Strategy for Lower Top, Lower Bottom Formations

- One could buy at-the-money put options when the first lower top, lower bottom formation is made as the price is then likely to move even lower with momentum, which would prevent any erosion in the time value of the put option.

Buying When Only the Lower Top is Breached

This kind of a trading set up is formed in a bearish market when the price is continuously making lower tops and lower bottoms, and the sentiment is completely negative. In such an environment, one could buy when the level of the immediate preceding lower top is breached during the next

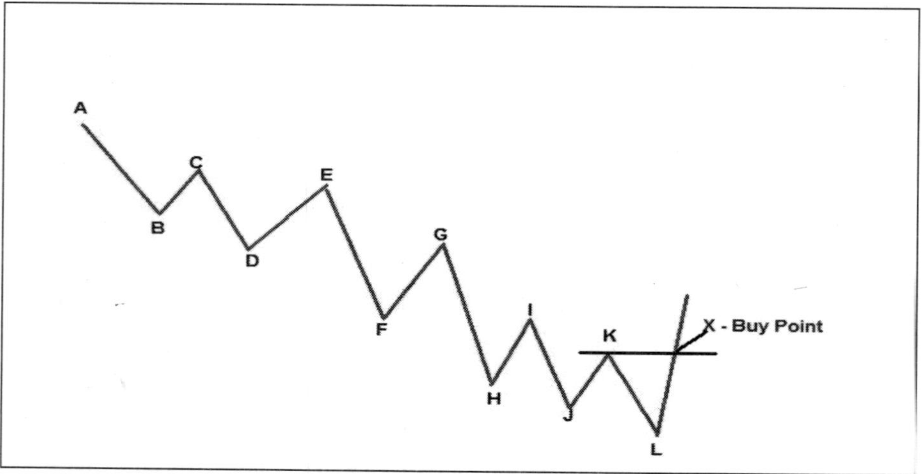

Figure 4.7: **Buy when the price level of Point K is crossed in the subsequent upmove from Point L, but only if it is also supported by a positive divergence**

upmove, without waiting for the formation of a higher bottom, provided it has a buy confirmation by way of a positive divergence, which is explained in Chapter 10 (Figure 10.2).

Figure 4.7 illustrates that the price is continuously making a series of lower bottoms, respectively at B, D, F, H, J and L. One could buy when the price level of the immediate preceding lower top i.e. the price level of Point K, is breached in the subsequent upmove from Point L without even waiting for the formation of a higher bottom, provided there is a buy confirmation from a positive divergence, which is explained in Chapter 10 (*see* Figure 10.2).

Option Trading Strategy When Only the Lower Top is Breached

- You should consider buying at-the-money call options when only the lower top is breached provided it has a buy confirmation by way of a positive divergence (explained ahead in Chapter 10) as the price is then likely to move even higher with a strong momentum, which would prevent any erosion in the time value of the call option.

Selling When Only the Higher Bottom is Breached

This kind of a trading set up is formed in a bullish market when prices are continuously making higher tops and higher bottoms, and when the sentiment is completely positive. In such an environment, one could sell when the level of the immediately preceding higher bottom is breached, even without waiting for the formation of a lower top, provided you have a sell confirmation by way of a negative divergence, which is explained in Chapter 10 (*see* Figure 10.3).

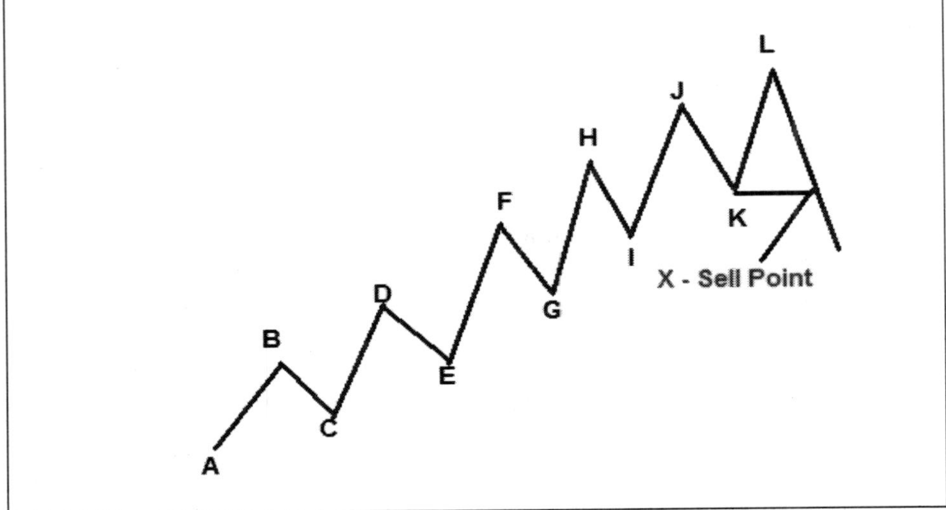

Figure 4.8: **Sell when the price level of Point K is breached in the subsequent down-move from Point L, provided it is also supported by a negative divergence**

In Figure 4.8, the price is continuously making a series of higher tops, namely points B, D, F, H, J and L, and one could sell when the price level of the immediate preceding higher bottom, i.e. the price level of Point K, is breached in the succeeding down move after Point L even without waiting for the formation of a lower top, provided there is also a sell confirmation by way of a negative divergence, which is explained in Chapter 10 (Figure 10.3).

Option Trading Strategy When Only the Higher Bottom is Breached

- You should consider buying at-the-money put options when only the higher bottom is breached provided it has a sell confirmation by way of a negative divergence (explained ahead in Chapter 10, as the price is then likely to move even lower with a strong momentum, which would prevent any erosion in the time value of the put option.

The Crux of Trading *via* Trends

- A trend once established remains in force and does not change direction at once.
- A trend is the trader's best friend and there is an old saying, "Stay with your best friend." In fact, the trend is the only friend which will never ditch a trader in the financial markets.
- Never try to predict intraday or small price movements, which are commonly referred to as *Aaj Kal Ka Hisab Kitab* in Hindi, since nobody can do this and you would only lose money attempting it.
- The market discounts everything before it happens, no matter what the event is.* Thus, one should stay with the trend and trade higher top, higher bottom and lower top, lower bottom formations with discipline and patience as this would lead you to wealth creation.

Let's now understand our trend trading strategies with real life market examples.

---

* The only exceptions are "black swan" events which are events or occurrences that are extremely difficult to predict. Such events are typically random and unexpected.

Example 1

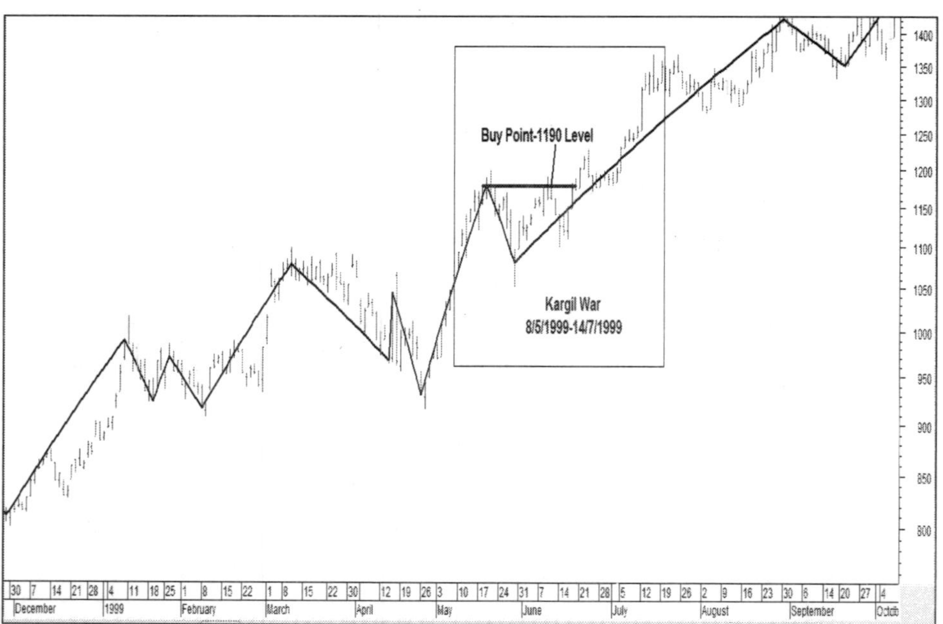

Figure 4.9: **Daily chart of Nifty in May 1999 — the uptrend continued despite the Kargil War**

As Figure 4.9 illustrates, Nifty was in an uptrend when the Kargil War broke out in May 1999. Indeed, Nifty made a new higher top, higher bottom formation after the Kargil War broke out — as highlighted in the inset box. This higher top, higher bottom formation gave a buy entry around 1,190 levels, and thereafter the Nifty rallied unchallenged to above 1,500 levels, thus demonstrating that:

- A trend once established remains in force and does not change direction at once.

- Market discounts everything and so no matter what the event is one should stay with the trend and trade higher top, higher bottom and lower top, lower bottom formations with discipline and patience.

Example 2

Figure 4.10 illustrates that Dow Jones was in downtrend when the 11 September 2001 attack took place in the US. Prior to the 11 September, the Dow Jones index was continuously making lower top, lower bottom formations, as highlighted in the inset box. This demonstrates that selling on the occurrence of a frightful event takes place only when the trend is already down. We witnessed selling across equities post-11 September attack as the trend was already clearly down but we did not witness selling in the Indian markets when the Kargil War broke out as the trend was then undisputedly up. This strengthens the saying the "trend is a trader's best friend."

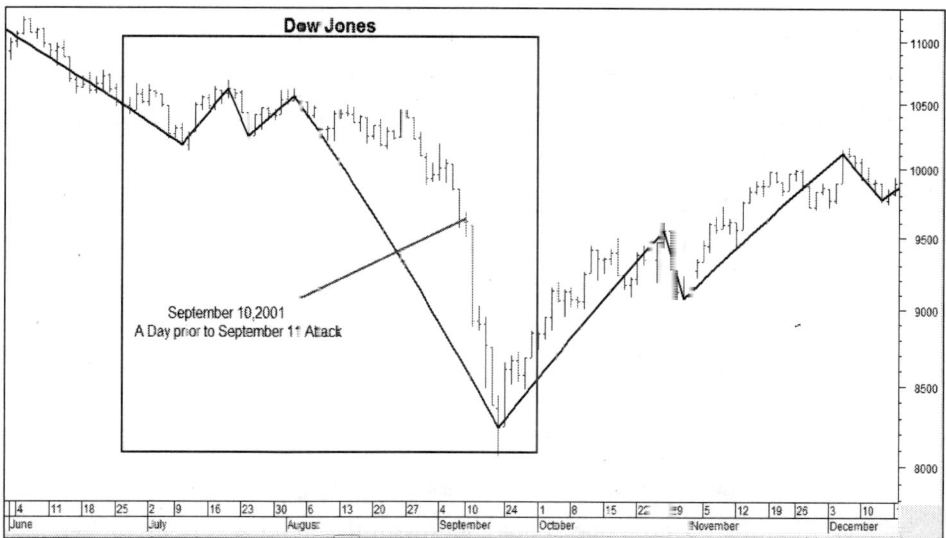

Figure 4.10: **Daily chart of Dow Jones: trading with the trend**

Example 3

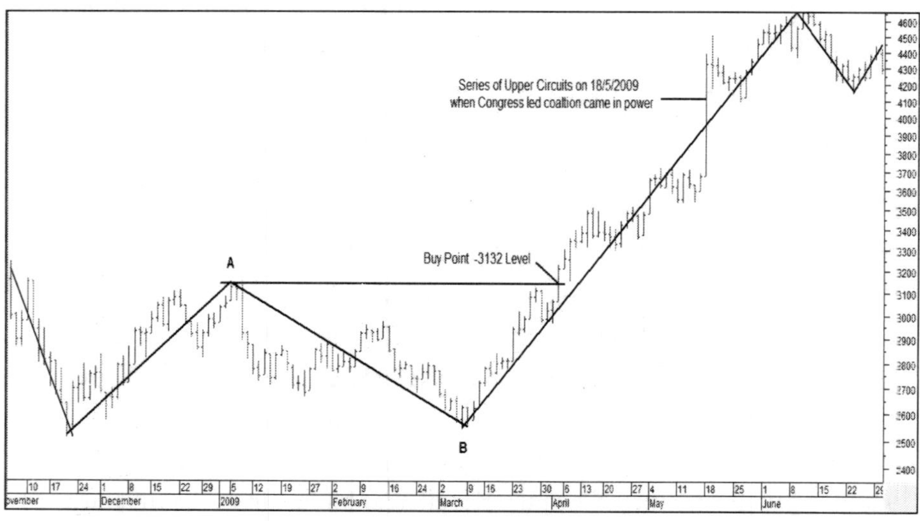

Figure 4.11: **Daily chart of Nifty; note how the index started rising even prior to the victory of the Congress-led coalition in India's 2009 general elections**

Figure 4.11 shows that Nifty was in an uptrend prior to the Congress-led coalition coming to power in India in May 2009. We can clearly observe that the Nifty started making higher tops and higher bottoms in the beginning of April 2009 at 3,132 levels, and thereafter rallied uninterrupted to above 4,650 levels. I still remember the series of upper circuits that Indian indices witnessed for the first time when the Congress-led coalition came to power. This happened because a number of funds had been sitting on cash, were not buying as they were waiting for the election results. But technical traders got a buy entry when the Nifty made its first higher top, higher bottom formation around 3,132 levels and they therefore enjoyed the cushion of a lower entry in the post-election rally.

This demonstrates that market discounts everything in advance, and no matter what the event is one should stay with the trend and trade higher top, higher bottom, or lower top, lower bottom formations as the case may be, with discipline and patience.

5

Trading Support and Resistance

Support

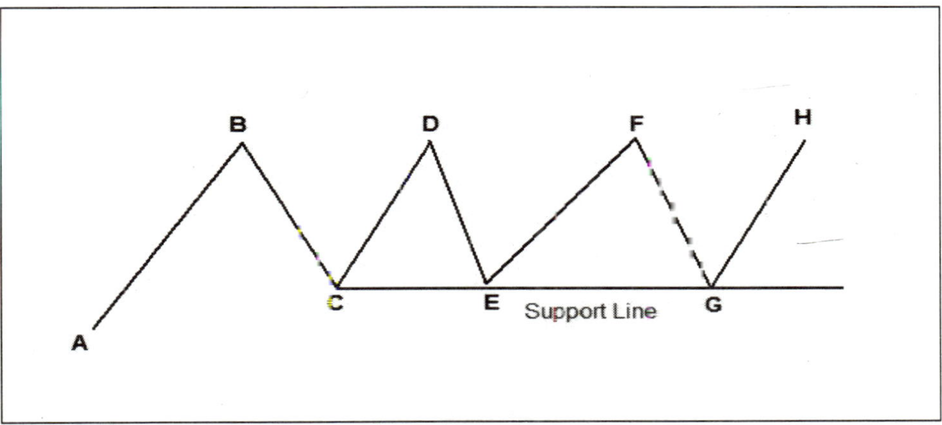

Figure 5.1: **Support levels and support line**

A **support level** is a price range where there is sufficient demand for a security, which thus prevents any further fall in its price. In other words, the price is more likely to rebound from a support level than fall below it.

If, on the other hand, the support level is breached then the price is likely to decline until it finds another, lower support level.

In Figure 5.1, points C, E and G are support levels and joining these points gives us a **support line.**

Resistance

A **resistance level** is a price range where there is a sufficient supply of a security available, which thus prevents any further rally in its prices. In other words, the price is more likely to fall back from a resistance level rather than breach it.

If, however, a resistance level is indeed breached, then the price is likely to rally further until it finds another, higher resistance level.

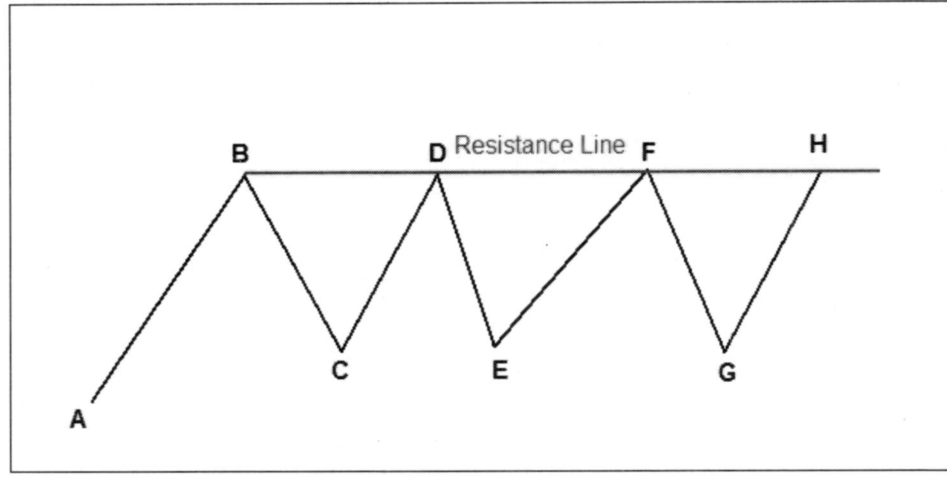

Figure 5.2: **Resistance levels and resistance line**

In Figure 5.2, points B, D, F and H are resistance levels and if one joins these points, we get a resistance line.

Once Breached, Support Becomes Resistance — and *vice versa*

Once a support is breached, it turns into a resistance. This is because when a support is breached the supply of the stock concerned in the market increases as the market psychology behind the stock's movements shifts and new levels of support and resistance are established.

Figure 5.3 illustrates the support line C-E-G being breached in the down move from H to I. Once the support line C-E-G is broken, the supply in the stock increases which pushes the stock price further down. The stock is now likely to find new levels of support and resistance, i.e. a new support at lower levels while old support now becomes the new resistance level. The reason why the support becomes a new resistance level is

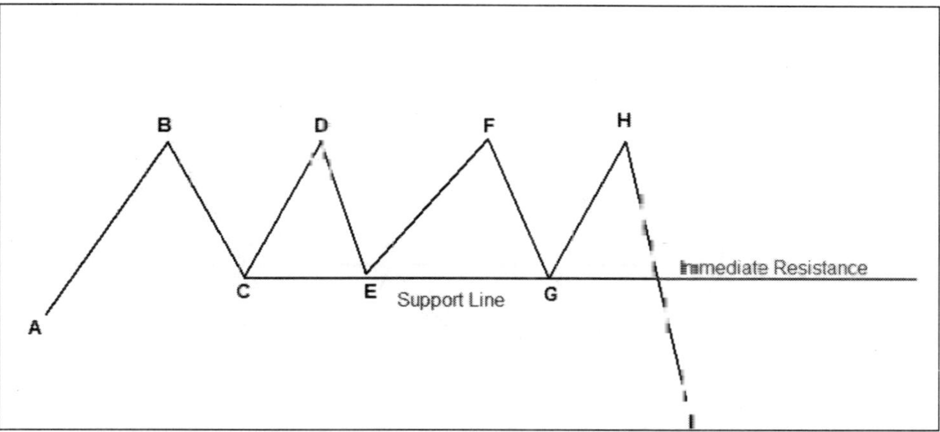

Figure 5.3: **A breached support level becomes the immediate resistance**

because on each and every rally the stock is likely to find strong supply around the previous support levels.

Figure 5.3 illustrates how once a support is breached it becomes an immediate resistance for the stock.

Similarly, once a resistance is breached, it becomes the immediate support. This is so because when a resistance is breached, the demand for the stock increases at the lower prices. Thus the market psychology behind the stock's movements shifts and new levels of support and resistance are established.

Figure 5.4 illustrates the resistance line B-D-F being breached in the up move from G to I. Once the resistance line B-D-F is taken off, the demand in the stock increases which pushes the stock price further up. The stock is likely to find new levels of support and resistance, i.e. a new resistance at higher levels while the old resistance becomes the new support level.

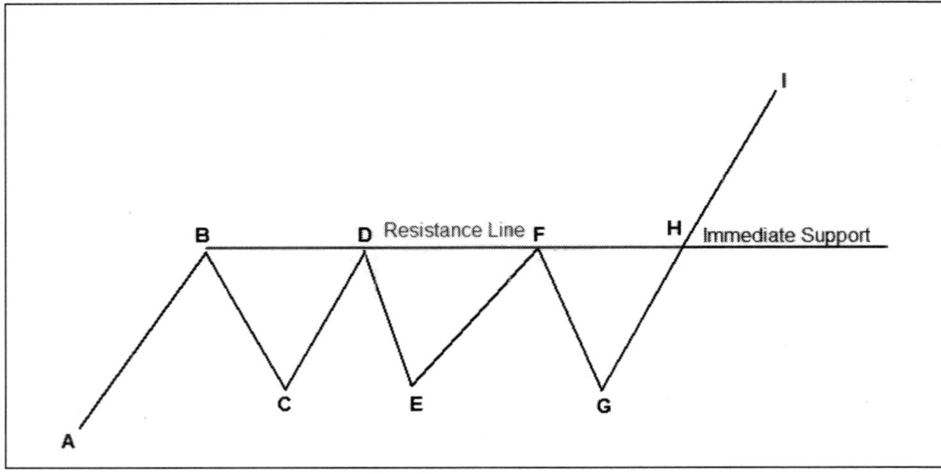

Figure 5.4: **A breached resistance becomes the next immediate support**

Figure 5.4 illustrates how once a resistance is breached it becomes an immediate support for the stock.

Support and resistance represent key junctures where the forces of demand and supply meet. In the stock market, prices are driven by demand and supply; an increase in demand drives prices higher, whereas an increase in supply drives prices lower. When supply and demand are equal, prices move sideways as both buyers and sellers struggle for control.

In practice, trading support and resistance is extremely profitable. There are two ways of trading support and resistance:

Strategy 1: Buying Near Support Levels and Selling Near Resistance Levels

Here one buys when prices are trading near to a support level with a stop loss just below the concerned support level.

Correspondingly, one sells when prices are trading near a resistance level, with a stop loss just above that level.

After initiating the trade, one should book profits when the stock price moves in the expected direction and presents a profitability of anywhere between 1.75 times to 2 times the original risk undertaken.

Original risk for buying = Buying price minus stop loss point.
Original risk for selling = Stop loss point minus selling price.

Strategy 2: Selling and Buying When Support and Resistance are Taken Off, Respectively

Supports do not always hold and a break below a support level signals that the supply has increased and sellers have taken control of the underlying asset. Such a decline below the support level indicates a new willingness to sell. Thus, one sells when a support level breaks, with a stop loss 2% above the support level.

Similarly, a resistance does not always hold and a break above a resistance level signals that demand has increased and buyers have taken control of the underlying asset. Such a rally above the resistance level indicates a new willingness to buy. In such a situation, one buys when resistance level breaks, with a stop loss 2% below the resistance level.

Unlike in the previous strategy, here one should book profits once the stock price moves in the expected direction and presents a profitability of anywhere between 2.50 times to 3 times the original risk undertaken.

Original risk for buying = Buying price minus stop loss point.
Original risk for selling = Stop loss point minus selling price.

As you would notice, in this case traders get a better risk reward ratio as compared to the risk reward ratio of the first strategy because in this case there is a change in the trend's direction with a break of support or resistance levels, as the case may be.

6

Four Profitable Strategies for Trading Trend Lines

Trend lines are essentially of two types:

1. Uptrend line, and
2. Downtrend line.

Uptrend Line

An uptrend line is a line drawn by connecting successive higher bottoms. This is illustrated in Figure 6.1.

So long as the price remains on or above this line, the uptrend is in force.

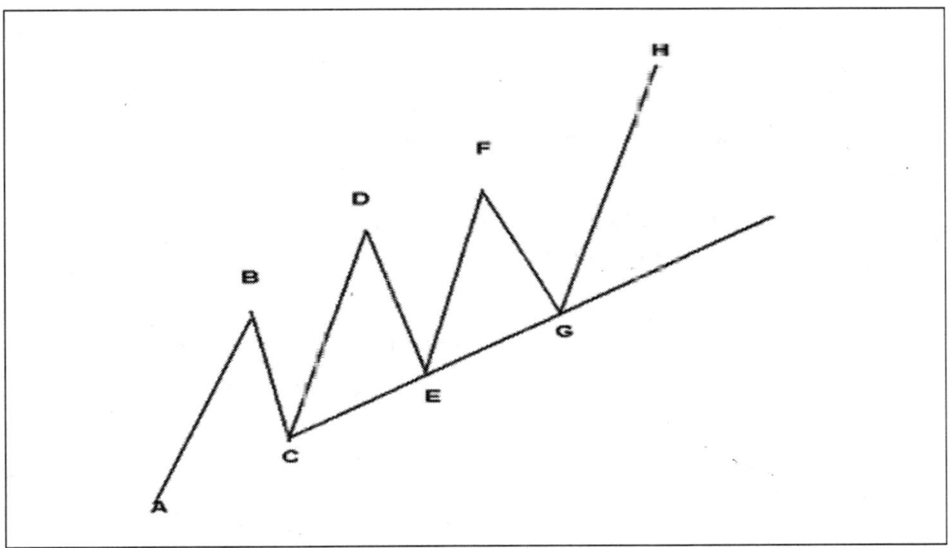

Figure 6.1: **Uptrend line formed by joining successive higher bottoms C, E and G**

Downtrend Line

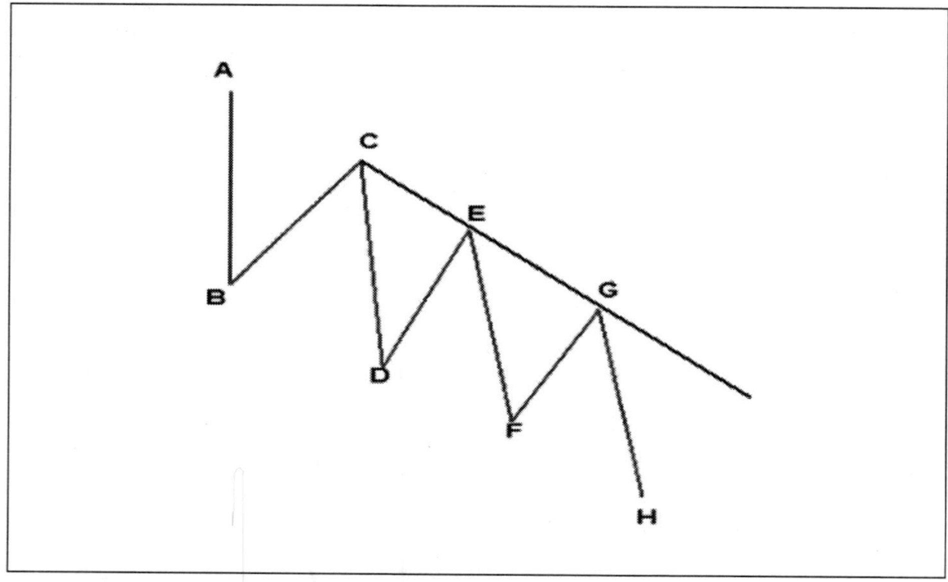

Figure 6.2: **Downtrend line formed by joining successive lower tops C, E and G**

A downtrend line is a line formed by connecting successive lower tops. This is illustrated in Figure 6.2.

So long as the price remains on or below this line, the downtrend is in force.

Trading Trend Lines

- Trend line theory holds that once a trend line is breached, the trend which was previously in force stands reversed.
- Thus, if an uptrend line is breached, it's a signal to sell.
- Correspondingly, if downtrend line is breached, it's a signal to buy.

- In practice, trading trendlines requires proficiency and to begin with one should focus on the four basic strategies given below for getting better trading decisions and profitability.

Strategy 1: Sell When the Uptrend Line of the Pullback Rally is Breached

A pullback rally is a bear market rally. It is also called a relief rally. As we now know, in a bear market prices make lower top, lower bottom formations. The typical characteristics of a pullback rally are as follows:

- It's unexpected;
- It's fast; and
- Most important, it's short-lived.

Hence one can easily identify a pullback rally from the characteristics defined above. Even then if one fails to differentiate a pullback rally from an actual bull market rally, i.e. when prices make higher top, higher bottom formations, then one should take into account the following two points:

- A reversal of trend from down to up is never unexpected as charts always suggest any such reversals fairly well in advance. Pullback rallies, on the other hand, are always unexpected.
- Bear markets are never short-lived and neither do they change direction overnight without giving any warning signals in advance. A pullback rally, on the other hand, is short-lived and it always ends overnight and, that too, without giving any warning signals.

One should sell when a pullback ends.

To identify the end of a pullback rally, draw an uptrend line on this pullback rally and a breach of this uptrend line is a final signal to the end of a pullback rally. This signifies that one should sell as the preceding downtrend is likely to resume.

The stop loss is initially placed just above the trend line. Experience shows that in most cases prices decline anywhere around 17% to 20% from the trend line breaking point and thereafter prices either demonstrate a sharp pullback or enter a long consolidation phase. I would therefore suggest booking profit when the price declines anywhere around 17% to 20% from the trend line breaking point.

Let's understand this better with the help of some real life market examples.

Example 1

Figure 6.3 shows that the stock of Jaypee Infratech was in a clear downtrend as prices were continuously making lower tops and lower bottoms.

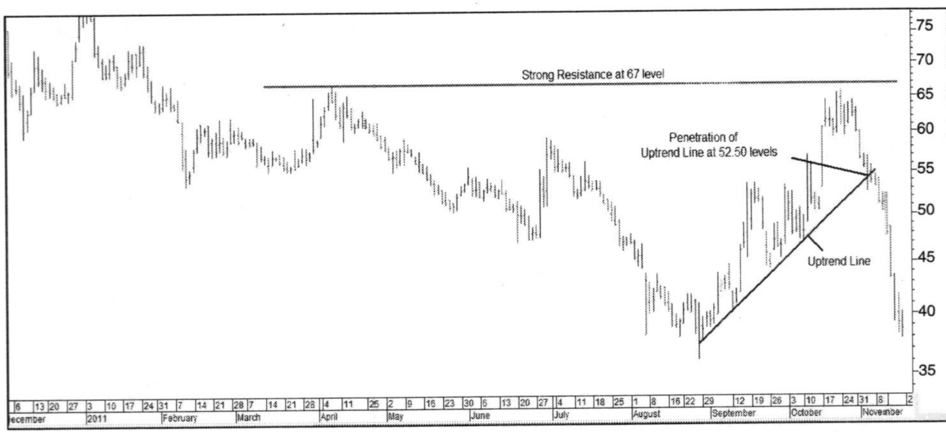

Figure 6.3: **Trading the end of the pullback rally in Jaypee Infratech which is in a clear downtrend**

The stock got listed at around ₹ 98 levels and thereafter it settled at around ₹ 37 in August 2011. From these levels, the first pullback rally started with all the media hype surrounding Formula One racing, better known as F1, coming to India. In this pullback rally, the stock failed to cross the strong resistance at around the level of ₹ 67. Thereafter, the uptrend line of the pullback rally was breached at ₹ 52.50 level on 3 November 2011. This downward penetration of the uptrend line signalled an end of the pullback rally, Now, since the stock was already in a downtrend prior to the pull-back, one could have gone short with a stop loss above ₹ 55. Thereafter, the stock fell to ₹ 38 level within nine trading sessions.

As explained above, one should take profit when prices decline anywhere around 17% to 20% from the trend line break point. Here the trend line breaking point was ₹ 52.50, hence one should have made an effort to take profit anywhere between ₹ 44 to ₹ 42 levels in the ongoing decline.

Example 2

Figure 6.4 shows the stock of Bajaj Hindustan in a clear downtrend as the price was continuously making lower tops and lower bottoms. In fact,

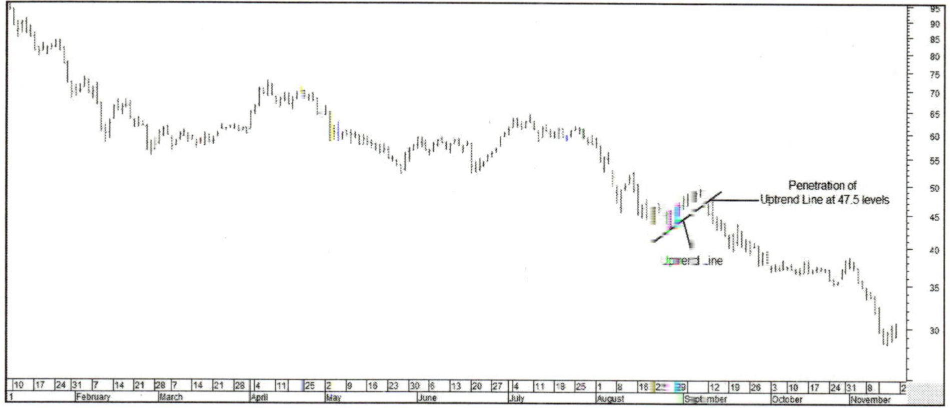

Figure 6.4: **Trading the end of the pullback rally in the downtrending Bajaj Hindustan**

the stock never participated in any market rally during the period under review. In a pullback rally in the month of August 2011, the price rose from a little less than ₹ 42 to around ₹ 50 levels, even though the stock was still making lower tops and lower bottoms. This pullback rally from ₹ 42 to ₹ 50 levels ended when the uptrend line of the rally was penetrated at ₹ 47.5 levels. This was the time to sell the stock with a stop loss above ₹ 48. After that, the stock fell to ₹ 37 levels within nineteen trading sessions.

As explained above, one should take profit when prices decline anywhere around 17% to 20% from the trend line break point. Here, the trend line breaking point was ₹ 47.50, hence one could have to book profit anywhere between ₹ 39.50 to ₹ 38 levels in the ongoing decline

Option Trading Strategy

- One could consider buying at-the-money put options as soon as the uptrend line of a pullback rally is breached because prices are likely to then crash with a downside momentum, which would prevent any erosion in the time value of the put option.

Strategy 2: Buy When the Downtrend Line of a Bull Market Corrective Wave is Breached

A corrective wave is better known as bull market correction. Remember, in a bull market prices make successively higher tops and higher bottoms formations. The typical characteristics of a bull market corrective wave are as follows:

- It's unexpected;
- It's fast; and
- Most important, it's a short lived decline.

One can therefore easily identify a corrective wave from the characteristics defined above. Even then if one fails to distinguish between a corrective wave and an actual bear market decline, wherein prices make lower top and lower bottom formations, then one should take into account the following two points:

- Reversal of trend from up to down is never unexpected as the charts invariably suggest it well in advance; whereas corrective waves are always unexpected.
- Bull markets are never short lived, and also they never change direction overnight without giving any warning signals in advance. Corrective waves, on the other hand, are short lived and always end overnight, and that too without giving any warning signal.

One should buy when such a correction ends.

To identify the end of a bull market correction, draw a downtrend line on the corrective wave, and an upside breach of this downtrend line is the signal for an end of corrective wave. This signifies that one should buy as the preceding uptrend is likely to resume.

The stop loss is initially placed just below the trend line. Experience shows that in most cases prices rally anywhere around 17% to 20% from the trend line breaking point and thereafter prices either decline severely or enter a long consolidation phase. I would therefore suggest booking profit when the price rallies anywhere around 17% to 20% from the trend line breaking point.

Let's now understand this with the help of some real life market examples.

Example 1

Figure 6.5 illustrates the stock of DLF in a clear uptrend as the price was continuously making higher tops and higher bottoms. During this uptrend, the stock price of DLF corrected from ₹ 425 to ₹ 260 levels in June-July 2009, just after the Congress-led coalition returned to power in India. This correction ended when its downtrend line was breached upward at ₹ 316 level. This was the time to buy the stock with a stop below the ₹ 303 level. From ₹ 316, the stock rallied almost vertically to ₹ 430 levels in nine trading sessions.

As suggested earlier, in this strategy one should take profit when prices rally anywhere around 17% to 20% from the trend line breaking point. Here the trend line breaking point was ₹ 316. Accordingly, one should have booked profits anywhere between ₹ 363 to ₹ 380 levels.

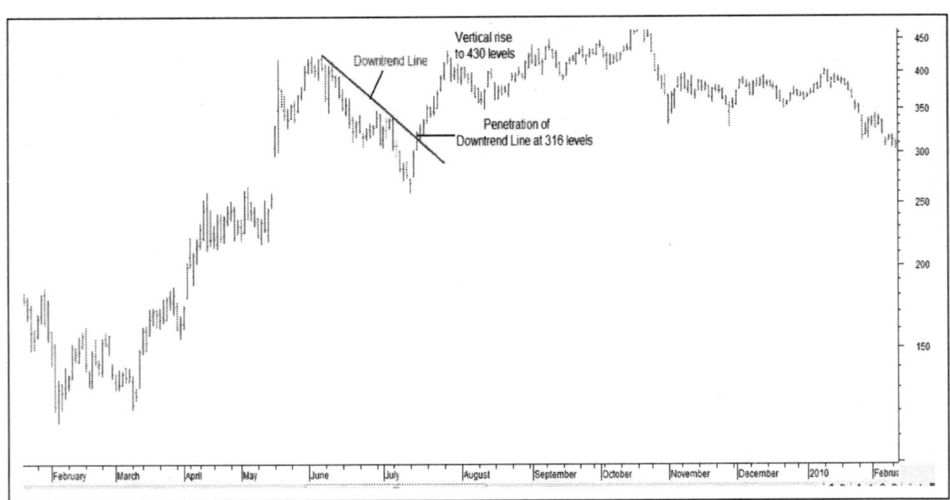

Figure 6.5: **Trading the upward break of the correction downtrend line in DLF**

Example 2

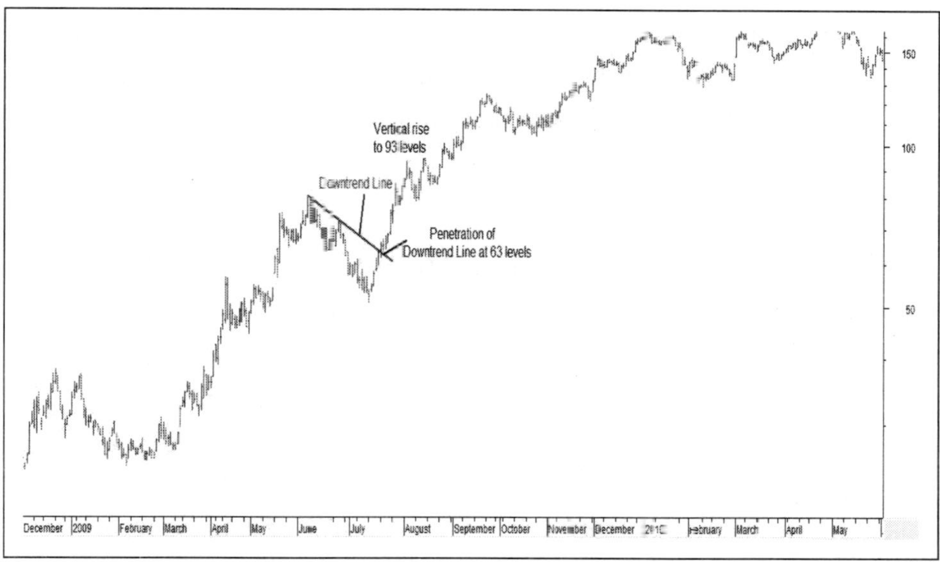

Figure 6.6: **Trading the upward break of the correction down trend line during an uptrend in Tata Motors**

Figure 6.6 illustrates the stock of Tata Motors in a clear uptrend as the price was continuously making higher tops and higher bottoms. Then, during a correction in this uptrend, the stock price corrected from ₹ 80 to ₹ 51 levels in June-July 2009, just after the Congress-led coalition came to power in New Delhi. The correction ended when its downtrend line was breached upward at ₹ 63 levels. This was the time to buy the stock with a stop below ₹ 60. From ₹ 63, the price then rallied almost vertically to ₹ 93 levels in twelve trading sessions.

As noted earlier, one should take profit when prices rally anywhere around 17% to 20% from the trend line break point. Here the trend line breaking point was ₹ 63, hence one should have booked profit anywhere in the ₹ 73 to ₹ 75 levels in the subsequent rally.

Option Trading Strategy

- One could consider buying at-the-money call options when the stock price closes above the downtrend line as the price is thereafter likely to rally with an upside momentum which would prevent any erosion in the time value of the call option.

Strategy 3: Buy When the Uptrend Line Is Breached and Thereafter the Price Again Closes Above the Trend Line, the Very Next Day or After a Few Days

Here, the first breach of an uptrend line is used as a signal of a shakeout which signifies that the weak hands are getting out of the market. The closing again above the trend line within a matter of days signifies that smart money is back and one could therefore buy with a stop loss placed below the recent lows made below the trend line. The stop loss is initially placed just below the trend line and one should only run buy side position until and unless trend a reversal takes place, i.e. the price reverses direction from ongoing higher top, higher bottom formation to lower top, lower bottom formation.

Again, experience shows that in most cases prices rally anywhere around 17% to 20% from the trend line breaking point and thereafter they either decline severely or enter a long consolidation phase. I would therefore suggest booking profit when the price rallies anywhere around 17% to 20% from the trend line breaking point.

Let's understand this with the help of some real life market examples.

Example 1

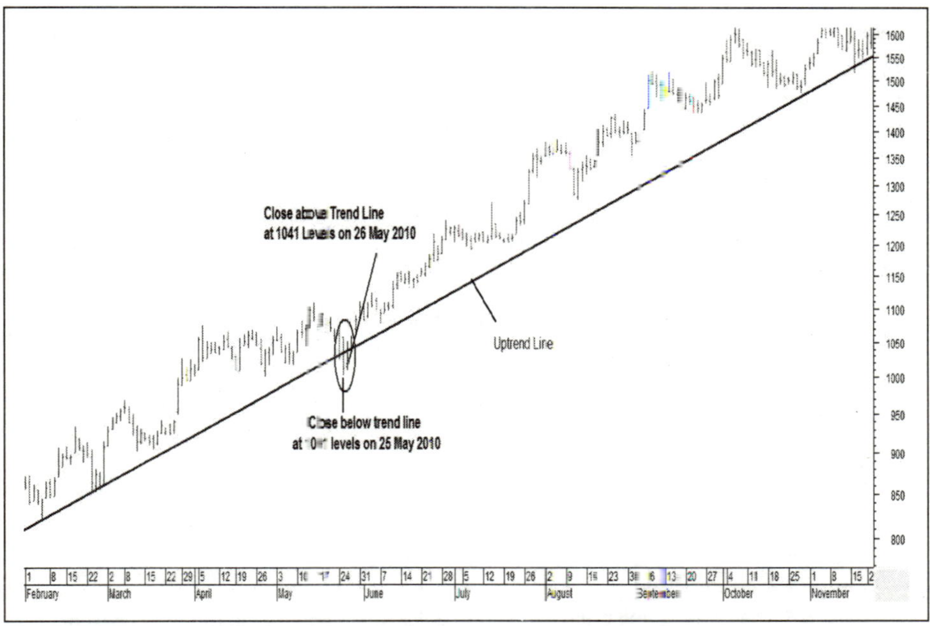

Figure 6.7: **The uptrend line breached — and quickly reclaimed in Bajaj Auto**

Figure 6.7 illustrates that the stock of Bajaj Auto was in a clear uptrend as prices were continuously making higher tops and higher bottoms. During this uptrend, the price closed below the trend line at ₹ 1,001 levels on 25 May 2010. The price, however, again closed above the trend line at ₹ 1,041 levels on 26 May. This was the time to buy the stock at ₹ 1,041 levels with a stop loss below ₹ 1,001, which was the low made below the trend line. Eventually, the stock price rallied to ₹ 1,600-plus levels by the beginning of November 2011.

As suggested earlier, in such a trade one should take profit when prices rally anywhere around 17% to 20% from one's buying point. Here the buying point was ₹ 1,041, hence one could have taken profit anywhere between ₹ 1,218 and ₹ 1,250 levels in the ongoing rally.

Example 2

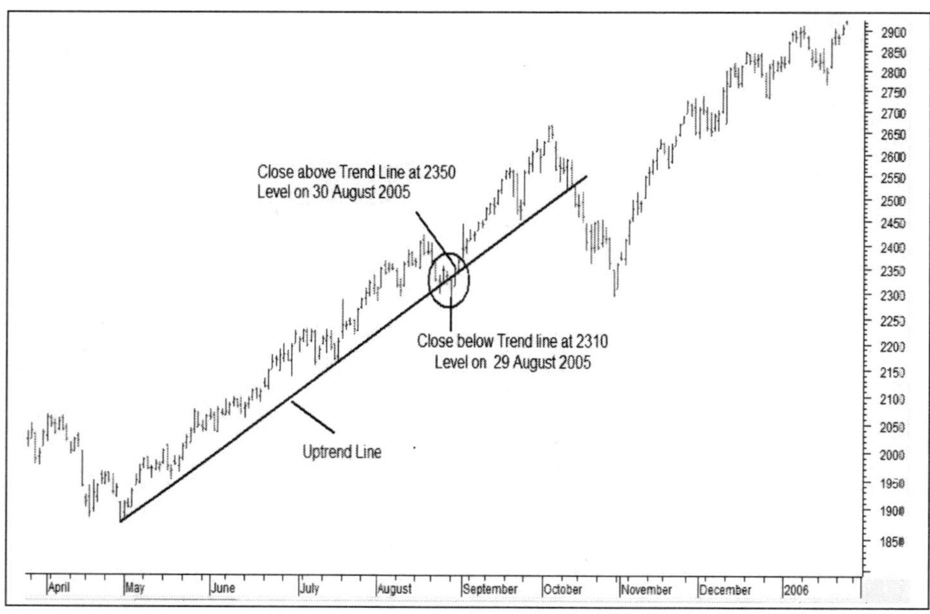

Figure 6.8: **The uptrend line breached — and quickly reclaimed — in the daily chart of Nifty futures**

Figure 6.8 shows Nifty futures in a clear uptrend as the price was continuously making higher tops and higher bottoms. During this uptrend, the price closed below the trend line at 2,310 levels on 29 August 2005 but again closed above the trend line at 2,350 level the very next day, i.e. on 30 August 2005. This was the time to buy Nifty futures at 2,350 levels with a stop loss below 2,287, which was the low made below the trend line. Eventually, Nifty futures rallied to 2,600-plus level by the beginning of October 2005.

As suggested above, in such a trade one should normally take profit when prices rally anywhere around 17% to 20% from the buying point. But this is a benchmark index and in case of indices one should take profit when prices rally anywhere around 7% to 8% from the buying point. Here buying point is 2,350, hence one should make an effort to take profit anywhere between 2,514-2,538 levels in the ongoing rally.

Option Trading Strategy

- You could consider buying at-the-money call options as the price would probably rally with an upside momentum which would prevent any erosion in the time value of the call option.

Strategy 4: Sell When the Price Again Closes Below the Downtrend Line After an Upward Breach, the Very Next Day or After Just a Few Days

The first breach of the downtrend line might suggest that the bears, i.e. the sellers, are losing control but if the price closes once again below the trend line the next day, or after a few days, it confirms that bears continue to have the upper hand. One could then sell with a stop loss at the high made above the trend line and one should run the sell side position until a trend reversal takes place, i.e. the price reverses direction from ongoing lower top, lower bottom formation to higher top, higher bottom formation.

Experience shows that in most cases prices decline anywhere around 17% to 20% from the selling point and thereafter prices either rally sharply or enter a time wise big consolidation phase. I would therefore suggest booking profit when the price declines anywhere around 17% to 20% from the selling point.

Let's understand this with the help of some real life market examples.

Example 1

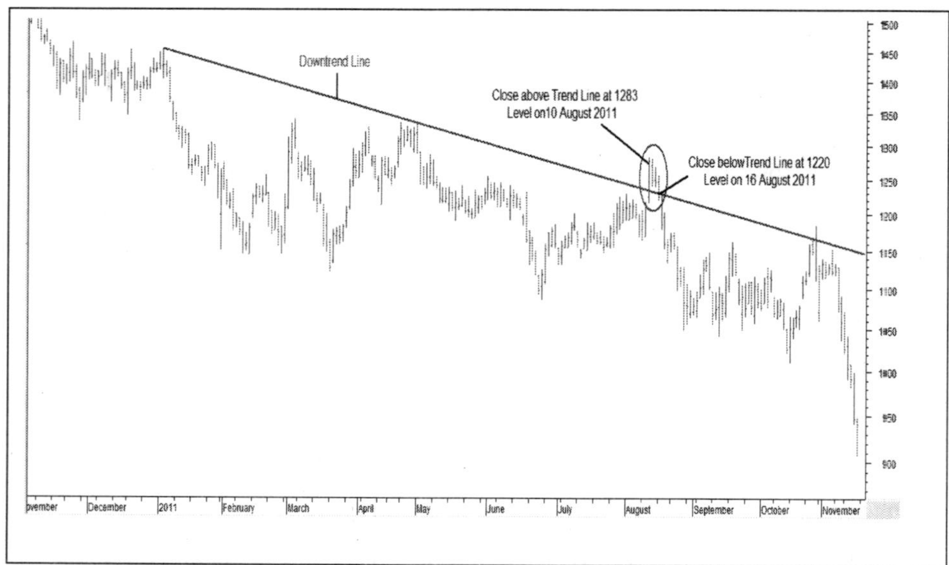

Figure 6.9: **Daily chart of Maruti Suzuki: sell when the stock again closes below the trend line after having briefly broken above it earlier**

Figure 6.9 illustrates that Maruti Suzuki was in a clear downtrend as the price was continuously making lower tops and lower bottoms. During this downtrend the price closed above the trend line at ₹ 1,283 levels on 10 August 2011 — but then again closed below the trend line at ₹ 1,220 levels on 16 August 2011. This was the time to sell Maruti Suzuki stock at around ₹ 1,220 level, with a stop loss above ₹ 1,284 which was the high made above the trend line. Eventually, Maruti Suzuki stock declined to below ₹ 1,000.

As suggested above, one should take profit when prices decline anywhere between 17% and 20% from your selling point. Here the selling point was ₹ 1,220, and so one should be booking profit anywhere between ₹ 1,013 and ₹ 976 levels in the ongoing decline.

Example 2

Figure 6.10: **Daily chart of Aban Offshore**

Figure 6.10 illustrates that Aban Offshore is in a clear downtrend as the price is continuously making lower tops and lower bottoms. During this downtrend, prices closed above the trend line at ₹ 818 levels on 31 December 2010 but then again closed below the trend line at ₹ 792 level on 5 January 2011. This was the time to sell Aban Offshore stock at around ₹ 792 levels with a stop loss above ₹ 834, the level of the high made above the trend line. Eventually, Aban Offshore stock declined to below ₹ 520 levels within twenty-five trading sessions.

As suggested above, one should take profit when the price declines anywhere between 17% and 20% from the selling point. Here the selling point was ₹ 792, hence one should make an effort to take profit anywhere between ₹ 658 and ₹ 634 levels in the ongoing decline.

Option Trading Strategy

- One could consider buying at-the-money put options because prices are likely to crash with a downside momentum which would prevent any erosion in the time value of the put option.

7

Trading Chart Patterns

Reading chart patterns is the backbone of technical trading. There is no specific formula to master them. Rather, the key to understanding chart patterns is sheer hard work. You can successfully interpret charts only by putting in lots of effort in identifying and studying hundreds of them but, believe me, this labour bears fruitful results and is very rewarding.

Prices always move in trends which could be either up or down. There is a mistaken belief that trend can also be sideways. However, the market's sideways movement is, in fact, the formation of continuation patterns which exist in both uptrends as well as downtrends.

Now, the price movement could be:

- Straight or curved.
- Short lived or long sustaining.
- Poorly defined or clearly defined.

As prices always move in trends, sooner or later either:

1. There is a change in the direction of the trend. A change in the trend's direction, however, typically does not happen at once. During the course of a change in the trend, certain patterns are formed which are called **reversal patterns**.
2. Alternately, a trend may take rest, i.e. the price consolidates at a certain level before moving further ahead in the direction of the existing trend. These patterns are better known as **continuation patterns**.

Reversal Patterns

The Head and Shoulders Top Formation

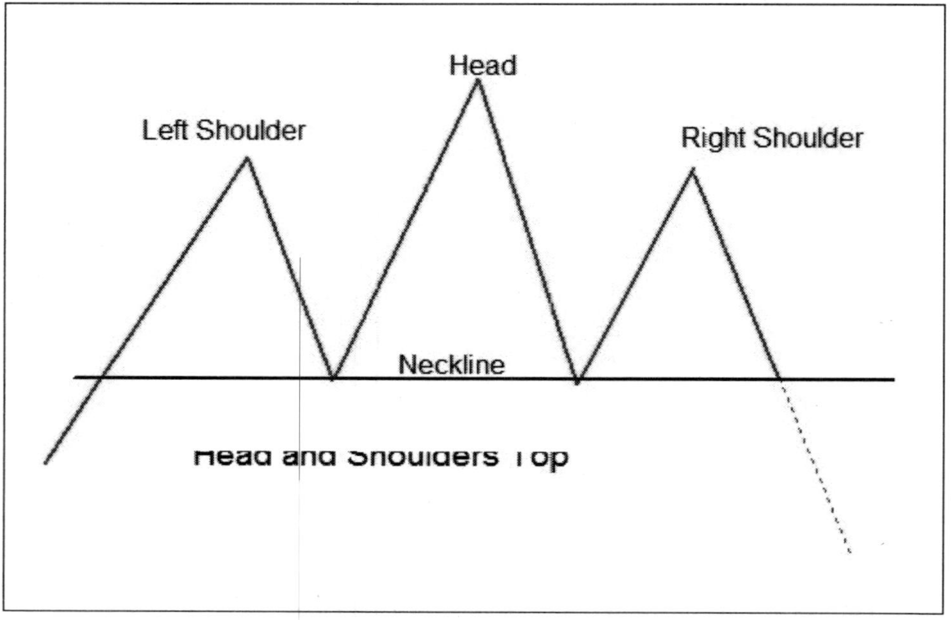

Figure 7.1: **A head and shoulders top formation**

Figure 7.1 illustrates the head and shoulders top formation. It consists of a left shoulder, a head, and a right shoulder. The formation of this pattern on a chart suggests a trend reversal from up to down.

The **left shoulder** is formed usually at the end of an extensive advance during which volume is often quite heavy. At the end of the left shoulder, there is a small correction and this correction usually occurs on lower volume.

The **head** is then formed with heavy volume on the upside but the subsequent correction happens with lower volume. At this point, in order to conform to the proper pattern, the price must come down to at least below the top of the left shoulder. However, even if the price falls somewhat lower than the bottom of the left shoulder, then too this pattern formation would be intact.

Finally, the **right shoulder** is formed by a rally, usually on lower volume than the previous rallies leading to this formation.

A **neckline** can now be drawn across the bottom of the left shoulder, the head and the right shoulder. A downward breaking of this neckline by the price declining from the right shoulder is the final confirmation and completes the head and shoulders top formation. This is, therefore, the signal to sell short.

Once the neckline is breached, you can initiate a position on the sell side.

Once the neckline is breached, a sell side position can be initiated. One should sell when the neckline is breached on closing basis. Theoretically, the stop loss should be placed above the top of right shoulder. However, I find such a stop loss enormously large and practically unviable because a substantial part of trading capital would erode in single trade when such large stop loss gets triggered.

Experience suggests that the stop loss should be placed 6% above the neckline. Thereafter, one should mark out the target which is arrived at by first measuring the vertical distance from the top of the head to the neckline. You then measure the same distance downward from the point where the price breached the neckline. This gives the minimum price

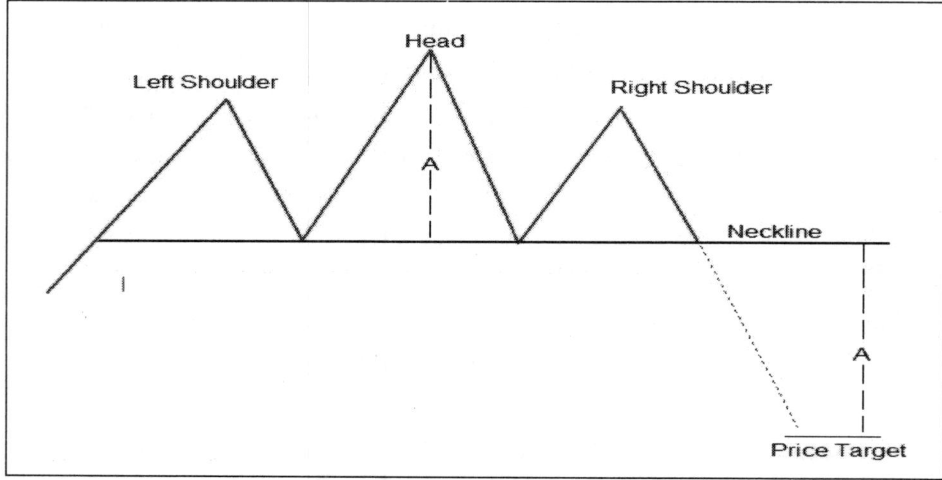

Figure 7.2: **How far can calculating the target after a head and shoulders top price fall?**

objective of how far the price could decline below the neckline after it is broken. This is illustrated in Figure 7.2

Caution

- Most head and shoulders patterns are not as perfectly symmetrical as illustrated in Figure 7.1. Often, one shoulder may appear to droop, i.e. be lower than the other.
- Many head and shoulders patterns consist of either multiple left shoulders, multiple right shoulders or both multiple left and right shoulders.
- Instead of being horizontal, the neckline might be sloping a little up or down. But if the neckline is up sloping, make sure that the lowest point on the right shoulder must be lower than the top of the left shoulder.
- The price moves lower after breaking the neckline, but often it pulls back thereafter to the neckline and, in some cases, the pullback goes

even higher than the neckline. Therefore, the stop loss for such trading should be placed at the top of the right shoulder.

Let's understand this with some real life market examples.

Example 1

Figure 7.3 illustrates a head and shoulders top formation on S&P 500 Index. Here the neckline was breached on 2 August 2011 at 1,254 levels on closing basis. As noted earlier, the stop loss should be placed 6% above the neckline. In this case, therefore, the stop loss should be placed at $1,331 levels (6% above the neckline level of $1,256 levels). The minimum price target of this breakdown was $1,147 which was met on 8 August 2011 when the market opened with a downside gap after America's AAA rating was downgraded on 6 August 2011

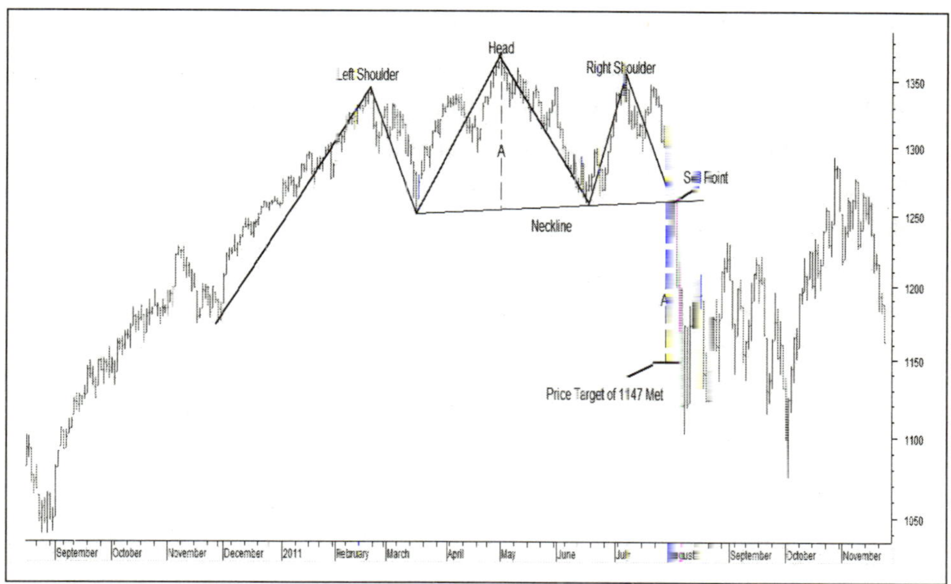

Figure 7.3: **The uptrend reverses after a head and shoulders top formation in the daily chart of S&P 500 Index**

Example 2

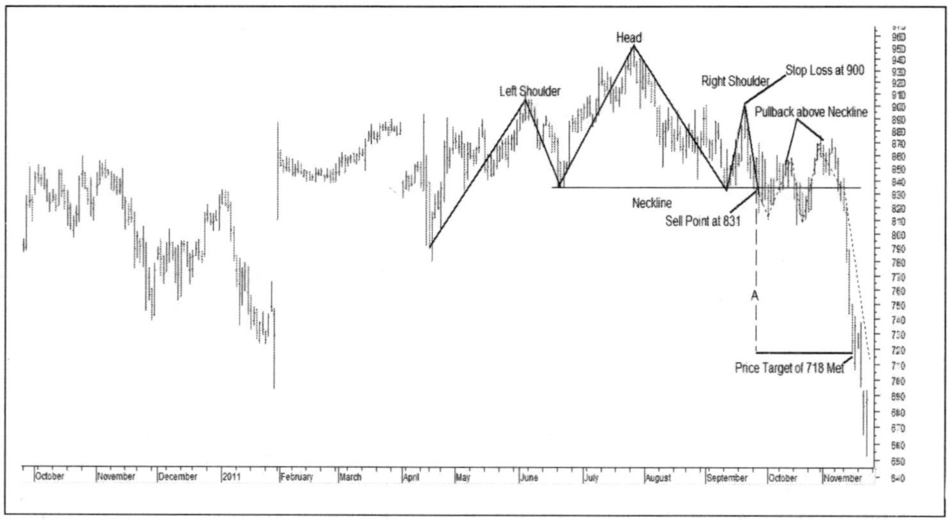

Figure 7.4: **The uptrend in Siemens reverses after the formation of a head and shoulders top**

Figure 7.4 illustrates a head and shoulders top formation in the daily price chart of Siemens. In this case, the neckline was breached on 28 September 2011 at ₹ 831 level on closing basis. Thereafter, there was a pullback rally till above the neckline on two occasions. It was a sell at ₹ 831 level with a stop loss at 6% above the neckline level — as explained earlier — hence here the stop loss should be placed at ₹ 885 level (6% above the neckline level of ₹ 835). The minimum price target of this breakdown was ₹ 718 which was met on 18 November 2011, and the price further slipped below ₹ 660 level in the next four trading sessions.

Example 3

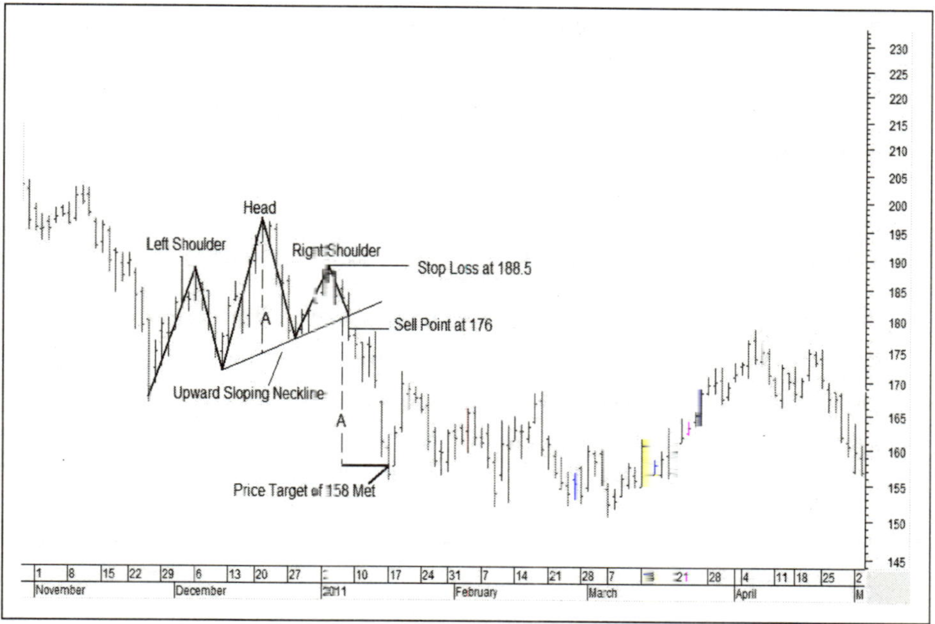

Figure 7.5: **Head and shoulders top formation in the daily chart of SAIL leads to a reversal of uptrend**

Figure 7.5 illustrates a head and shoulders top formation in the chart of SAIL. Here the neckline was up sloping. However, as you can observe the lowest point on the right shoulder was lower than the top of the left shoulder.

The neckline was breached on 7 January 2011 at ₹ 176 level on closing basis. It was a sell at these levels with a stop loss at 6% above the neckline, i.e. at ₹ 190 levels — 6% above neckline level of ₹ 179. The minimum price target of this breakdown was ₹ 158 which was duly met on 17 January 2011.

Option Trading Strategy for Head and Shoulders Top Formation

- One could consider buying at-the-money put options when the neckline is breached as the price is then likely to fall with a downside momentum which would prevent any erosion in the time value of the put option.

The Head and Shoulders Bottom Formation

Figure 7.6 illustrates the head and shoulders bottom formation which is simply the inverse of a head and shoulders top formation. This formation too consists of a left shoulder, a head, and a right shoulder but it suggests a trend reversal from down to up.

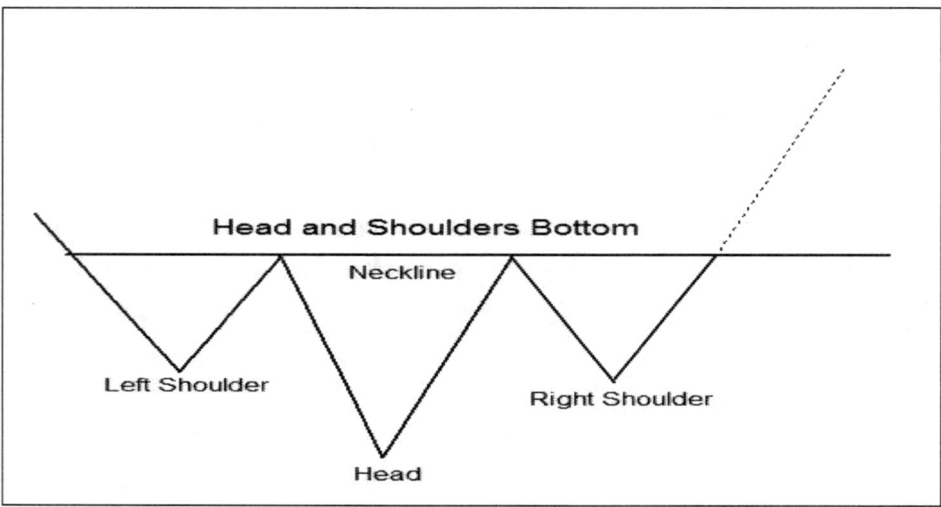

Figure 7.6: **A head and shoulders bottom formation**

The **left shoulder** is formed usually at the end of an extensive decline during which the volume is often quite heavy. At the end of the left shoulder, there is a small rally and this rally usually occurs on low volumes.

The **head** is then formed with a correction on lower volume, followed by a rally, usually on higher volume than the previous rallies.

Finally, the **right shoulder** is formed by a rally usually with higher volume than the previous rallies in this formation. At this point, in order to conform to the proper rules, volumes should pick up as the price rallies from the bottom of the head, and then rises even more dramatically on the rally from the right shoulder.

A **neckline** can now be drawn across the top of the left shoulder, the head and the right shoulder (*see* Figure 7.7). An upside breach of this neckline on a rally from the right shoulder is a final confirmation and completes the head and shoulders bottom formation. This is, therefore, the signal to buy.

If the upward breach of the neckline occurs on low volumes, then one must avoid taking a buy position as such a breakout could be false and the price might retest the lows. A high volume breakout, on the other hand, would give confidence in the breakout.

Once the neckline is breached, a buy position can be initiated. Remember, one should buy when the neckline is breached on closing basis. Theoretically, the stop loss should be placed below the bottom of right shoulder. However, such a stop loss as often too large and practically unviable because a substantial part of one's trading capital could erode in single trade when such large stop loss gets triggered.

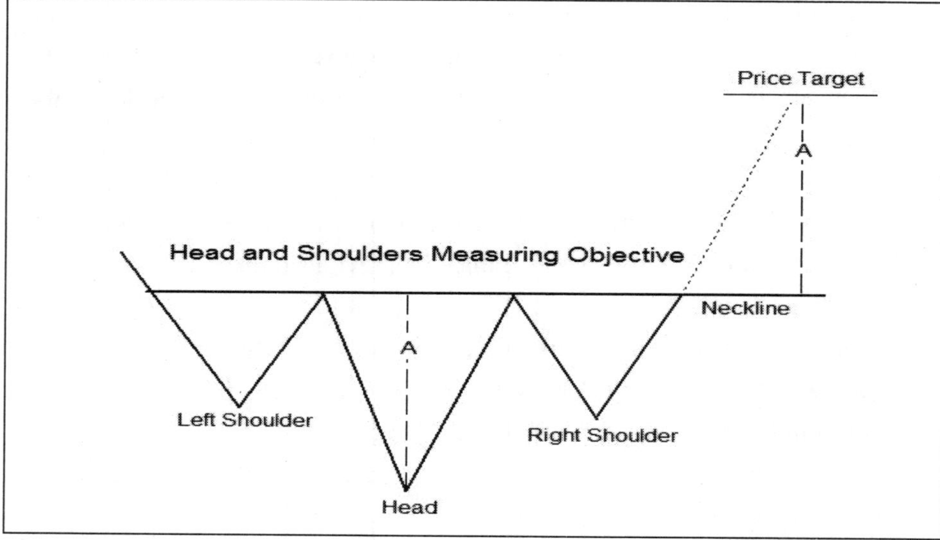

Figure 7.7: **Measuring the price target after the formation of a head and shoulders bottom formation**

Experience suggests that the stop loss is better placed 6% below the neckline. Thereafter one should mark out target which is defined by measuring the vertical distance from the bottom of the head up to the neckline (*see* Figure 7.7). Then measure the same distance up from the point where the price breached the neckline. This gives the minimum target of how far the price could rally following the upside break of the neckline.

Let's understand this with some real life market examples.

Example 1

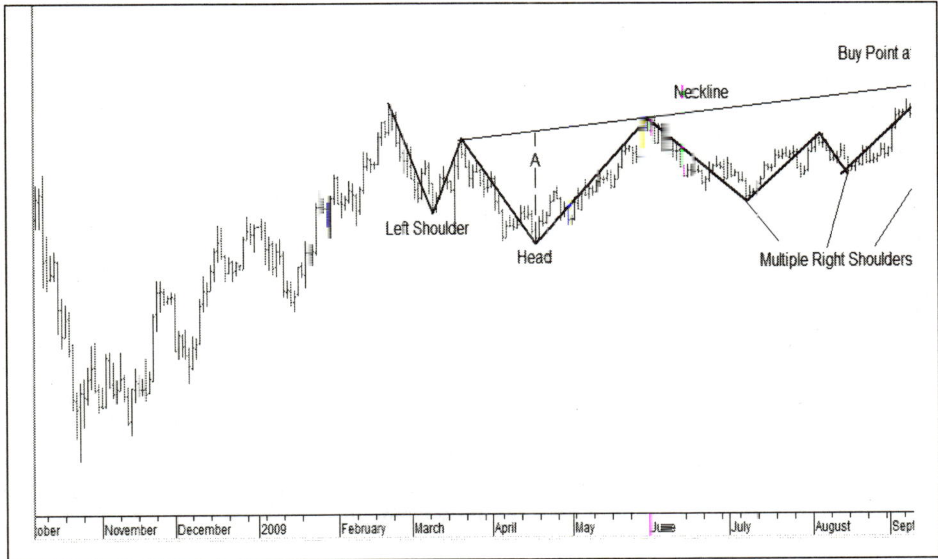

Figure 7.8: **A head and shoulders bottom formation in the daily chart of gold cash ($)**

Figure 7.8 illustrates a head and shoulders bottom formation on gold in dollar denomination. Here the neckline was up sloping and we can observe that the lowest point on the right shoulder was lower than top of the left shoulder. The rising gold price breached the neckline on 6 October 2009 at $1,041 level on closing basis. As already suggested, the stop loss should be placed 6% below the neckline and hence the stop loss in this case should be placed at $976 levels, i.e. 6% below neckline level of $1,039 levels.

The minimum price target of this breakout of $1,157 was met on 23 November 2009 — and thereafter the price of gold rallied further to $1,225 in the next eight trading sessions.

Example 2

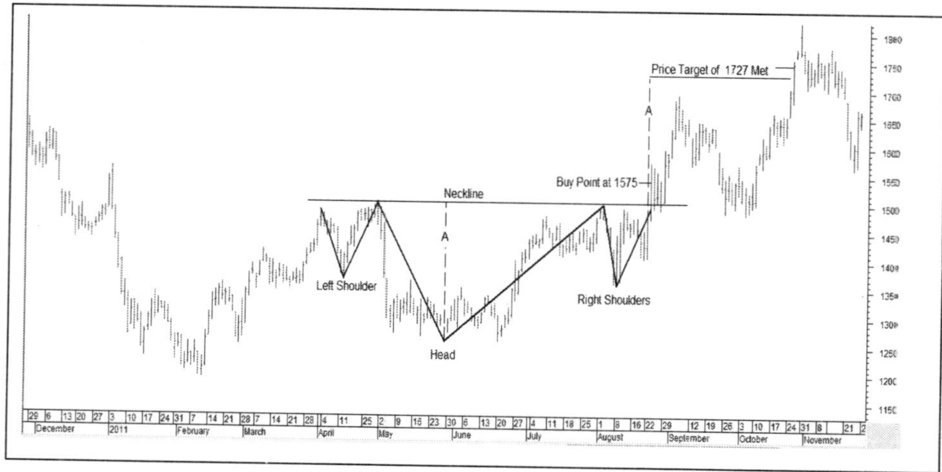

Figure 7.9: **A head and shoulders bottom formation in the daily chart of Bajaj Auto reverses the downtrend**

Figure 7.9 illustrates a head and shoulders bottom formation in the chart of Bajaj Auto futures. The neckline was breached by the rising price on 23 August 2011 at ₹ 1,575 levels on closing basis. It was a buy at these levels. As already suggested, the stop loss should be placed 6% below the neckline and hence the stop loss in this case should be placed at ₹ 1,408 levels, i.e. 6% below neckline level of ₹ 1,498 levels.

The minimum price target of this breakout is ₹ 1,727, which was duly met on 25 October 2011.

Example 3

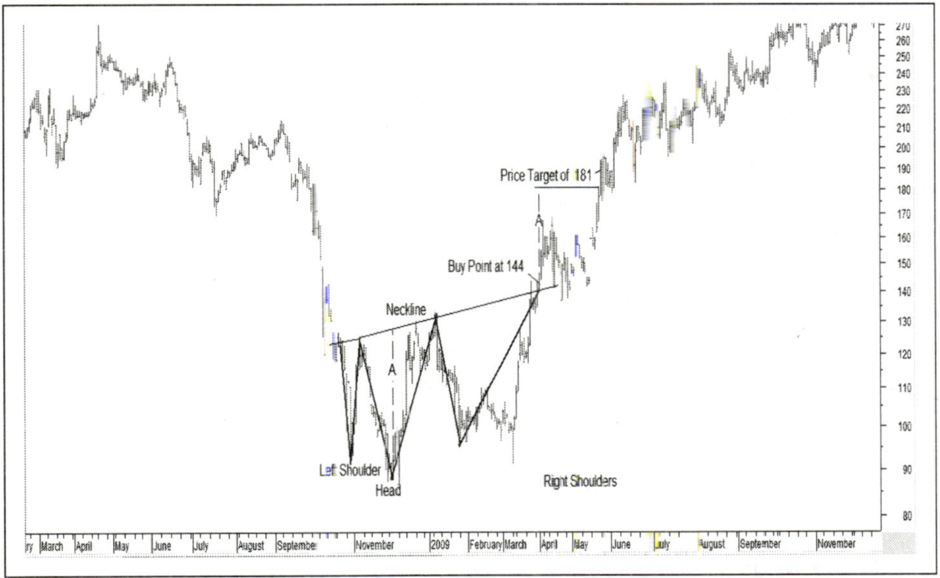

Figure 7.10: **A head and shoulders bottom formation in the daily chart of Biocon futures leads to a trend reversal from down to up**

Figure 7.10 illustrates a head and shoulders bottom formation in the chart of Biocon futures. The neckline was up sloping and we can observe that the lowest point on the right shoulder was lower than the left shoulder's top. The rising price breached the neckline on 1 April 2009 at ₹ 144 levels on closing basis. It was a buy at these levels. As suggested, the stop loss should be placed 6% below the neckline, thus in this case at ₹ 133.50 levels (6% below the neckline level of ₹ 142). The minimum price target of this breakout was ₹ 181 which was met on 25 May 2009. Eventually, the price doubled from the minimum target levels without making any significant correction *en route*.

Option Trading Strategy for Head and Shoulders Bottom Formation

- You could consider selling at-the-money put options when the neckline is breached by the rising price. You should, however, avoid buying at-the-money call option because in most cases the price consolidates after the breakout and this can erode the time value of a call option.

- If the immediate lower bottom below the neckline is breached after you've sold at-the-money put options, then you should close the position with a loss. You could then consider buying at-the-money put options since a pattern failure has taken place and the price might thereafter crash with a downside momentum.

Double Top Formation

Figure 7.11 illustrates a double top formation which on charts visually looks like the letter "M". A double top formation, as the name suggests, consists of two tops — a left top and a right top — and signals a trend reversal from up to down.

The **left top** is formed usually at the end of an extensive advance during which the volume is often quite heavy. At the end of the left top, there is a small correction and this correction usually occurs on low volume.

The **right top** is then formed by a rally, typically on a lower volume than the previous rallies leading up to this formation.

A **neckline** can now be drawn across the bottoms of the left top and the right top. A downward break of this neckline on a decline from the right top is the final confirmation and completes the double top formation. This formation is the signal to sell short.

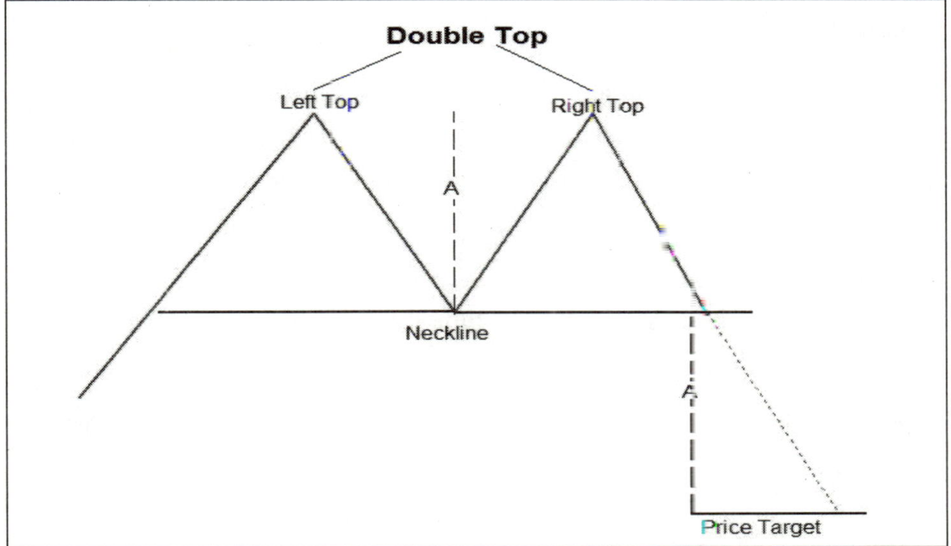

Figure 7.11: **Double top formation — and how to set a price target**

Once the neckline is breached, a sell side position can be initiated. One should sell when the neckline is breached on closing basis. Theoretically, the stop loss should be placed above the second top. In practice, however, such a stop loss could be very far and unviable because a substantial part of one's trading capital would erode in a single trade by the time such a distant stop loss gets triggered.

Experience suggests that the stop loss should be placed 4% above the neckline. Thereafter, one should mark out the price target for the trade. The target is defined by first measuring the vertical distance from the peak of the two tops down to the neckline (*see* Figure 7.11). Then the same distance is measured downward from the point where the price breached the neckline. This gives the minimum target of how far the price could decline following a breach of the neckline.

Caution

- Never anticipate or assume the formation of a double top pattern until and unless the neckline is actually breached because in an uptrend each new rally after a reaction could appear to be making a double top.
- The two tops must be separated by a deep and long reaction. If the two peaks are close together in time then it signifies consolidation, rather than reversal.
- Volume during the rise to the second peak must be lower than that during the rise to the first peak.

Let's now understand double top formations with some real life market examples.

Example 1

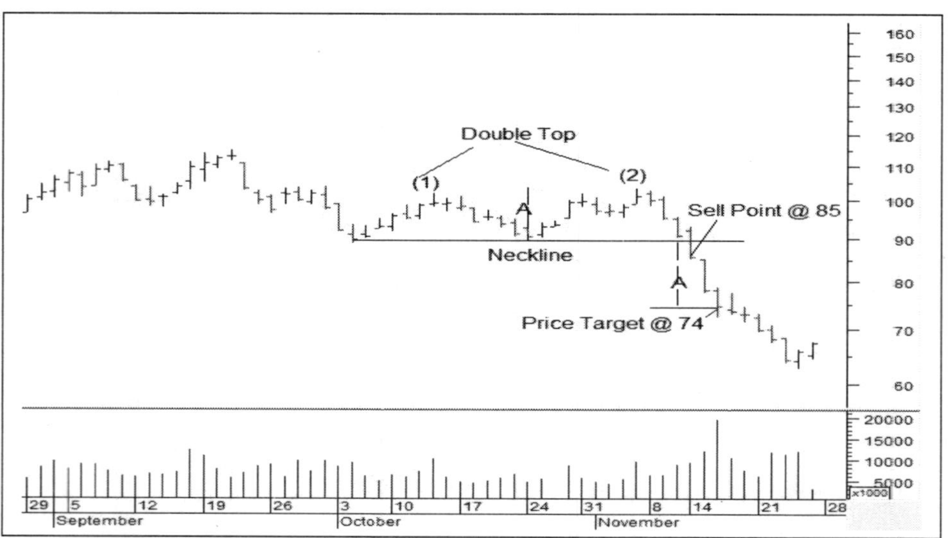

Figure 7.12: **Double top formation in the daily chart of HDIL signals the reversal of the trend from up to down**

Figure 7.12 illustrates the formation of a double top in HDIL stock. The left top was made on 13 October 2011 at ₹ 102 levels and the right top on 4 November 2011 at ₹ 103 level. The neckline was at ₹ 90 levels and got breached on closing basis on 14 November 2011 at ₹ 85 levels. It was a sell at these levels. As explained earlier, the stop loss could be placed at ₹ 93.60 level, i.e. 4% above the neckline level of ₹ 90. The minimum price target of this breakdown was ₹ 74 which was met in the next two trading sessions and thereafter the prices crashed nearly vertically to ₹ 65 levels within seven trading sessions of the sell signal being generated.

Example 2

Figure 7.13 illustrates a double top formation in the futures chart of Educomp Solutions.

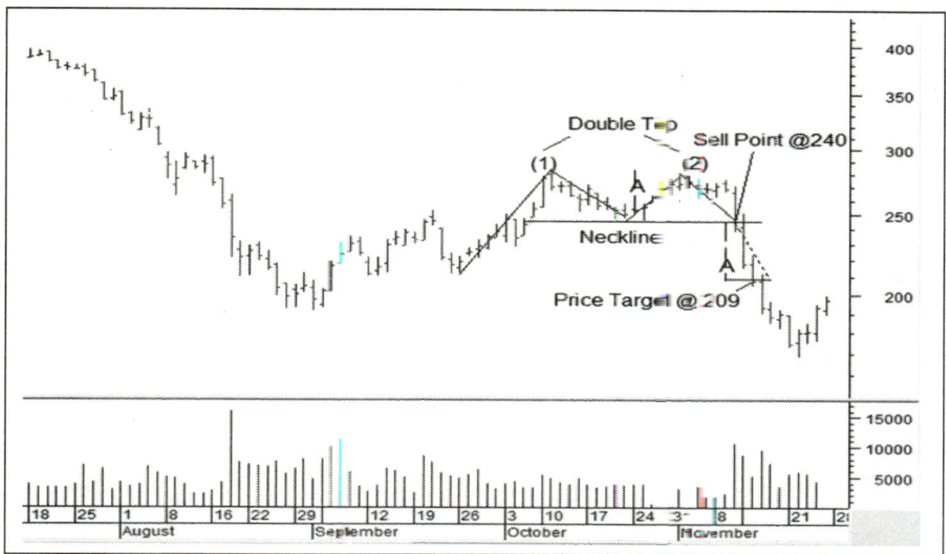

Figure 7.13: **Double top formation in the daily chart of Educomp Solutions futures. Note how the uptrend gets reversed thereafter**

The left top was made on 11 October 2011 at ₹ 284 and the right top on 1 November 2011 at ₹ 279 level. The neckline was at ₹ 245 level and was breached on 11 November 2011 when the price closed at ₹ 241, triggering a sell signal at these levels. As explained earlier, the stop loss should be at 4% above the neckline level, in this case at ₹ 254.80 levels. The minimum price target of this breakdown was ₹ 209 which was swiftly met in the next two trading sessions. Thereafter, the price crashed nearly vertically to ₹ 173 within seven trading sessions of the sell signal being generated.

Option Trading Strategy for Double Top Formation

- One should consider buying at-the-money put option when the neckline is breached as the price is then likely to crash with a momentum which would generally prevent any erosion in the time value of the put option.

Double Bottom Formation

Figure 7.14 illustrates a double bottom formation, which is simply the inverse of the double top formation and which on charts looks like the letter "W". It consists of a left bottom and a right bottom and suggests a reversal of the trend from down to up.

The **left bottom** is formed usually at the end of an extensive decline during which the volume is often quite heavy. At the end of the left bottom, there is a small rally but this rally usually occurs with low volume.

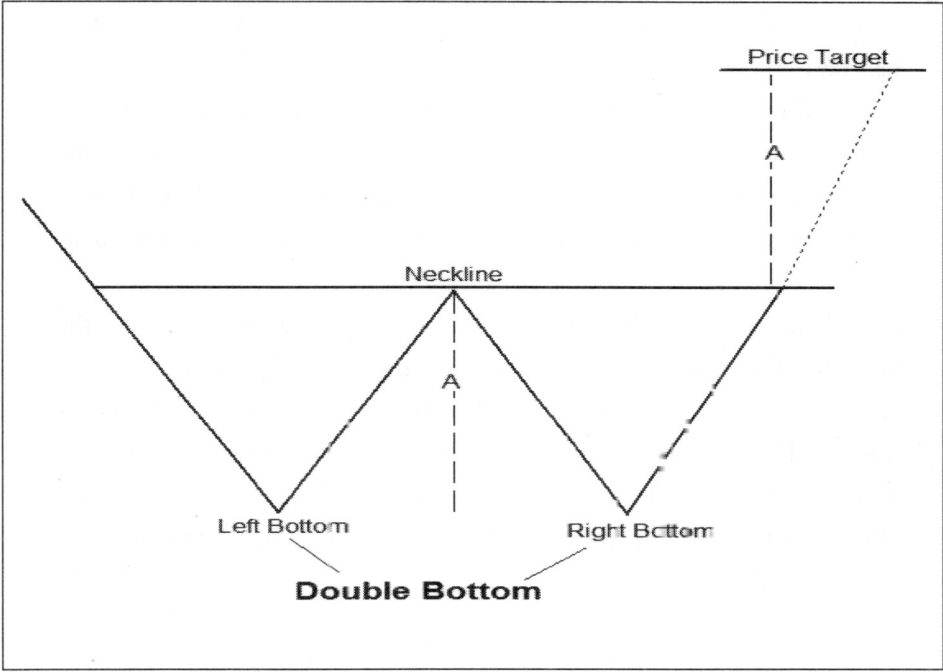

Figure 7.14: **Double bottom formation and the price target after a neckline break**

The **right bottom** is then formed by a rally, usually on higher volume than the previous rallies in this formation. In order to conform to the rules of this pattern, volumes should pick up even more dramatically at this point as the price rallies from the right bottom.

A **neckline** can now be drawn across the top of the left and right bottoms. An upside break of this neckline on a rally from the right bottom is the final confirmation and completes the double bottom formation. This is the signal to buy.

Once the neckline is breached by the rising prices, a buy side position can be initiated. Remember, one should buy only when the neckline is breached on closing basis. Theoretically, the stop loss should be placed below the second bottom. However, such a stop loss is very distant and often unviable in practice a substantial part of your trading capital could get eroded in a single trade were such a large stop loss to get triggered.

Experience suggests that the stop loss is better placed 4% below the neckline. Thereafter one should mark out the target. To arrive at the target price, first measure the vertical distance from the bottom to the neckline (*see* Figure 7.14). Then measure the same distance upwards from the point where the price breached the neckline. This gives the minimum objective of how far the price could rally following a breach of the neckline.

Caution

- If the breach of the neckline occurs on low volumes, avoid taking long positions as such a breakout could be false and the price might well retest the earlier lows. A high volume breakout, on the other hand, would give confidence in the breakout.

- Never assume the formation of the double bottom pattern. Wait until the neckline is actually breached, because in any downtrend after a pullback each new decline would seemingly appear to be making a double bottom.

- The two bottoms must be separated by a deep and long reaction. If the bottoms are close together in time then it signifies consolidation instead of reversal.

Let's understand this with the help of some real life market examples.

Example 1

Figure 7.15 illustrates the formation of a double bottom on DLF's chart. The left bottom was made on 25 May 2010 at ₹ 254.75 and the right bottom on 9 June 2010 at ₹ 254.50 levels. The neckline was at ₹ 292 levels and was breached on closing basis on 21 June 2010 at ₹ 290 levels. This triggered a buy at these levels with a stop loss 4% below the neckline level, namely at ₹ 280 30. The minimum price target of this breakout was around ₹ 318 which was met on 14 July 2010.

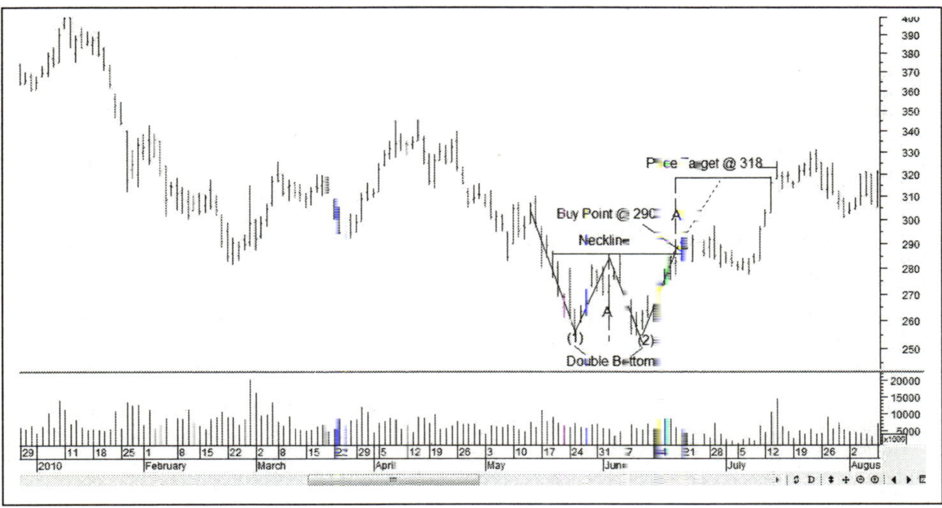

Figure 7.15: **The trend changes to up after a double bottom formation in DLF's daily chart**

Example 2

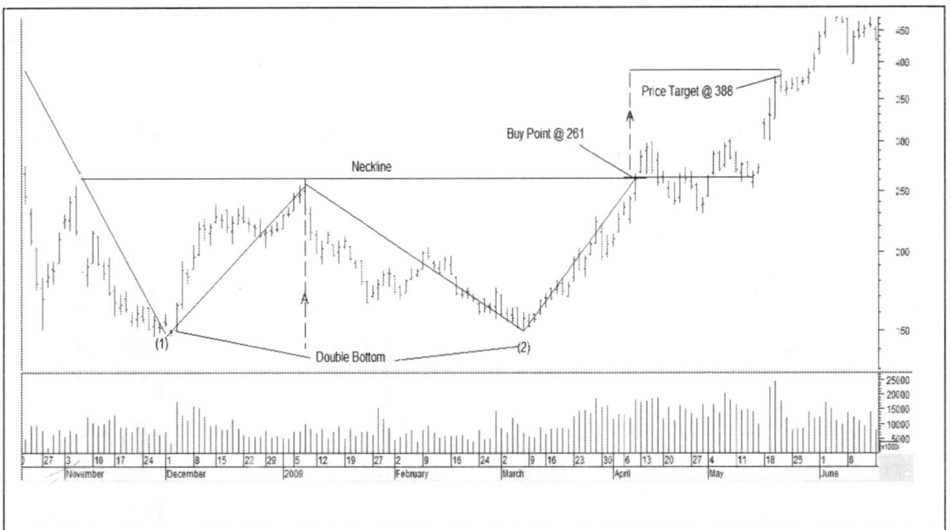

Figure 7.16: **The trend reverses to up after a double bottom formation in the daily chart of Tata Steel**

Figure 7.16 illustrates a double bottom formation in Tata Steel's chart. Here, the left bottom was made on 2 December 2008 at ₹ 146.5 and the right bottom on 6 March 2009 at ₹ 148.7 levels. The neckline was at ₹ 261 levels which was breached on closing basis on 9 April 2009 with a closing at ₹ 262 levels. It was a buy at these levels with a stop loss 4% below the neckline at ₹ 250.55 levels. The minimum price target of this breakout was ₹ 388 which was met on 21 May 2009, and thereafter the price rallied vertically to ₹ 498 levels without making any significant correction. The beauty of this example is that the two bottoms were separated by a deep and long reaction, a feature which strengthens the confidence for buying on breakout.

Option Trading Strategy for Double Bottom Formation

- One can consider selling at-the-money put options when the neckline is breached on the upside. One should, however, avoid buying at-the-money call option because in most cases the price consolidates after the breakout. In such situations, the time value of call options might get eroded.

- If the immediate lower bottom below the neckline is breached after you've sold at-the-money put options, then you should immediately close the position and accept the loss. Thereafter, you can consider buying at-the-money put options since a pattern failure has taken place and the price might crash with a downside momentum.

Triple Top Formation

Figure 7.17 illustrates the triple top formation which, as the name suggests, consists of three successive tops. This formation suggests a trend reversal from up to down.

The **left top** is formed usually at the end of an extensive advance during which the volume is often quite heavy. At the end of the left top, there is a small correction which typically occurs on low volume.

The **middle top** is then formed by a rally, usually on lower volume than the previous rallies in the formation.

Finally, the **right top** is then formed by a rally, again usually on lower volume than the previous rallies in the formation.

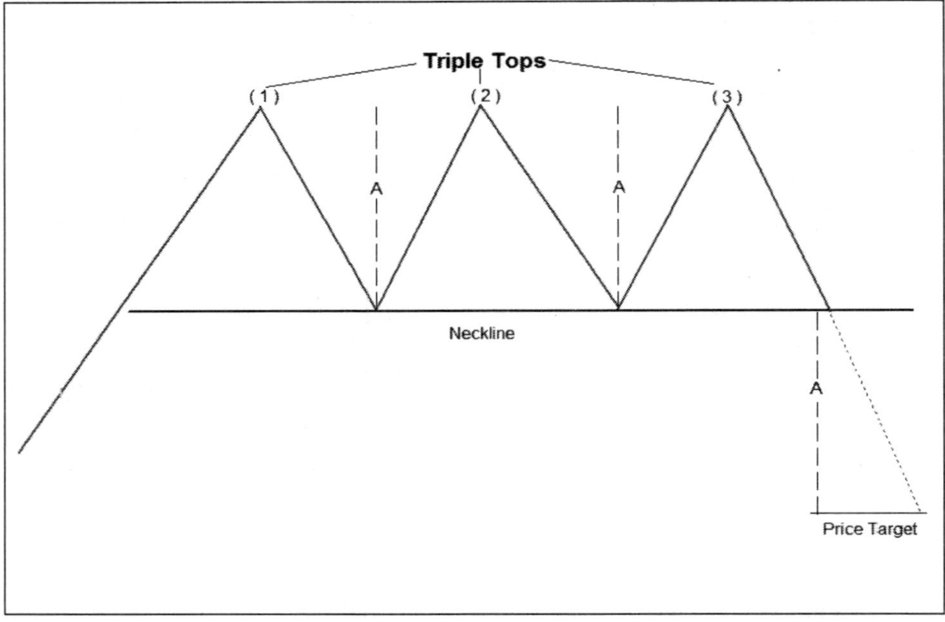

Figure 7.17: **Triple top formation**

A **neckline** can then be drawn joining the bottoms of the three tops. A downward break of this neckline on a decline from the right top is the final confirmation and completes the triple top formation. This is therefore the signal to sell short.

Once the neckline is breached, a sell side position can be initiated. Remember, one should sell only when the neckline is breached on a closing basis. Theoretically, the stop loss should be placed above the right top. However, such a stop loss is often too loose and unviable in practice because a substantial part of one's trading capital could get eroded in single trade when such a large stop loss gets triggered.

Experience suggests that the stop loss is better placed 4% above the neckline. Thereafter one should mark out price target by first measuring the vertical distance between the peaks of the three tops to the neckline (*see* Figure 7.17). You then measure the same distance downward from the point where the price breached the neckline. This gives the minimum price objective for the falling price following the downward break of the neckline.

Caution

- Never assume or anticipate the formation of a triple top pattern. Wait until the neckline is clearly breached.
- The three peaks need not be separated by deep and long reactions as in the case of double top formations. Also, the intervening valleys need not bottom out exactly at the same level; either the first or the second may be deeper.
- Volume is usually lower on the advance to the second top, and lower still on the advance to the third one.

Let's now understand triple top formation with the help of some real life market examples.

Example 1

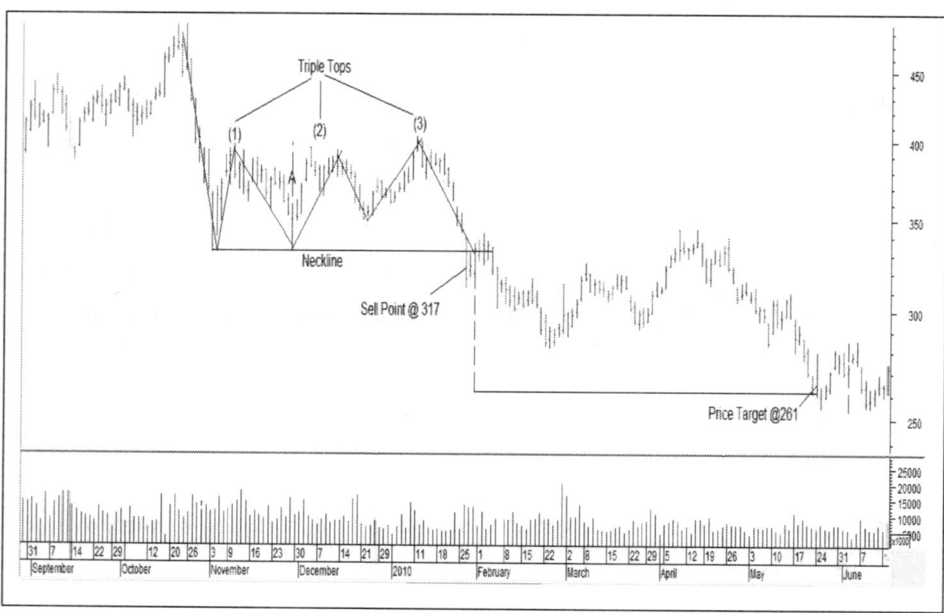

Figure 7.18: **Triple top formation in the daily chart of DLF signals a trend reversal from up to down**

Figure 7.18 illustrates a triple top formation in DLF's price chart. The left top was made on 10 November 2009 at ₹ 397.70, the middle top on 11 December 2009 at ₹ 396, and the right top was made on 11 January 2010 at ₹ 403.50 levels. The neckline was at ₹ 332 levels.

The neckline was breached on 27 January 2010 with the price closing at ₹ 317. This triggered a sell at these levels with a stop loss at 4% above the neckline level, i.e. at ₹ 345.30 levels. The minimum price target of this breakdown was ₹ 261 which was duly met on 24 May 2010.

Note that in this case the intervening valley did not bottom out at exactly the same level — the first valley was deeper. As explained above, that all these bottoms be at the same level is not a pre-requisite for triple top formations.

Example 2

Figure 7.19 illustrates the formation of a triple top in BHEL. The left top was made on 29 September 2011 at ₹ 336, the middle top on 13 October 2011 at ₹ 344, and the right top was made on 4 November 2011 at ₹ 339 levels. The neckline was thus at ₹ 311 levels.

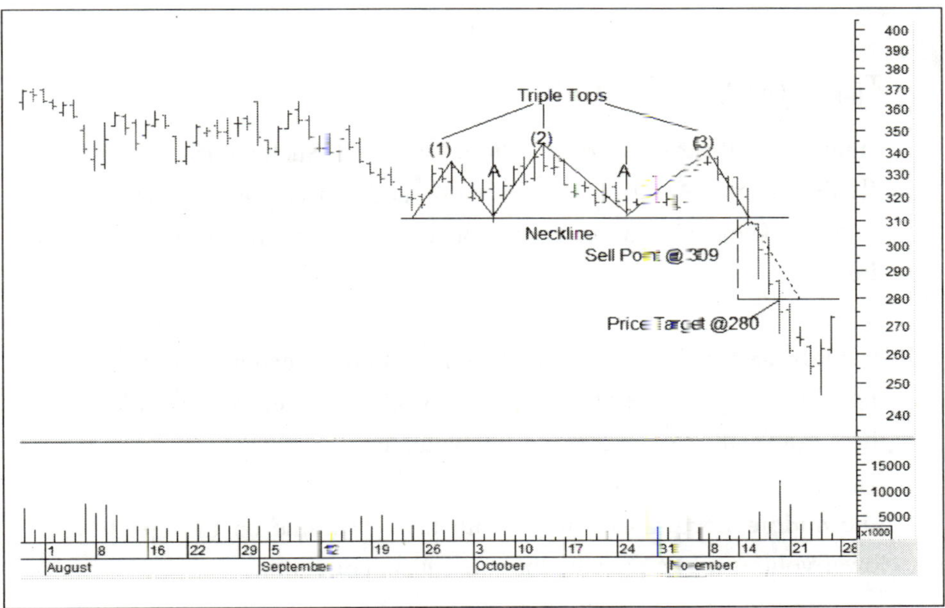

Figure 7.19: **Triple top formation in BHEL's daily chart reverses the trend**

The neckline was breached on 15 November 2011 when the stock closed at ₹ 309. It was a sell at these levels with a stop loss at 4% above the neckline level of ₹ 311, i.e. at ₹ 323.50 levels (4% above the neckline level of ₹ 311). The minimum price target of this breakdown was ₹ 280, which was met in the next three trading sessions.

Option Trading Strategy for Triple Top Formation

- One should consider buying at-the-money put options when the neckline is breached as the price could then crash with a downside momentum which would prevent any erosion in the time value of the put option.

Triple Bottom Formation

Figure 7.20 illustrates a triple bottom formation. Such a formation is simply the inverse of a triple top formation and consists of three successive bottoms. The triple bottom formation suggests trend reversal from up to down.

The **left bottom** is formed usually at the end of an extensive decline during which volumes are often quite heavy. Once the left bottom is formed, there is a small rally, usually on low volume.

The **middle bottom** is formed with heavy volume on the upside and lower volume accompanying the subsequent correction.

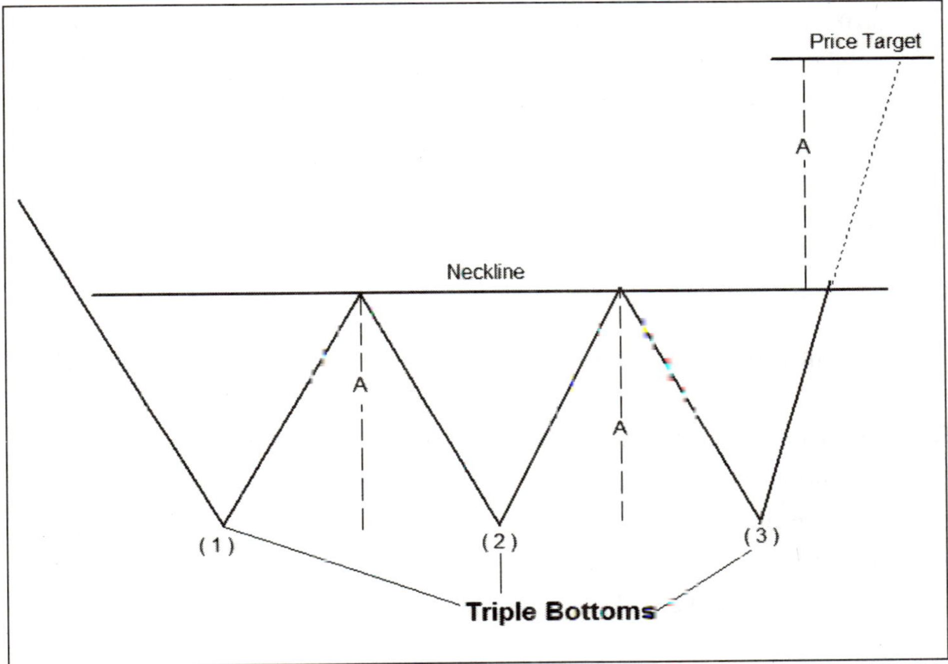

Figure: 7.20: **Triple bottom formation**

The **right bottom** is then formed by a rally usually on higher volume than during the previous rallies in this formation. At this point, in order for the formation to conform volumes should increase as the price rallies from the middle bottom, and then increase even more dramatically on a rally from the right bottom.

A **neckline** can now be drawn across the tops of the three bottoms. A break of this neckline on a rally from the right bottom is the final confirmation and completes the triple bottom formation. This is the signal to buy.

Once the neckline is broken with good volumes, a buy position can be initiated. If the neckline is broken on low volumes, however one must avoid taking a buy position as the breakout could be false and prices might retest the lows. A high volume breakout, on the other hand, would give confidence in the breakout.

Once the neckline is breached by the rising price, a buy side position can be initiated. One should buy only when the neckline is breached on closing basis.

As explained earlier, the stop loss should be placed 4% below the neckline. Thereafter one should mark out the price rise target. The minimum target is defined by measuring the vertical distance from the triple bottom up to the neckline (*see* Figure 7.20). Then you mark out the same distance upward from the point where the price breached the neckline. This gives the minimum target of how far the price could rally following the breaking of the neckline.

Caution

- Never assume or anticipate the formation of a triple bottom. Wait until the neckline is actually breached.
- The three bottoms need not be separated by deep and long pullbacks as in the case of double bottom formations.
- Volume is usually high on the second advance, and even higher on the third advance.

Let's now understand this with some real life market examples.

Example 1

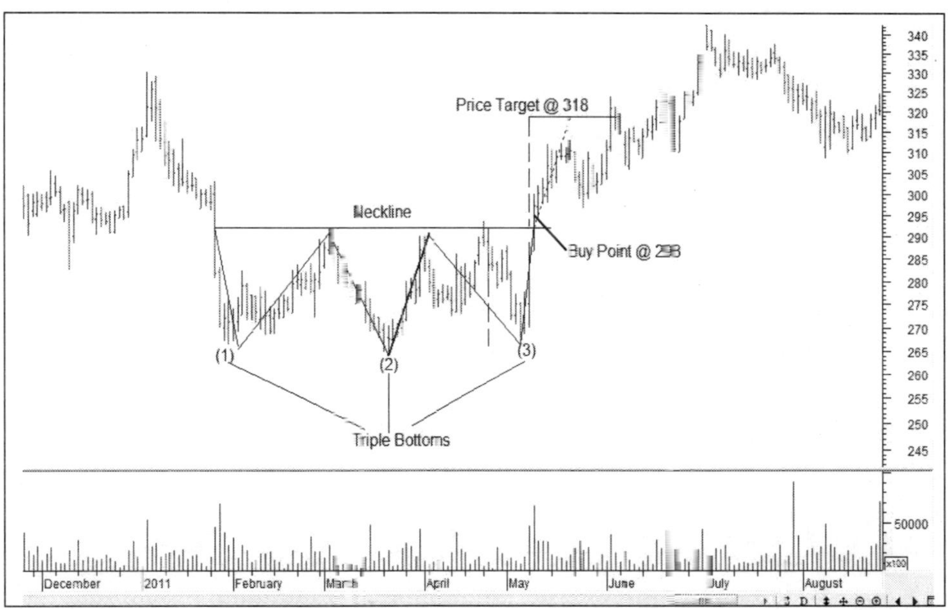

Figure 7.21: **Triple bottom formation in Hind Uniliver's daily chart signals the reversal of the downtrend**

Figure 7.21 shows a triple bottom formation on the Hind Unilever chart. The left bottom was made on 28 January 2011 at ₹ 256, the middle bottom on 22 March 2011 at ₹ 265, and the right bottom on 5 May 2011 at ₹ 266 levels. The neckline was at ₹ 292 level and was breached when the price closed on 10 May 2011 at ₹ 290. It was a buy at these levels with a stop loss at 4% below the neckline level, namely at ₹ 280.30 levels. The minimum price target of this breakout was ₹ 318 which was met on 2 June 2011 and thereafter the price rallied further to around ₹ 348 without making any significant correction.

Example 2

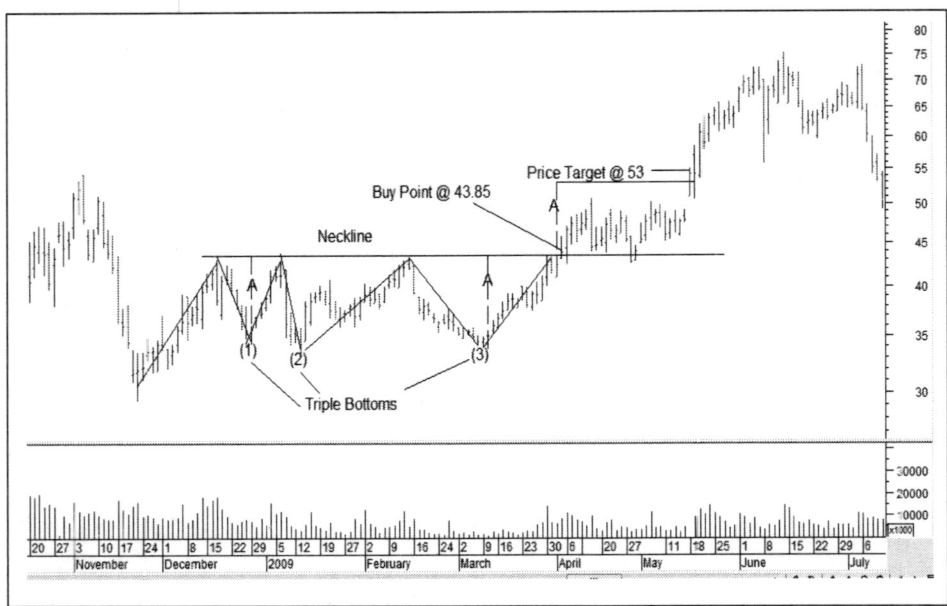

Figure 7.22: **Triple bottom formation in Chambal Fertilizers' daily chart signals the reversal of the downtrend**

Figure 7.22 illustrates a triple bottom formation in Chambal Fertilizers. The left bottom was made on 29 December 2008 at ₹ 34.25, the middle bottom on 13 January 2009 at ₹ 33.30, and the right bottom on 9 March 2009 at ₹ 33.85 levels. The neckline was at ₹ 43.50 level and was breached on closing basis, on 2 April 2009 at ₹ 43.85. It was a buy at these levels with a stop loss at 4% below the neckline level at ₹ 41.75. The minimum price target of this breakout was ₹ 53 which was met on 18 May 2009 and thereafter the price rallied higher to ₹ 73 levels without making any significant correction.

Option Trading Strategy for Triple Bottom Formation

- One can consider selling at-the-money put options once the neckline is breached on the upside. On the other hand, one should avoid buying at-the-money call option because in most cases the price goes into a consolidation phase after the breakout; hence the time value of a call option can get eroded.
- If the immediate lower bottom below the neckline is breached after you've sold at-the-money put options, then you should close the position with a loss. Thereafter, you could consider buying at-the-money put options since a pattern failure has clearly taken place and the price might then crash with a downside momentum.

Broadening Tops Formation

Broadening formations appear much more frequently at tops than at bottoms and for that reason we will limit our discussion to the broadening tops formation alone.

Broadening top formations have bearish implications.

A **broadening top** is powerful reversal chart pattern which occurs frequently in the later part of an overextended bull rally. It consists of three successive peaks, each higher than the previous one and, between them, two bottoms with the second bottom being lower than the first.

Figure 7.23 illustrates three successive higher peaks namely Point 1, Point 3 and Point 5 and two bottoms, namely Point 2 and Point 4. The bottom at Point 4 is lower than the bottom at Point 2. Broadening tops signify that prices are lacking support from the "smart money." There have been major crashes, globally, in equities and commodities following such patterns.

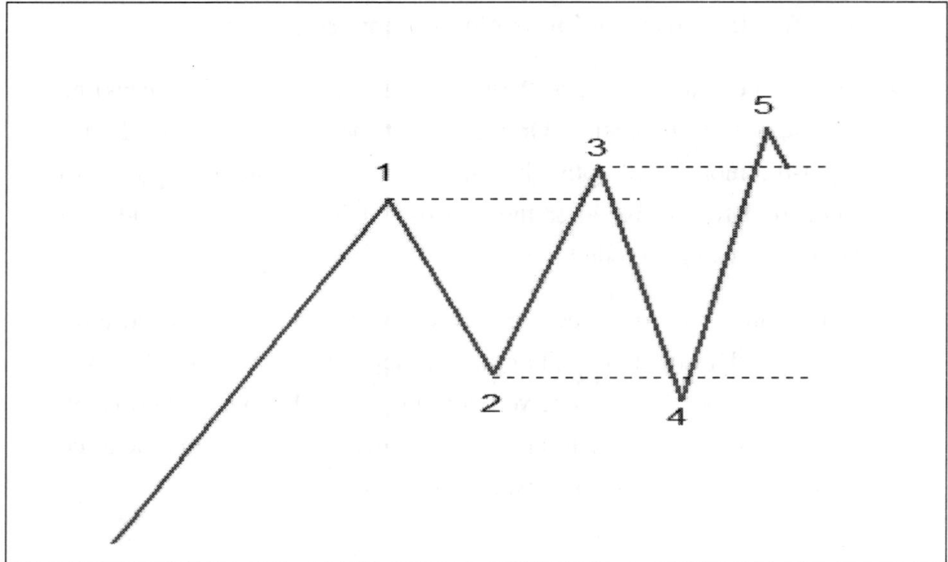

Figure 7.23: **Broadening tops**

The best method for trading a broadening top formation is to wait for a break of the first bottom in the formation, namely Bottom 2 in Figure 7.23, after the third and final peak has formed. Theoretically, the stop loss should be placed above the last top, i.e. Point 5. However, such a stop loss can be enormously large and unviable in practice because a substantial part of one's trading capital would erode in a single trade when such a large stop loss gets triggered.

Experience suggests that the stop loss is better placed 6% above the first bottom in the formation, namely Point 2 in Figure 7.23.

The price target for a broadening top formation is two-thirds of the vertical distance from the starting point of the bull move to the highest peak of the broadening top formation.

Quite often well informed selling is completed during the early stages of the formation. Eventually in the later stages, the participation is from the less informed retail segment.

I recommend trading broadening top formations because the momentum builds very fast on the sell side of the market — and we are all here to catch precisely such momentum.

Now, let's understand this with some real life market examples.

Example 1

Figure 7.24 depicts an extended bull rally on Nasdaq 100 Index from 610 levels on 24 July 1995 to 4,780 levels on 27 March 2000. At the top —

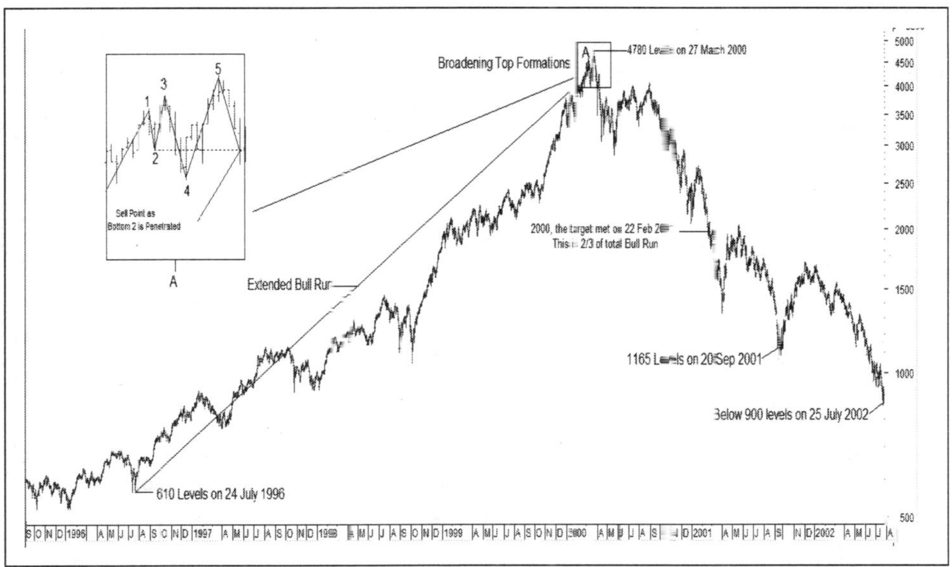

Figure 7.24: **Broadening tops formation on the daily chart of Nasdaq leads to a reversal of trend from up to down**

as illustrated in the inset Box A — a broadening top formation occurred where Points 1, 3 and 5 were three successive higher peaks and Bottom 4 was lower than Bottom 2. As noted earlier, one should sell when the price level of Bottom 2 is broken after peaks 3 and 5 are in place. Here Bottom 2 was breached on 30 March 2000 at 4,250 levels. Thus, it was a sell at 4,250 with a stop loss at 6% above the first bottom in the formation, namely Bottom 2, i.e. at 4,505 levels. The price target level of this breakdown was 2,000, which was met on 2 February 2001. Thereafter, Nasdaq declined to around 1,165 levels by 20 September 2001, and subsequently it even touched sub-900 levels on 25 July 2002.

Example 2

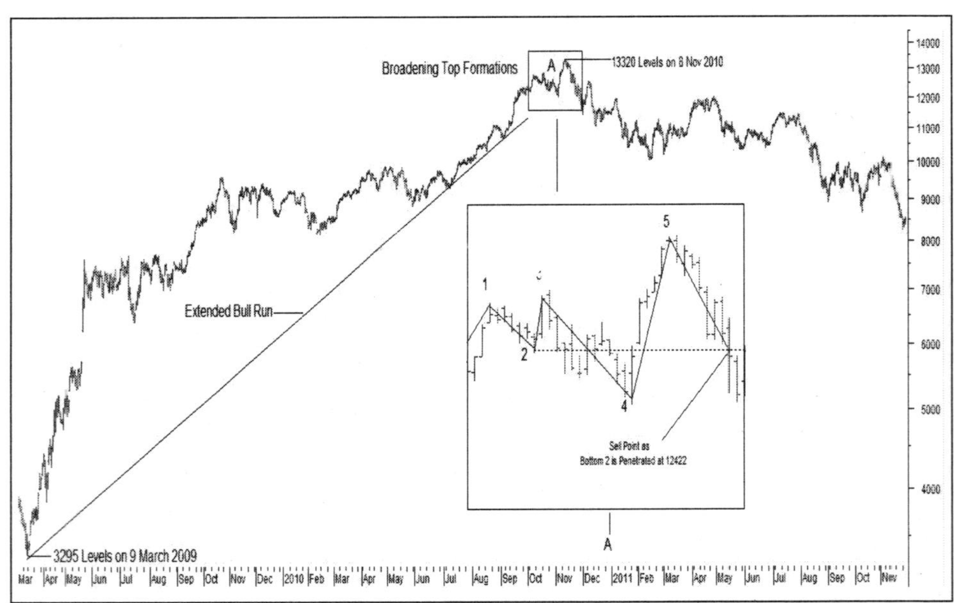

Figure 7.25A: **Reversal of trend of Bank Nifty futures after the formation of broadening tops**

Figure 7.25A shows an extended bull rally in the Bank Nifty futures post the great 2009 crash when everyone felt that the market itself might end. Instead, Bank Nifty futures rallied from 3,295 (9 March 2009) to 13,320 levels (8 November 2010). At the top, as highlighted in the inset Box A, a broadening tops pattern then formed; Point 1, Point 3 and Point 5 were three successive higher peaks, and Bottom 4 was lower than Bottom 2. As explained, one should sell when the level of Bottom 2 is breached after Point 3 and Point 5 are in place. Here Bottom 2 was breached on 18 November 2010 at 12,422. Thus, Bank Nifty futures were a sell at 12,422 levels with stop loss at 13,168, i.e. at 6% above the first bottom in the formation, namely Bottom 2. The target price level of this breakdown was 6,637. But after making a low of around 7,750 on 20 December 2011, the price rallied and generated a trend reversal signal, namely a reversal of trend from down to up at around 8,775 level on 10 January 2012. (This trend reversal signal would become clearer once you go through Chapter 10, Figure 10.4.)

As the trend reversed from down to up at 8,775 levels, traders who went short in Bank Nifty at 12,422 levels due to the broadening tops pattern formation should have closed their sell side position at 8,775 levels, still with a decent profit.

One should not forget that the price often overshoots the target in a rising market, and falls short of the target in a declining market.

Example 3

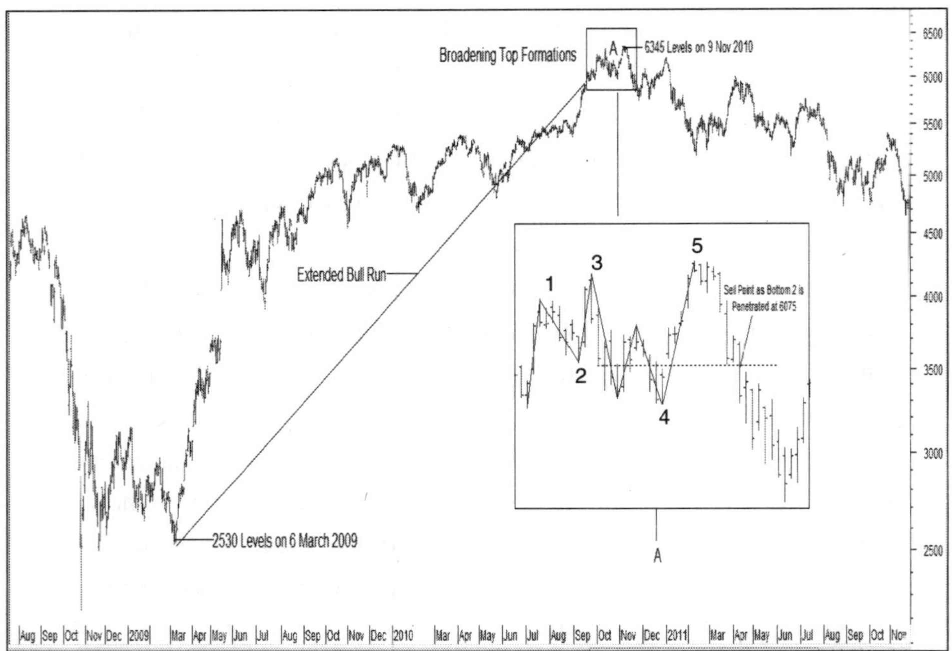

Figure 7.25B: **Broadening tops formation reverses the uptrend in the daily chart of Nifty Futures**

Figure 7.25B illustrates an extended bull rally in Nifty futures post the daunting 2009 crash which struck the world. Nifty futures, however, witnessed a rally from 2,530 levels (on 6 March 2009) to 6,345 levels (on 9 November 2010). At the top — as illustrated in the inset Box A in Figure 7.25B — a broadening tops pattern was formed where Point 1, Point 3 and Point 5 were three successive higher peaks and Bottom 4 was lower than Bottom 2. Bottom 2 was then breached on 16 November 2010 at 6,075 levels. It was thus a sell at these levels with a stop loss at 6,440 levels, i.e. 6% above the first bottom in the formation, namely Bottom 2 (6,075). The price target of this breakdown was 3,802 level. But after making a low of around 4,540 on 20 December 2011, the price rallied and generated a trend reversal signal, i.e. the trend reversed from down to up, at around 4,877 level on 10 January 2012. (This trend reversal signal, i.e. reversal of trend from down to up would become clearer once you go through Chapter 10 on Indicators, Figure 10.5).

Once the trend reversed from down to up at 4,877 levels, traders who went short in Nifty around 6,075 levels due to the broadening tops pattern formation should have closed their sell side position at these levels. This trade would still have given them a decent profit.

Please always remember that the price often overshoots the target in a rising market and falls short of target in a declining market.

Option Trading Strategy for Broadening Tops Formation

- One can consider buying at-the-money put options when the price level of Bottom 2 is breached on the downside after Top 3 and Top 5 are in place as prices would then usually fall with a downside momentum which prevents any erosion in the time value of a put option.

Rounding Tops Formation

Rounding tops are formed when there is a gradual change in the direction of the trend as a result of a step-by-step shift in the balance of power between the buyers and the sellers.

Accordingly, a rounding tops formation suggests a trend reversal from up to down.

A typical characteristic of this pattern is that volume increases with the increase in selling pressure and declines as the selling pressure eases. The trend then becomes neutral with very little trading activity as the

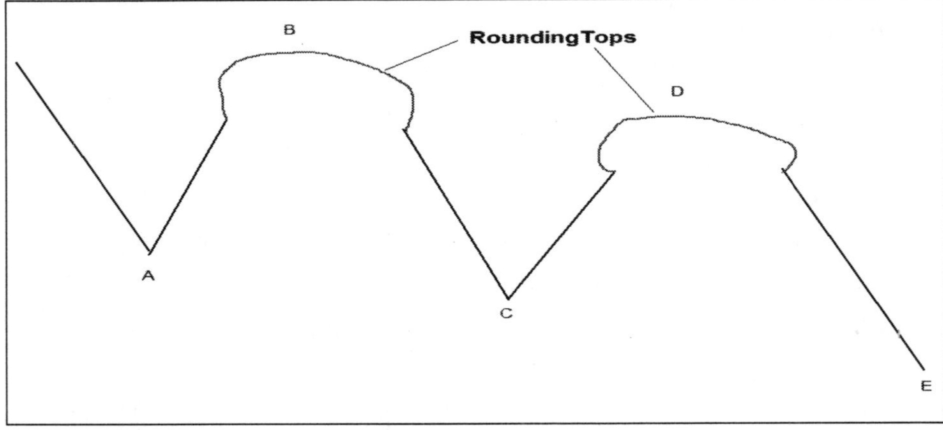

Figure 7.26: **Rounding tops formation signals a reversal of the trend from up to down**

volume dries up. This is the point where one should consider selling as the price thereafter is likely to decline with a downside momentum.

Figure 7.26 illustrates distribution in the form of rounding tops B and D, which is technically considered very bearish.

The best method for trading a rounding tops formation is to sell after a breakdown from the first rounding top, with a stop loss above the highs of the first rounding top.

Most important, one should hold the short position with patience and discipline as a number of rounding tops might be formed before the climax selling finally comes about.

Thus patience, discipline and, above all, confidence in the pattern are the key to success when trading rounding top formations.

Let's understand this with some real life market examples.

Example 1

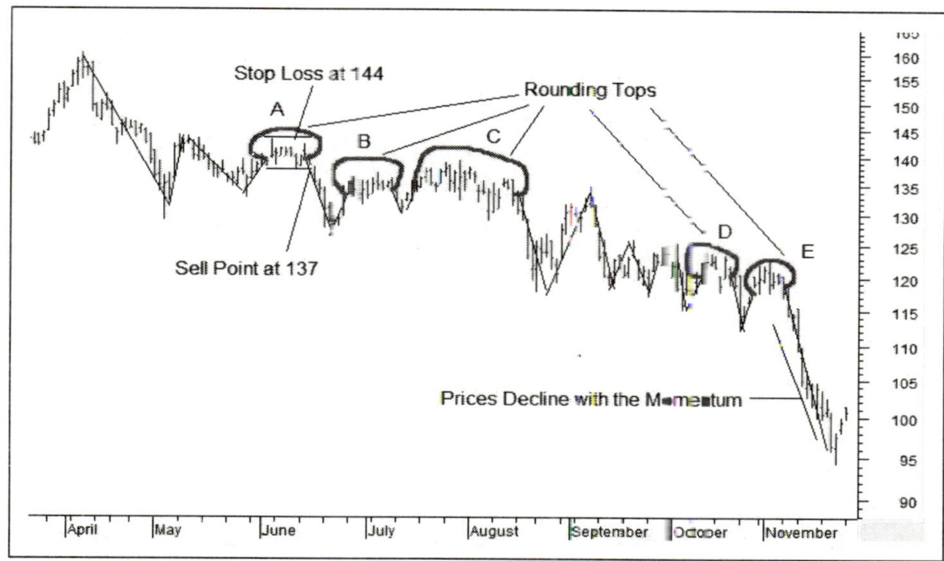

Figure 7.27: **Bearish rounding tops formation in the daily chart of Andhra Bank futures signals distribution**

Figure 7.27 shows the futures of Andhra Bank continuously making lower tops and lower bottoms, indicating distribution in the form of rounding tops which is technically considered very bearish.

One could have gone short at ₹ 137 levels on 16 June 2011 which was the breakdown level from first rounding top, i.e. Point A, with a stop loss above ₹ 144 levels. Thereafter, the price made a number of rounding tops, namely points B, C, D and E. Finally the price crashed below ₹ 100 level by November 2011. It's worth noting that it took five months for the price to crash from ₹ 137 to a sub- ₹ 100 level, demonstrating how patience, discipline and, above all, confidence about the pattern is the key to success.

Example 2

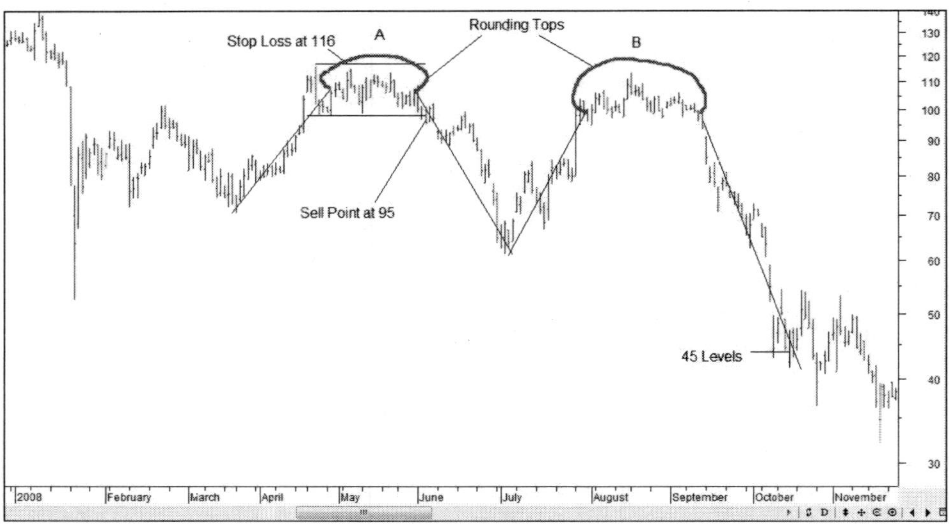

Figure 7.28: **Bears take over after a rounding tops formation in the daily chart of Polaris futures signals distribution**

Figure 7.28 illustrates the price chart of Polaris futures. The first rounding top was at A and the price breakdown thereafter occurred at ₹ 95 levels on 4 June 2008. One could have gone short at ₹ 95 levels with a stop loss above ₹ 116. Thereafter, the price made another rounding top, namely B. Finally, the price crashed to ₹ 45 levels by mid-October 2008 after breaking down from the second rounding top. In other words, it took four months for the price to crash from ₹ 95 to ₹ 45 levels.

Option Trading Strategy for Rounding Tops Formation

- One could consider selling at-the-money call options when the price breaks down from the first rounding top. One should, however, avoid buying at-the-money put options because in most cases the price consolidates after breaking down from the first rounding top and a number of rounding tops might be formed before the selling climax occurs. Hence, the time value of a put option is likely to get eroded.
- If the highs above the first rounding top are breached after you've sold at-the-money call options, then you should take the loss and close the position. Eventually, you can consider buying at-the-money call options since a pattern failure has taken place and the price might therefore rally with an upside momentum.

Rounding Bottoms Formation

Rounding bottoms are formed as a result of a gradual change in trend direction. They are produced by a step-by-step shift in the balance of power between the buyers and sellers.

Accordingly, a rounding bottoms formation suggests a trend reversal from down to up.

A typical characteristic of this pattern is that volume increases as the price rallies and reduces with a decline in prices. The trend then becomes neutral with little trading activity as volume dries up. This is the point where one should consider buying since the price is likely to then accelerate with a strong momentum.

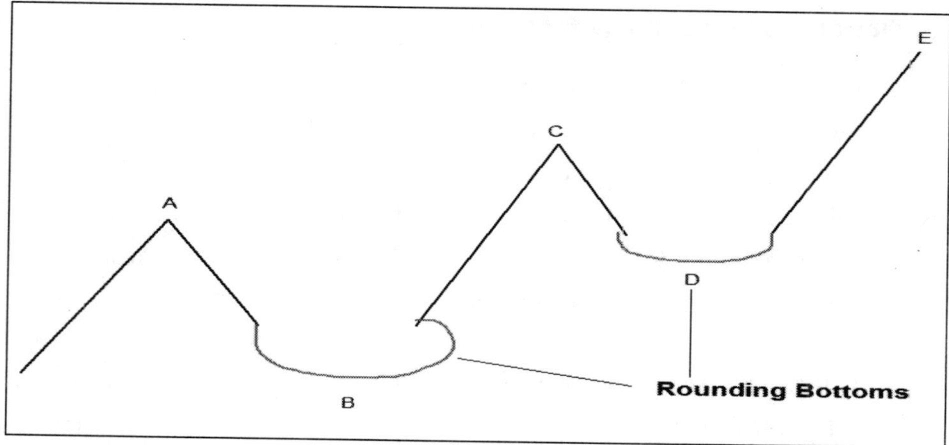

Figure 7.29: **Rounding bottoms formation signals accumulation which is a signal of the reversal of trend from down to up**

Figure 7.29 illustrates accumulation in the form of rounding bottoms B and D. Accumulation is technically considered very bullish.

The best method for trading a rounding bottoms formation is to buy after the price breaks out from the first rounding bottom with a stop loss below the lows of the first rounding bottom.

Most important, one should hold the long position with patience and discipline as a number of rounding bottoms might be formed before any decisive run up in price is observed. Patience, discipline, and, above all, confidence in this pattern are the key to success.

Let's understand this with some real life market examples.

Example 1

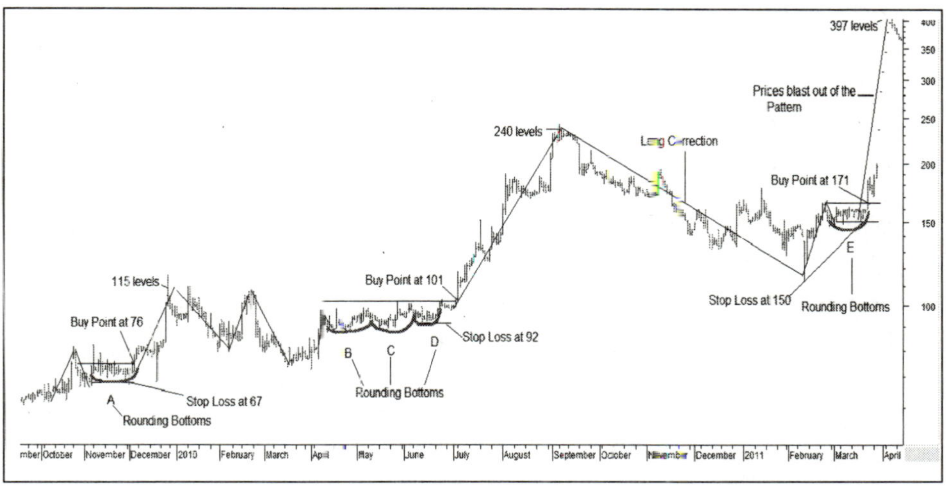

Figure 7.30: **Rounding bottoms formation in the daily chart of Andhra Paper signals the reversing of trend to up**

Figure 7.30 is a price chart of Andhra Paper. The price made the first rounding bottom at A. The breakout from this occurred at ₹ 76 levels on 3 December 2009. One could have gone long at this level with a stop loss below ₹ 67. Thereafter, the price rallied with an upside momentum to ₹ 115 levels by the end of December 2009.

Three simultaneous triple rounding bottoms, namely B, C and D were then formed between April 2010 to June 2010. This is a very rare occurrence and the subsequent breakout occurred at ₹ 101 levels on 2 July 2010. One could then have gone long at ₹ 101, with a stop loss below ₹ 92. Thereafter, the price rallied with an upside momentum to ₹ 240 levels by the beginning of September 2010.

Another rounding bottom E was formed by the beginning of March 2011 and a breakout from that occurred at ₹ 171 levels on 23 March 2011. One could then have gone long at ₹ 171, with a stop loss below ₹ 150. Thereafter, the price rallied with a series of upper circuits to ₹ 397 by the first week of April 2011.

Example 2

Figure 7.31 illustrates their rounding bottoms, i.e. A, B and C being formed on OCL Iron and Steel stock. In this case the breakout occurred only after the rounding bottom C was formed at ₹ 5.14 levels on 26 March 2009. One could have gone long at this level with a stop loss below ₹ 3.80. The price thereafter rallied with a series of upper circuits to ₹ 16 level by the first week of May 2009 and, ultimately, to ₹ 20-plus levels by the end of May 2009.

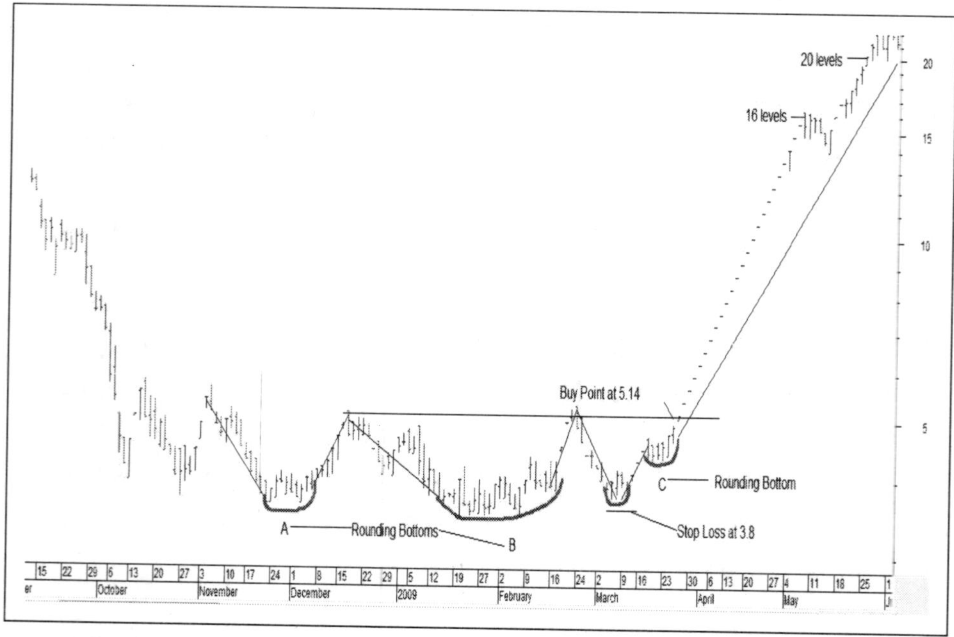

Figure 7.31: **Rounding bottoms in the daily chart of OCL Iron and Steel reverse the trend from down to up**

Option Trading Strategy for Rounding Bottoms Formation

- One should consider selling at-the-money put options when the price breaks out from the first rounding bottom. You should, however, avoid buying at-the-money call options because in most cases the price first consolidates as a number of rounding bottoms might be formed before the final run up in the price. So the time value of the call option might get eroded.

Caution

If the lows of the first rounding bottom is breached after you sell at-the-money put options, you should promptly close the position with a loss. Eventually, you can consider buying at-the-money put option as a pattern failure has taken place and the price might then decline further with a downside momentum.

Continuation Patterns

Triangles

Triangles are formed as a result of indecision on the part of both buyers and sellers as prices have already seen a run up or a run down.

Triangles act as a period of consolidation from where prices continue to move in the direction of the original trend.

Triangles are basically of three types:

1. Symmetrical triangle;
2. Ascending right-angle triangle; and
3. Descending right-angle triangle.

Symmetrical Triangles

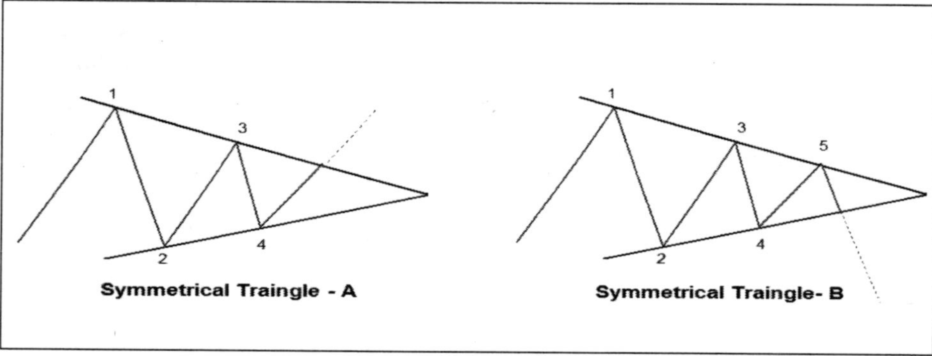

Figure 7.32: **Symmetrical triangles: note that they must have at least four reversal points**

These are regularly found on charts and are formed by a down slanting line and an up slanting line coming together. By definition, a symmetrical triangle must have at least four reversal points, as illustrated in Figure 7.32. An upside breakout is illustrated in Symmetrical Triangle A and a downside breakout is illustrated in Symmetrical Triangle B.

One can buy on upside breakout from a symmetrical triangle. Hypothetically, the stop loss should be placed below the lows of the immediate bottom, namely Point 4 in Figure 7.32 (Symmetrical Triangle-A). In practice, however, such a stop could be too distant and unviable because a substantial part of one's trading capital could get eroded in single trade when such a loose stop loss gets triggered.

Experience suggests that the stop loss would be better placed 5% below the breakout point. Theoretically, after initiating a buy side position one should continue only with buy side positions until and unless a trend reversal takes place, i.e. the price reverses direction from the ongoing higher top, higher bottom formation to lower top, lower bottom formation.

Experience, however, shows that in most cases prices rally anywhere around 7% to 8% from the breakout point and thereafter they decline severely. I would therefore suggest profit booking when the price rallies anywhere around 7% to 8% from the breakout point

Correspondingly, one can sell upon a downside breakout from a symmetrical triangle. Hypothetically, the stop loss should be placed above the highs of the latest top, i.e. Point 5 in Figure 7.32 (Symmetrical Triangle-B). In practice, however, such a stop loss is very loose and practically unviable because a substantial part of one's trading capital could erode in a single trade when such a large stop loss gets triggered.

Experience suggests that the stop loss should be placed 5% above the breakout point. Theoretically, after initiating a sell side position one should run only sell side positions until and unless a trend reversal takes place, i.e. the price reverses direction from the ongoing lower top, lower bottom formation to higher top, higher bottom formation.

Experience, however, shows that in most cases prices decline anywhere around 7% to 8% from the breakout point — and thereafter they rally sharply. I would therefore suggest booking profit when the price declines anywhere around 7% to 8% from the breakout point.

Unlike in the case of reversal patterns where trade is initiated when the price cracks upside / downside breakout levels on closing basis, in the case of continuation patterns the trade is initiated immediately on an upside / downside breakout without waiting for prices to crack the breakout levels on closing basis. This is because in case of breakout from continuation patterns, prices move swiftly and significantly from breakout level in the direction of the breakout.

Experience suggests that breakouts from symmetrical triangles should be traded with extreme caution as most times traders lose money in trading such breakouts. This would become clearer from the following four points:

- First, success rate of these breakouts is relatively low, i.e. approximately 40%.

- Second, breakouts from symmetrical triangles result in price moves of around 7% to 8% in the direction of the breakout. A price move of around 7% to 8% from the breakout level is unattractive for initiating trade, especially when one takes into account the stop loss of 5%.

- Third, prices often witness sudden reversals of direction after attaining target levels and that too without giving any warning signal in advance. Traders who are not quick in taking profit end up as victims of such sudden reversals of price which result in stop losses getting triggered.

- Fourth, traders who fail to exit a trade either at their target or stop loss levels find themselves trapped in their own trade, namely either in a "seller trap" or a "buyer trap" which is explained next with the help of Figure 7.33 and Figure 7.34.

Example 1

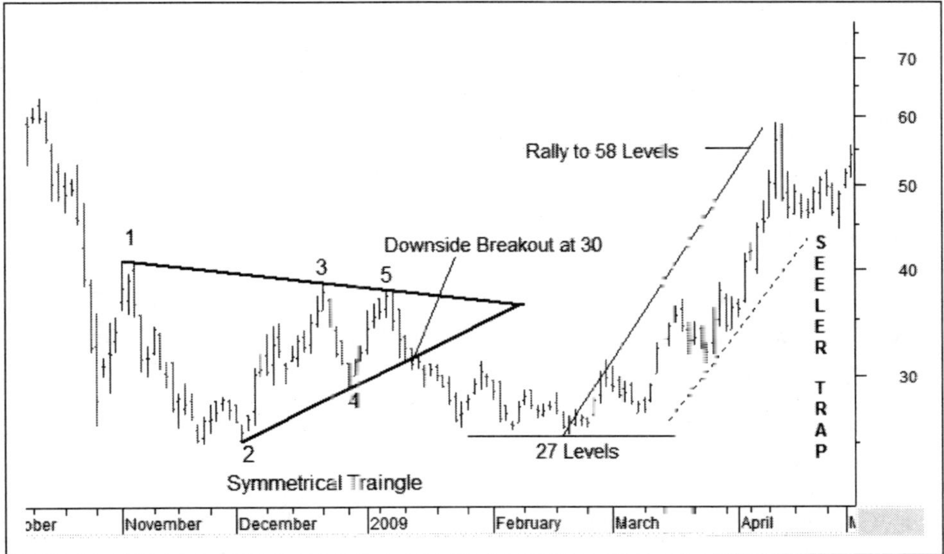

Figure 7.33: **Symmetrical triangle formation in the daily price chart of Tata Motors**

Figure 7.33 illustrates the price chart of Tata Motors consolidating in a symmetrical triangle with five reversal points prior to a breakout on the downside. The breakout occurred at ₹ 30 levels on 13 January 2009.

As already explained:

- One can sell at the breakout level, i.e. at ₹ 30 levels without waiting for the price to close below the breakout level.
- Stop loss for this trade should be placed at ₹ 31.50 levels, i.e. 5% above the breakout level.
- One should take profit when prices decline anywhere around 7% to 8% from the breakout level. Here the breakout level is ₹ 30, hence one should take profit anywhere between ₹ 28 and ₹ 27.60 levels.

After making a low of around ₹ 27, the stock price swiftly zoomed up to around ₹ 58 levels in a short span of two months. Those traders who were not fast enough in taking profit in the recommended target range ultimately got trapped on the wrong side of the market, namely in the seller's trap.

Example 2

Figure 7.34 is the price chart of Reliance Capital consolidating in a symmetrical triangle with four reversal points prior to a breakout on the upside. The breakout occurred at ₹ 557 levels on 27 June 2011.

As explained above:

- One can buy at the breakout level, i.e. at ₹ 557 levels in this case, without waiting for the price to close above the breakout level.

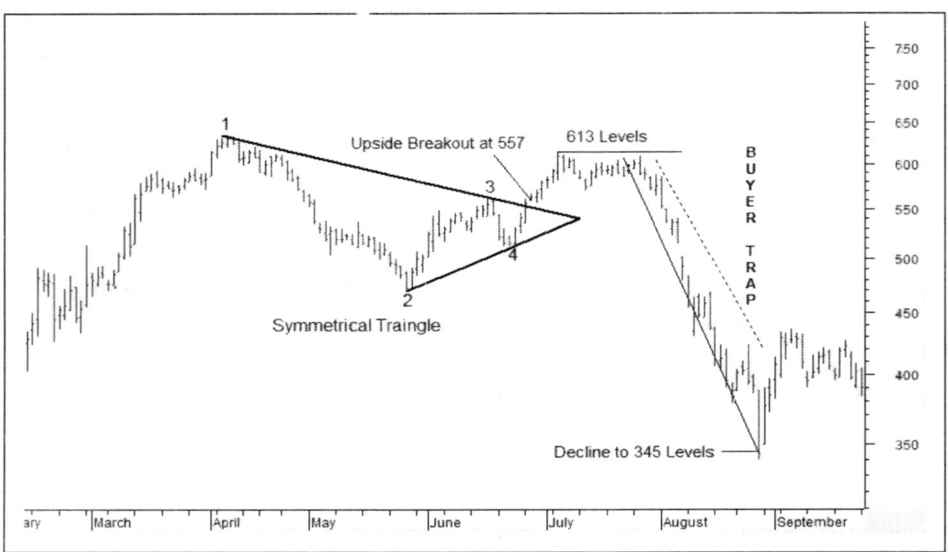

Figure 7.34: **Symmetrical triangle formation in the daily price chart of Reliance Capital**

- Stop loss for this trade should be placed at ₹ 529 levels, i.e. 5% below the breakout level.
- One should take profit when prices rally anywhere around 7% to 8% from the breakout level. Here the breakout level is ₹ 557, hence one should try and take profit between ₹ 596 and ₹ 601 levels.

After making a high of around ₹ 613, the price declined sharply to around ₹ 345 levels in a short span of two months. Traders who were not alert enough in taking profit in the recommended target range ultimately got trapped on the wrong side of the market, a classic case of buyer trap.

Ascending Right-Angle Triangle

An ascending right-angle triangle is formed by the meeting of a horizontal top line and an up sloping bottom line and, by definition, must have at least four reversal points within it as illustrated in Figure 7.35.

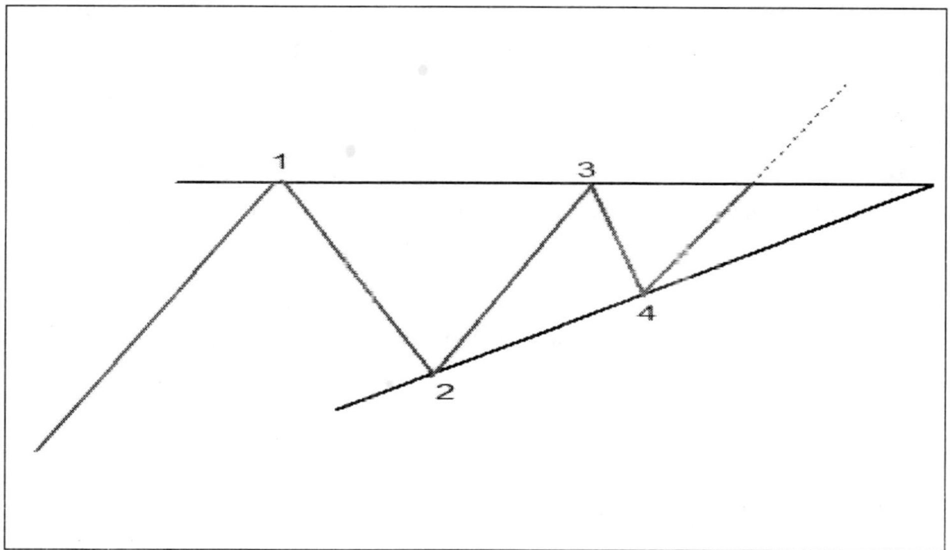

Figure 7.35: **Ascending right-angle triangle**

If the demand continues to increase and the available supply is completely absorbed, then an upside breakout takes place and this is the time to buy. In other words, one should buy on an upside breakout from a right angle ascending triangle. Hypothetically, the stop loss should be placed below the lows of the latest bottom, i.e. Point 4 in Figure 7.35. In practice, however, such a stop losing could be very loose and unviable because a substantial part of trading capital could erode in a single trade when such a distant large stop loss gets triggered.

Experience suggests that the stop loss should be placed 5% below the breakout point. After initiating a buy side position, one should only run buy side positions until and unless a trend reversal takes place, i.e. the price reverses direction from the ongoing higher top, higher bottom formations to lower top, lower bottom formations.

Experience also shows that in most cases prices rally anywhere around 25% to 30% from the breakout point — and thereafter they decline sharply. I would therefore suggest booking profit when the price rallies anywhere around 25% to 30% from the breakout point.

Breakouts from ascending right-angle triangles should only be considered valid if the price was already making higher tops and higher bottoms before the formation of the triangle, i.e. the earlier trend was up; otherwise there is 90% probability of a false breakout.

Let's understand this with the help of some real life market examples.

Example 1

Figure 7.36: **Ascending triangle in the daily chart of TCS futures**

Figure 7.36 illustrates the price of TCS consolidating in an ascending right-angle triangle after an extensive price rally. The breakout occurred at ₹ 796 levels on 16 June 2010.

As explained above:

- One should buy at the breakout level, i.e. in this case at ₹ 796 levels, without waiting for prices to close above the breakout level.
- Stop loss for this trade should be placed at ₹ 756 levels, namely at 5% below the breakout level.
- One should take profit when prices rally anywhere around 25% to 30% from the breakout level. Here the breakout level is ₹ 796, so one should make an effort at taking profit anywhere between ₹ 995 and ₹ 1034 levels.

The stock's price, in fact, rallied to ₹ 1,050-plus levels and gave substantial time for taking profits.

Example 2

Figure 7.37: **Ascending triangle in the daily chart of Tata Motors**

Figure 7.37 illustrates the price of Tata Motors consolidating in an ascending right-angle triangle and then making a first higher top, higher bottom formation in 2009 after the breakout from the triangle. The trend was up at the time of the breakout. The breakout occurred at ₹ 32 level on 13 March 2009.

As explained above:

- One should buy at the breakout level, i.e. at ₹ 32 levels in this case, without waiting for prices to close above the breakout level.
- Stop loss for this trade should be placed at ₹ 30.40 level, i.e. 5% below the breakout level.

One should take profit when the price rallies anywhere around 25% to 30% from the breakout level. Here the breakout level is ₹ 32, hence one should make an effort in taking profit anywhere between ₹ 40-41.60 levels.

Stock prices in fact rallied to ₹ 75-plus levels and gave substantial time for taking profit.

Option Trading Strategy for Ascending Right-Angle Triangle Formation

- One should consider buying at-the-money call options on a breakout from the said pattern as prices are likely to rally with a strong momentum which would prevent erosion in the time value of the call option.

Descending Right-Angle Triangle

A descending right-angle triangle is formed by the meeting of a horizontal bottom line and a down sloping upper boundary and, by definition, must have within it at least four reversal points as illustrated in Figure 7.38.

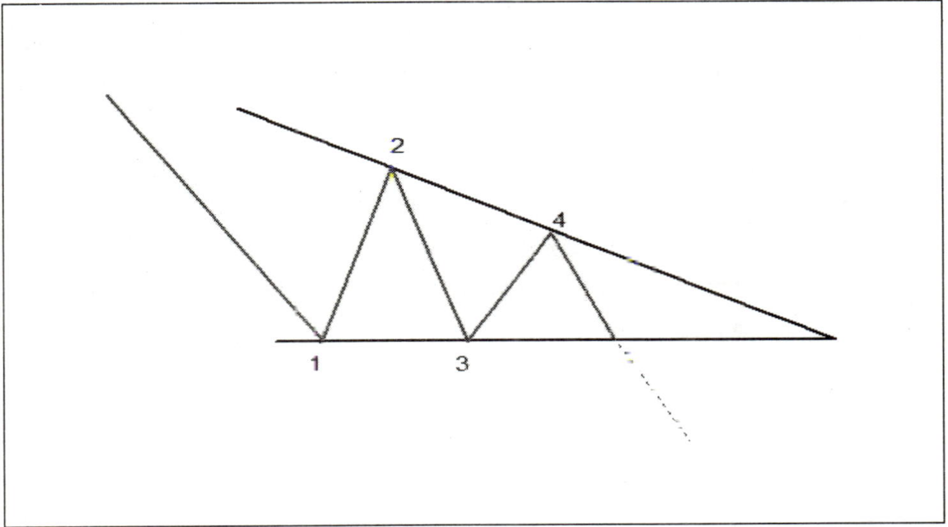

Figure 7.38: **Descending right-angle triangle**

This formation occurs when the demand at a particular price is met by fresh supply continually coming into market. Eventually, the demand is exhausted and the price breaks out of the triangle on the downside and this is the time to sell. Thus, one should sell on the downside breakdown from a right-angle descending triangle. Theoretically, the stop loss should be placed above the highs of the last top prior to the breakdown, which is Point 4 in Figure 7.38. In practice, however, I find such a stop loss very loose and unviable because a substantial part of one's trading capital could erode in a single trade when such a large stop loss gets triggered.

Experience suggests that the stop loss could be better placed 5% above the breakout point. Again, theoretically, after initiating sell side position one should only run sell side position until and unless a trend reversal takes place, i.e. the price reverses direction from ongoing lower top, lower bottom formation to higher top, higher bottom formation.

Experience, however, shows that in most cases prices decline anywhere around 25% to 30% from the breakout point and thereafter rally sharply. I would therefore suggest booking profit when the price declines anywhere around 25% to 30% from the breakout point.

Experience further suggests that breakdowns from descending right-angle triangles should only be considered valid if prices were already making lower-tops and lower-bottoms prior to the formation, i.e. the trend was already down; otherwise there is 90% probability of a false breakdown.

Let's now understand this with some real life market examples.

Example 1

Figure 7.39: **Descending right-angle triangle in the daily chart of Sesa Goa. The preceding downtrend continues after the price breaks out of the triangle**

Figure 7.39 shows the price of Sesa Goa consolidating in a descending right-angle triangle after an extensive prices decline. The breakdown occurred at ₹ 255 levels on 5 August 2011.

As explained above:

- One should sell at the breakdown level, i.e. at ₹ 255 levels in this case, without waiting for prices to close below the breakout level.
- Stop loss for this trade should be placed at ₹ 268 level, i.e. 5% above the breakdown level.

One should take profit when prices decline anywhere around 25% to 30% from the breakdown level. Here the breakdown level is ₹ 255, hence one should be taking profits anywhere between ₹ 191 and ₹ 178 levels.

Stock prices, in fact, declined to ₹ 175 levels and gave one substantial time for taking profit.

Example 2

Figure 7.40 illustrates the price of BHEL consolidating in a descending right-angle triangle after an extensive decline. The breakdown occurred at ₹ 380 levels on 27 July 2011.

As explained above:

- One should sell at the breakdown level, in this case at ₹ 380 levels, without waiting for prices to close below the breakout level.

- Stop loss for this trade should be placed at ₹ 399 levels, i.e. 5% above the breakdown level.

One should take profit when prices decline anywhere around 25% to 30% from the breakdown level. Here the breakdown level was ₹ 380. Accordingly, one should take profit anywhere between ₹ 285 and ₹ 266 levels.

Figure 7.40: **The price continues to fall after breaking out from the descending triangle in the daily chart of BHEL**

In fact, the stock's price declined to ₹ 255 levels and gave one substantial time for taking profit.

Option Trading Strategy for Descending Right-Angle Triangle Formation

- One should consider buying at-the-money put options on breakdown from the said pattern as prices are then likely to decline with a strong momentum which would prevent erosion in the time value of the put option.

Rectangles

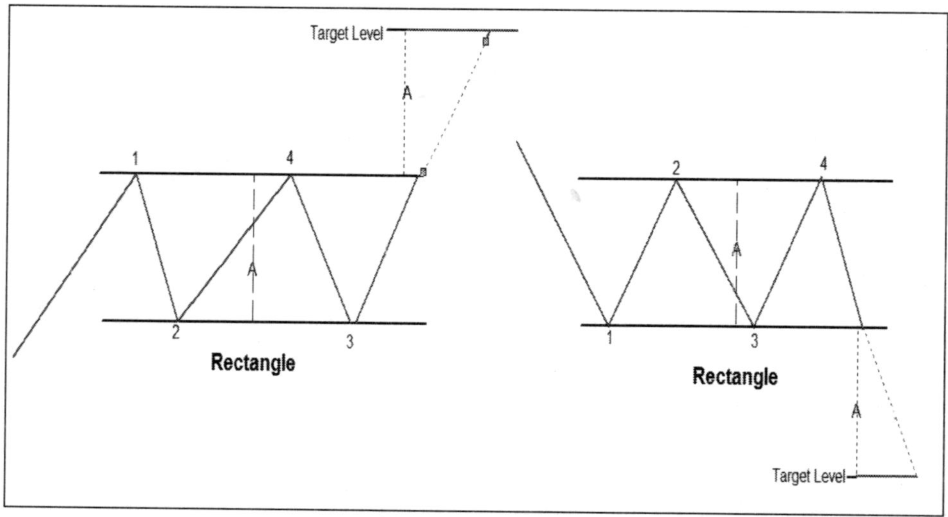

Figure 7.41: **Rectangles are continuation patterns; note how they need contain at least four reversal points**

Rectangles are formed as the result of a battle between groups of buyers and sellers of approximately equal strength and, by definition, must have at least four reversal points as illustrated in Figure 7.41.

A rectangle formation occurs when initially there is both a certain amount of demand at a price and also a certain amount of supply at that price. Eventually, either the demand is exhausted and the price breaks out of the triangle on the downside, or the supply is fully absorbed and the price breaks out of the triangle on the upside.

One should buy on an upside breakout from a rectangle. Theoretically, the stop loss should be placed below the bottom of the rectangle. In practice, however, this hypothetical stop loss can be too distant from the price and unviable in practice because a substantial part of one's trading capital could erode in a single trade by the time such a distant stop loss gets triggered.

Experience suggests that stop loss should be placed 5% below the breakout point. One should take profit when prices rally to a target point which is derived by adding the width of the rectangle to the point of breakout as shown by Dotted Line A in Figure 7.41.

Experience also shows that upside breakouts from rectangles should be considered valid only if prices were already making higher tops and higher bottoms, namely if the earlier trend was up. Otherwise, there is 90% probability of a false breakout.

Correspondingly, one should sell in case of a downside breakdown from a rectangle. The stop loss should be placed above the top of the rectangle. In practice, however, this hypothetical stop loss is usually too distant and unviable in practice because a substantial part of one's trading capital could erode in a single trade by the time such a loose stop loss gets triggered.

Experience suggests that stop loss should be placed 5% above the breakout point. One should take profit when prices decline to the target point, which is derived by adding the width of the rectangle to the point of breakout as shown by Dotted Line A of the right hand rectangle in Figure 7.41.

Experience, also shows that Breakdowns from rectangle should only be considered valid if prices were already making lower tops, lower bottoms prior to its formation, i.e. if the trend was already down. Otherwise, there is a 90% probability of false breakdown.

Let's now understand this with some real life market examples.

Example 1

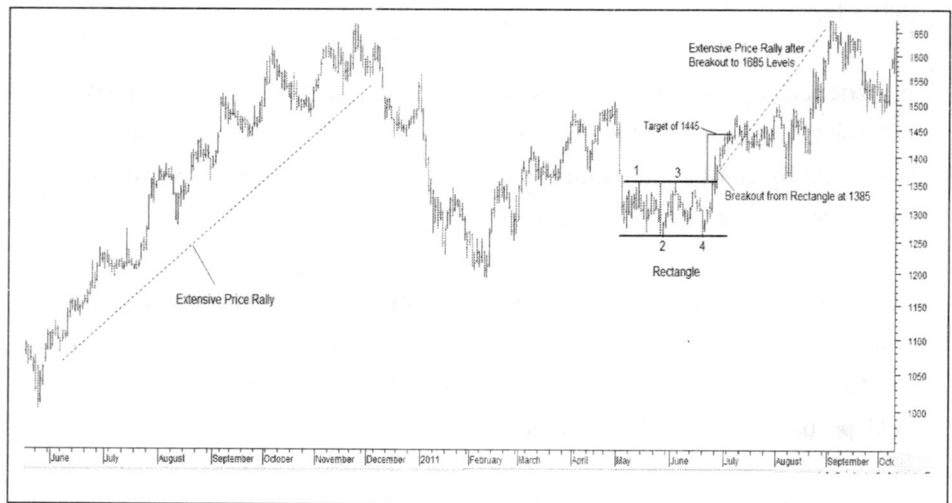

Figure 7.42: **Breakout from a rectangle formation in the daily chart of Bajaj Auto**

Figure 7.42 shows the price of Bajaj Auto futures consolidating in a rectangle after an extensive price rally. The breakout occurred at ₹ 1,385 levels on 28 June 2011 in the direction of the ongoing uptrend.

As explained above:

- One should buy at the breakout level, in this case at ₹ 1,385 levels, without waiting for prices to close above the breakout level.
- Stop loss for this trade should be placed at ₹ 1,315 levels, i.e. 5% below the breakout level.

One should take profit when prices rally to a target point which is derived by adding the width of the rectangle to the point of breakout as shown Figure 7.42. Accordingly, in this case one should be taking profit anywhere around ₹ 1,445 levels.

The stock's price, in fact, rallied to around ₹ 1,685 levels in a short span of little less than three months and gave substantial time for taking profit.

Example 2

Figure 7.43 illustrates the price of Central Bank of India consolidating in a rectangle after an extensive price decline.

First, an upside breakout occurred at ₹ 108 levels against the direction of the ongoing trend, which was down. As explained above, one should trade breakouts only in the direction of the original trend. This upside breakout, however, was against the direction of the ongoing trend because the original trend was down but the direction of the breakout was up. Hence, one should clearly avoid buying on this upside breakout from

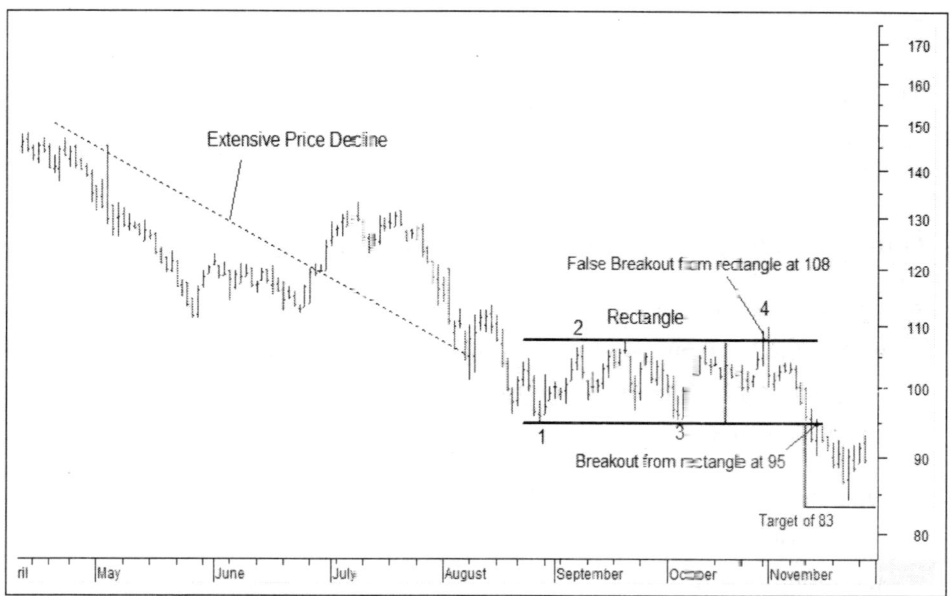

Figure 7.43: **A false upward breakout from a rectangle formation in the daily chart of Central Bank of India, followed by a continuation of the down trend**

a rectangle pattern. Indeed, ultimately this upside breakout turned out to be a false one as prices thereafter demonstrated a downside breakdown. The breakdown occurred at ₹ 95 levels on 15 November 2011 in the direction of the downtrend.

As explained above:

- One should sell at breakout level, in this case at ₹ 95 levels without waiting for prices to close below the breakout level.
- Stop loss for this trade should be placed at ₹ 99.75 levels, i.e. 5% above the breakout level.

One should take profit when the price declines to the target point which is derived by adding the width of the rectangle to the point of breakout as shown Figure 7.43. Thus, in this case one should take profit anywhere around ₹ 83 levels.

The stock's price, in fact, declined to around ₹ 83 levels in the next seven trading sessions.

Options Trading Strategy for Rectangle Formation

- One can consider buying at-the-money call options, if both the direction of the breakout and the ongoing trend are up. In such a situation, the price might rally with an upside momentum which would prevent any erosion in the time value of the call option.
- One should consider buying at-the-money put options if both the direction of the breakout and the ongoing trend are down. In such a situation, the price might decline with a downside momentum which would prevent erosion in the time value of the put option.

Flags

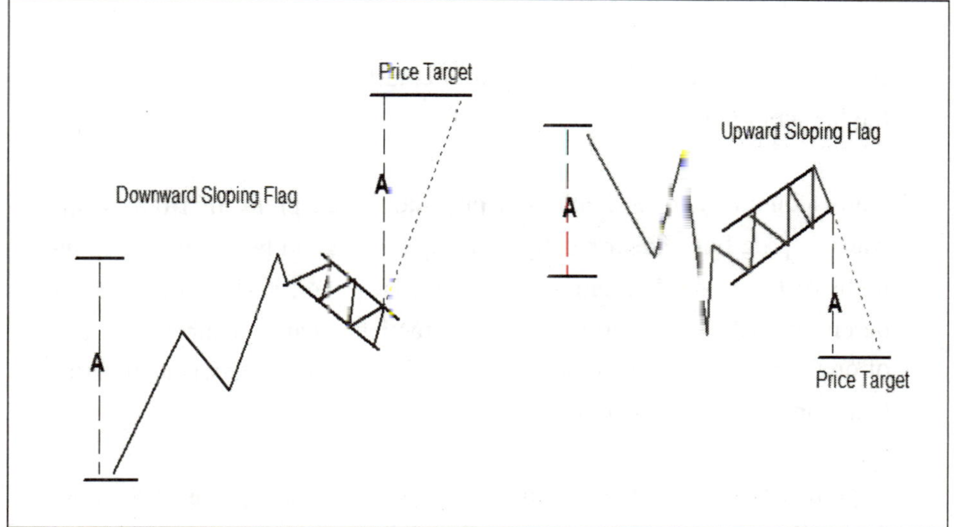

Figure 7.44: **Flags — Downward sloping and upward sloping flags**

Flags are excellent continuation patterns to trade, having a success rate of more than 85%.

Flags are formed by:

- A downward sloping, compact parallelogram when the trend is up.
- An upward sloping compact parallelogram, when the trend is down.

Figure 7.44 illustrates both downward sloping and upward sloping flags.

One should buy on an upside breakout from a downward sloping flag. In such a case, theory suggests that the stop loss should be placed below the lows of the downward sloping flag pattern. However, such a stop loss can be very distant and therefore unviable in practice because a substantial part of one's trading capital could erode in a single trade when such a loose stop loss gets triggered.

Experience suggests that the stop loss could be better placed 5% below the breakout point.

Correspondingly, one should sell on a downside breakout from an upward sloping flag. Theoretically, the stop loss should be placed above the highs of the upward sloping flag pattern. However, such a stop loss can be enormously loose and unviable in practice because a substantial part of one's trading capital could get eroded in a single trade when such distant stop loss gets triggered.

Experience suggests that the stop loss could be better placed 5% above the breakout point.

One should take profit when prices reach the target point which is derived by adding the height of the move preceding the flag formation, namely the extent of line A, to the breakout point of the flag, as illustrated in Figure 7.44.

Caution

- Flag formation always takes place after an extensive up or down move.
- Volumes should decline throughout the formation of the flag pattern.
- Prices should break out of the flag pattern within three weeks.

Let's now understand flags with some real life market examples.

Example 1

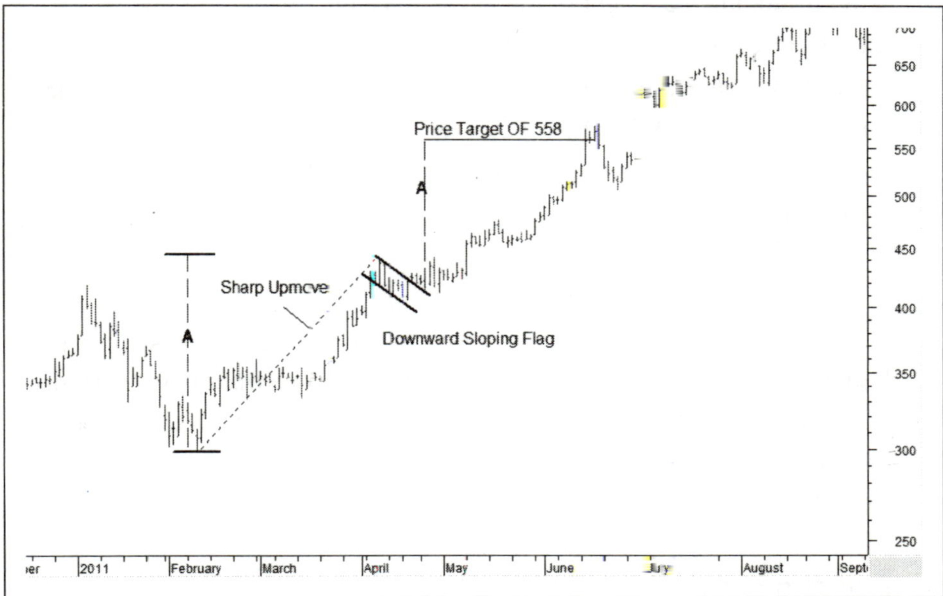

Figure 7.45: **The ongoing uptrend continues after the formation of a downward sloping flag in the daily chart of Bata futures**

Figure 7.45 illustrates an extensive price rally in Bata futures from ₹ 300 to ₹ 435 levels. Thereafter, a downward sloping flag was formed. An upward breakout from this flag occurred on 20 April 2011 at ₹ 425 levels.

As explained above:

- One should buy at the breakout level, namely at ₹ 425 levels in this case, without waiting for prices to close above the breakout level.
- Stop loss for this trade should be placed 5% below the breakout level, i.e. at ₹ 403.75 levels.

One should take profit when prices rally to the target point which is derived by adding the height of the move preceding the flag formation, i.e. the extent of line A, to the breakout point of the flag, as illustrated in Figure 7.45. Hence, in this case one should be taking profit around the target price of ₹ 558 levels, which was achieved in a little less than two months. The price further rallied to ₹ 700-plus levels without making any significant correction.

Example 2

Figure 7.46 illustrates an extensive price decline in Bharti Airtel from ₹ 410 to ₹ 335 levels in five trading sessions during October 2009. Thereafter, an upward sloping flag was formed. A downside breakout from this flag occurred on 26 October 2009 at ₹ 333 levels.

As explained above:

- One should sell at the breakout level, in this case at ₹ 333 levels, without waiting for prices to close below the breakdown level.
- Stop loss for this trade should be placed at ₹ 349.65 levels, i.e. 5% above the breakdown level.

One should take profit when prices decline to the target point which is derived by adding the height of the move preceding the flag formation, i.e. the extent of line A, to the breakout point of the flag as illustrated in Figure 7.46. Accordingly, in this case the profit taking point was around the target price of ₹ 255 levels.

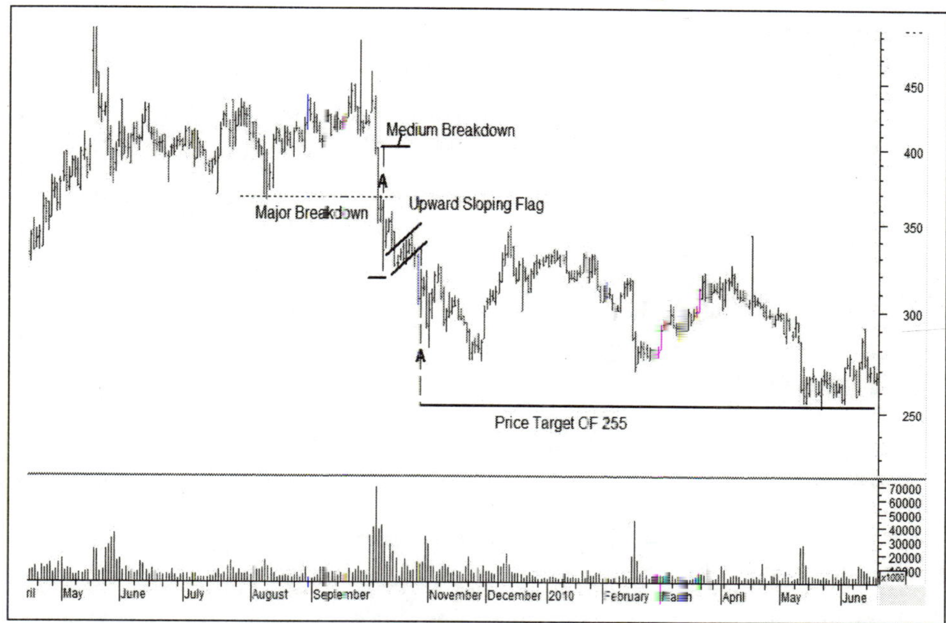

Figure 7.46: **The downtrend continues after the formation of an upward sloping flag in the daily chart of Bharti Airtel**

Option Trading Strategy for Flags

- One should consider buying at-the-money call option if the breakout is from a downward sloping flag as prices might rally with an upside momentum which would prevent any erosion in the time value of the call option.

- One should consider buying at-the-money put options if the breakout is from an upward sloping flag as prices might thereafter decline with a downside momentum which would prevent any erosion in the time value of the put option.

Pennants

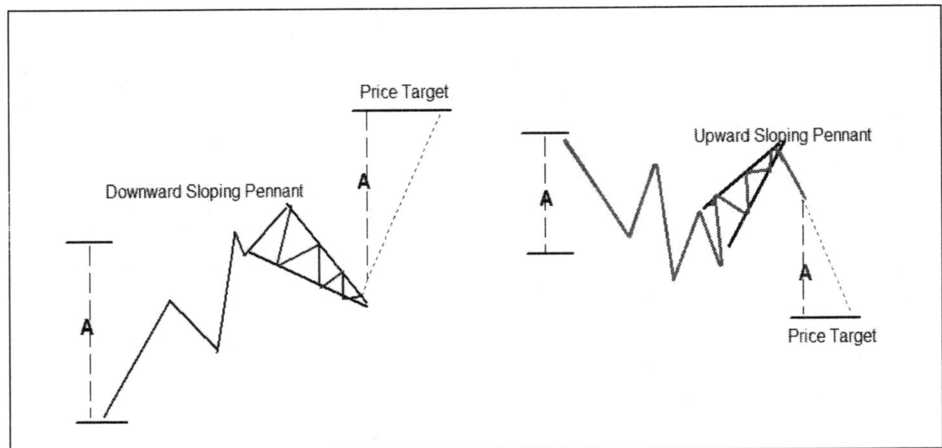

Figure 7.47: **Downward and upward sloping pennants**

Pennants are continuation patterns having success rate of more than 85% and are formed by:

- Downward sloping converging lines when the trend is up.
- Upward sloping converging lines when the trend is down.

Figure 7.47 illustrates both downward sloping and upward sloping pennants.

One should buy on an upside breakout from a downward sloping pennant. In such a case, theory suggests that the stop loss should be placed below the lows of the downward sloping flag pattern. However, such a stop loss can be enormously distant and unviable in practice because a substantial part of one's trading capital could erode in a single trade when such a loose stop loss gets triggered.

Experience suggests that the stop loss would be better placed 5% below the breakout point.

Correspondingly, one should sell on a downside breakout from an upward sloping pennant. Theoretically, the stop loss should be placed above the highs of the upward sloping flag pattern. However, such a stop loss is likely to be far away and unviable in practice because a substantial part of one's trading capital could get eroded in a single trade when such a distant stop loss gets triggered.

Experience suggests that the stop loss could be better placed 5% above the breakout point.

One should take profit when prices reach the target point which is derived by adding the height of the move preceding the pennant formation, i.e. the extent of line A, to the breakout point of the pennant as illustrated in Figure 7.47.

Caution

- Pennant formations always take place after an extensive up or down move.
- Volumes should decline throughout the formation of the pennant.
- Prices should break out of the pennant pattern within three weeks.

Now let's understand pennants with some real life market examples.

Example 1

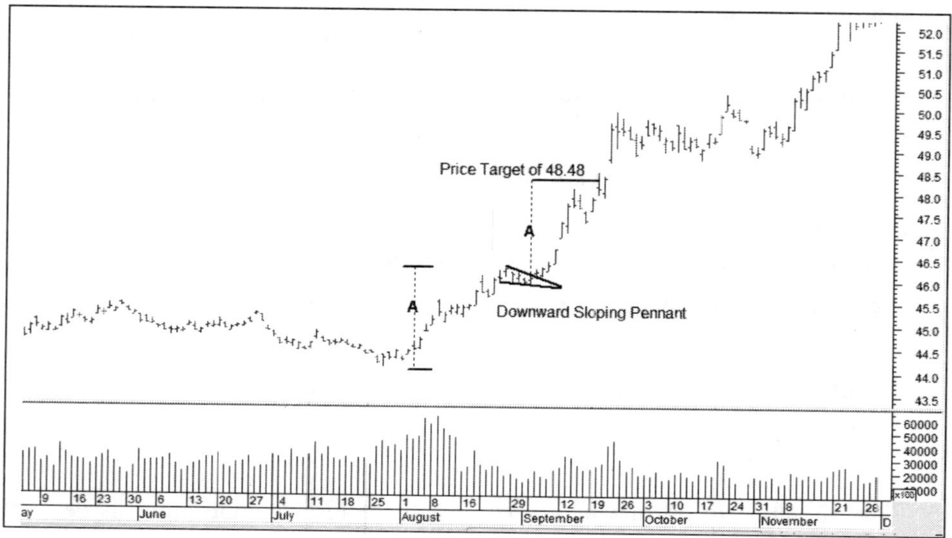

Figure 7.48: **The uptrend continues after the price breaks out from the downward sloping pennant in the daily chart of US dollar and Indian rupee**

Figure 7.48 illustrates an extensive rally in the US dollar from ₹ 44.09 to ₹ 46.27 levels in less than twenty trading sessions. Thereafter, a downward sloping pennant was formed. An upside breakout from this pennant occurred on 6 September 2011 at ₹ 46.17 levels.

Now, as explained above:

- One should buy at the breakout level, in this case at ₹ 46.17 levels, without waiting for prices to close above that level.
- Stop loss for this trade should be placed 5% below the breakout level, i.e. at ₹ 43.86 levels.

One should take profit when prices rally to the target point, which is derived by adding the height of the move preceding the pennant formation, i.e. the extent of line A, to the breakout point of the pennant as illustrated in Figure 7.48. Accordingly, in this trade one should be taking profit around the target price of ₹ 48.48 levels, which was achieved in ten trading sessions. Thereafter, the price further rallied to ₹ 52-plus levels without making any significant correction in the next two months.

Example 2

Figure 7.49 illustrates an extensive price decline in Bajaj Hindustan from ₹ 64 to ₹ 47 levels in less than a month in August 2011. Thereafter, an upward sloping pennant was formed. A downward breakout from this pennant occurred on 12 September 2011 at ₹ 47 levels.

Now, as explained above:

- One should sell at the breakout level, in this case at ₹ 47 levels, without waiting for prices to close below it.

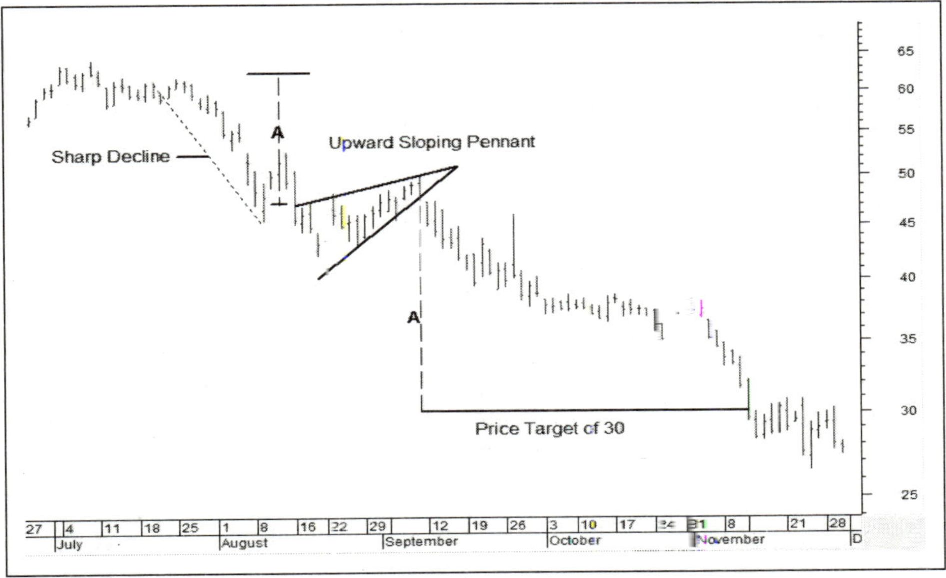

Figure 7.49: **The downtrend continues after the price breaks out of an upward sloping pennant in the daily chart of Bajaj Hindustan**

- Stop loss for this trade should have been placed at ₹ 49.35 levels, i.e. 5% above the breakdown level.

One should take profit when prices decline to the target point which is derived by adding the height of the move preceding the pennant formation, i.e. the extent of line A, to the breakout point of the pennant as illustrated in Figure 7.49. Accordingly, in this case one should be taking profit around the target price of ₹ 30, which was achieved in the next two months.

Option Trading Strategy for Pennants

- One should consider buying at-the-money call options if there is an upside breakout from a downward sloping pennant since prices are then likely to rally with an upside momentum which would prevent any erosion in the time value of the call option.
- One should consider buying at-the-money put options if the price breaks downward from an upward sloping pennant since then prices are likely to decline with a downside momentum, preventing any erosion in the time value of the put option.

8

Trading Gaps

Gaps represent an area on a price chart where no trading has taken place. For example, if a stock price reaches a high of ₹ 90 on Monday, opens at ₹ 95 on Tuesday and moves straight up from ₹ 95 to ₹ 99 levels, then no trading has occurred in the ₹ 90 ₹ 95 area. This no-trade area appears as a "gap" on the price charts.

Gaps could be either upside gaps or downside gaps:

- An upside gap is produced when the previous day's highest price is lower than the following day's lowest price.
- A downside gap is produced when the previous day's lowest price is higher than the following day's highest price.

Gaps are bound to occur in financial markets which are volatile by nature as prices fluctuate on milli-second basis. Theoretically, one can define any number of gaps but typically there are two types of gaps.

1. Normal gaps; and

2. Breakaway gaps.

Normal Gaps

Most gaps get filled up very quickly. Such gaps are known as normal gaps.

These normal gaps have no bearing on buying and selling decisions and one should not be influenced by them.

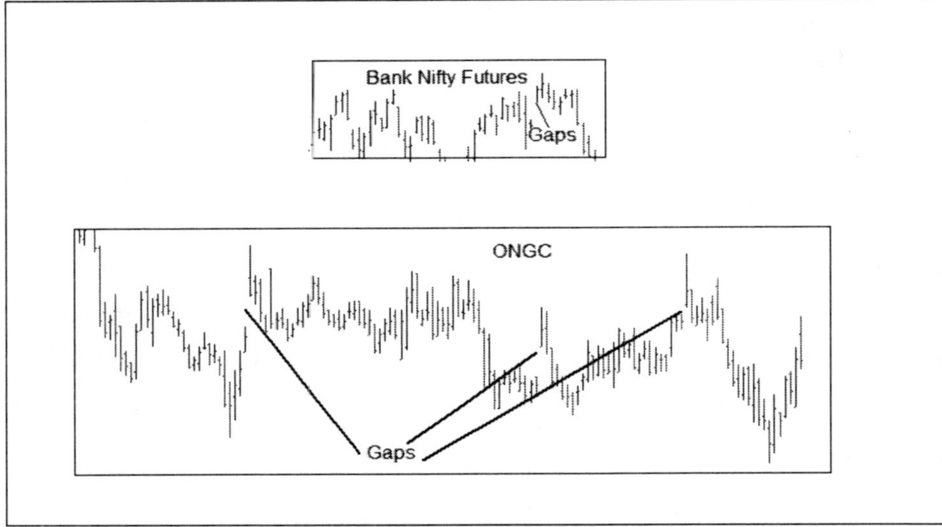

Figure 8.1: **Normal gaps in the charts of ONGC and Bank Nifty futures**

Figure 8.1 illustrates normal gaps in ONGC and Bank Nifty futures.

Breakaway Gaps

Gaps which result in a breakout from reversal or consolidation patterns are known as breakaway gaps.

Breakaway gaps signify that the breakout in question is genuine and that a move in the direction of the breakout would be powerful. Accordingly, one should initiate trade in the direction of the breakout and, often, prices do not return to "fill the gap" in a short period.

Usually, such gaps are formed on breakouts from ascending or descending right-angle triangles.

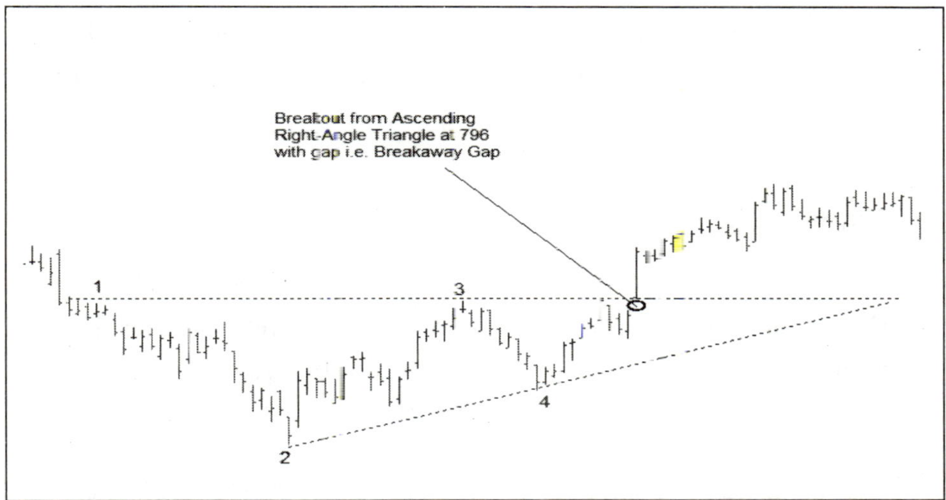

Figure 8.2: **Upward breakout with a gap from an ascending right-angle triangle in TCS futures. This is an example of a breakaway gap.**

Figure 8.2 illustrates an upside breakout from a right-angle ascending triangle in TCS futures accompanied by a breakaway gap. This was a genuine breakaway gap as it was not filled in the short term.

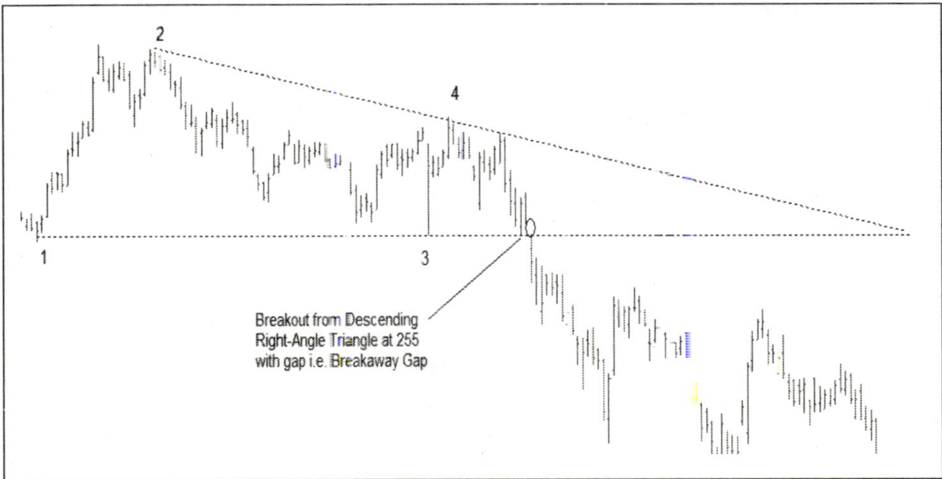

Figure 8.3: **Breakaway gap in Sesa Goa after which the price breaks out downwards from a descending right-angle triangle**

Figure 8.3 illustrates a downward breakout from a right-angle descending triangle in Sesa Goa accompanied by a breakaway gap. This gap was not filled in the short tenure.

Trading Gaps

Gaps are a regular phenomena in price charts. One should not worry about their occurrence. Gaps offer a particularly powerful trading signal when the price breaks out of a trading range with a gap. In such a case, one should always trade in the direction of the breakout, especially when the breakout is accompanied by a gap. Most important, at the time of the breakout one should never assume that the price would necessarily return and fill the gap.

Options Trading Strategy for Breakaway Gaps

- One should consider buying at-the-money call options if the breakout is upwards as the price might then rally with momentum, which would prevent any erosion in the time value of the call option.
- One should consider buying at-the-money put options if the price breaks out downwards as the price then might decline with a momentum which would prevent any erosion in the time value of the put option.

9

Trading Retracements

Stock prices move in a trend, which could be either up or down.

Each up move is followed by a "correction" in the opposite (downward) direction.

Conversely, each down move is followed by an upward "pullback."

On a chart where a stock's price is generally headed upward, retracements are the small dips in price that the stock experiences during its overall upward move (*see* Figure 9.1).

Conversely, when the price is falling, retracements are the small rallies, or pullbacks, in price that the stock experiences during its overall downward move as illustrated in Figure 9.1.

These corrections and pullbacks are better known as retracements. Most market traders prefer buying on declines and selling on rallies. Equally, most market analysts and financial news channels recommend buying "Stock XYZ on declines" or selling "Stock XYZ on rallies." In other

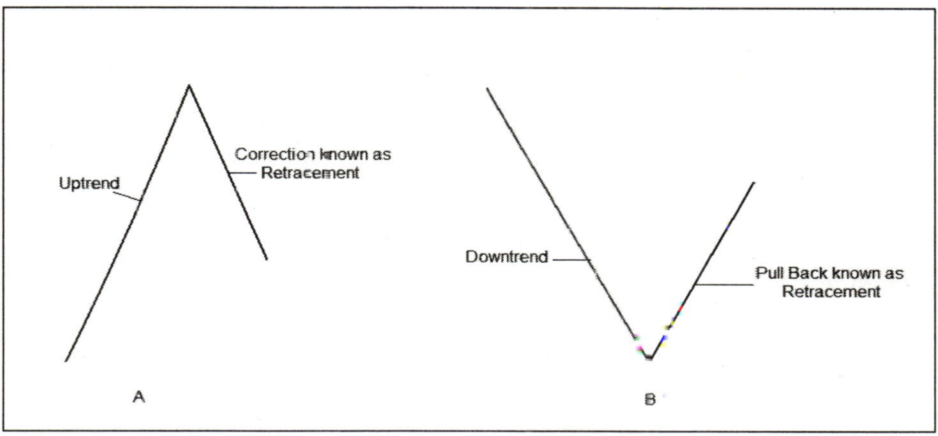

Figure 9.1: **Retracements — correction and pull back**

words, both traders and market analysts prefer initiating trades on retracements. However, one cannot buy blindly on any price decline and similarly, one cannot sell blindly on any price rally. Actually both traders and market analysts use the Retracement Theory to buy on declines and sell on rallies.

Retracement Theory and Fibonacci Retracement Levels

Retracement theory is based on the Fibonacci retracements levels.

Fibonacci retracement is a very popular tool used by many technical traders to identifying support, resistance, stop losses and target levels.

Fibonacci retracement is based on the key numbers identified by mathematician Leonardo Fibonacci in the thirteenth century The Fibonacci sequence of numbers is as follows: 0, 1, 1, 2, 3, 5, 8, 13, 21, 34, 55, 89, 144, etc. Each number in this sequence is simply the sum of the two preceding numbers and the sequence continues infinitely. However, this sequence of numbers is not as important as the mathematical relationships between the numbers in the series.

One of the remarkable characteristics of the Fibonacci sequence of numbers is that each number is approximately 1.618 times greater than the preceding number. This common relationship between every number in the series is the foundation of the common ratios used in retracement studies.

Thus, the key Fibonacci ratios 23.6%, 38.2%, 50%, 61.8% and 100% are derived from mathematical relationships among the Fibonacci sequence of numbers.

The ratio 23.6% is arrived at by dividing one number in the series by the number that is three places to its right. For example: 8÷34 = 0.2352.

The ratio 38.2% is arrived at by dividing one number in the series by the number that is found two places to the right. For example: 55÷144 = 0.3819.

The ratio 61.8% is arrived at by dividing any number in the series by the number that immediately follows it. For example: 8÷13 = 0.6153, and 55÷89 = 0.6179.

In addition to the ratios described above, many traders also like using the 50% levels. The 50% retracement level is not really a Fibonacci ratio, but is used because many times stock prices find support and / or resistance at the 50% retracement level.

In technical analysis, Fibonacci retracement levels are created by taking two extreme points — usually a major peak and a trough — on a stock chart and dividing the vertical distance by the key Fibonacci ratios of 23.6%, 38.2%, 50%, 61.8% and 100%. Once these levels are identified, horizontal lines are drawn and used to identify possible support and resistance levels as this theory says Fibonacci ratios can be used to determine critical support and resistance levels (*see* Figure 9.2).

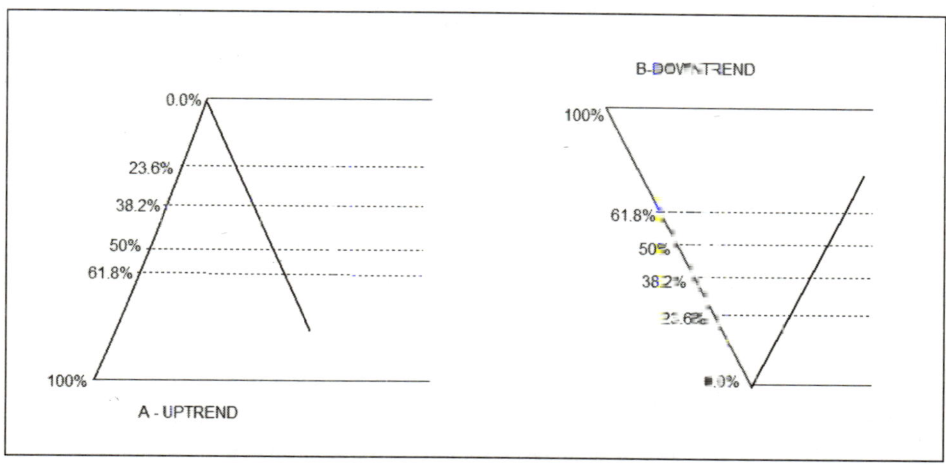

Figure 9.2: **Fibonacci retracement levels**

Retracement theory suggests buying upon prices correcting to a Fibonacci support level when the market is in an uptrend and selling upon price rallying to a Fibonacci resistance level when the market is in a downtrend.

For reasons that are unclear, these ratios seem to play an important role in the stock market, just as they do in nature.

Buying Correction Retracements in an Uptrend

Once a support is established (as explained in Chapter 5) at any one of the key Fibonacci ratios, namely 23.6%, 38.2%, 50%, 61.8% or 100%, a buy position can be initiated whenever prices approach the support in a correction during an ongoing uptrend. The stop loss is initially placed below the key Fibonacci ratio level at which support develops as shown in Figure 9.3.

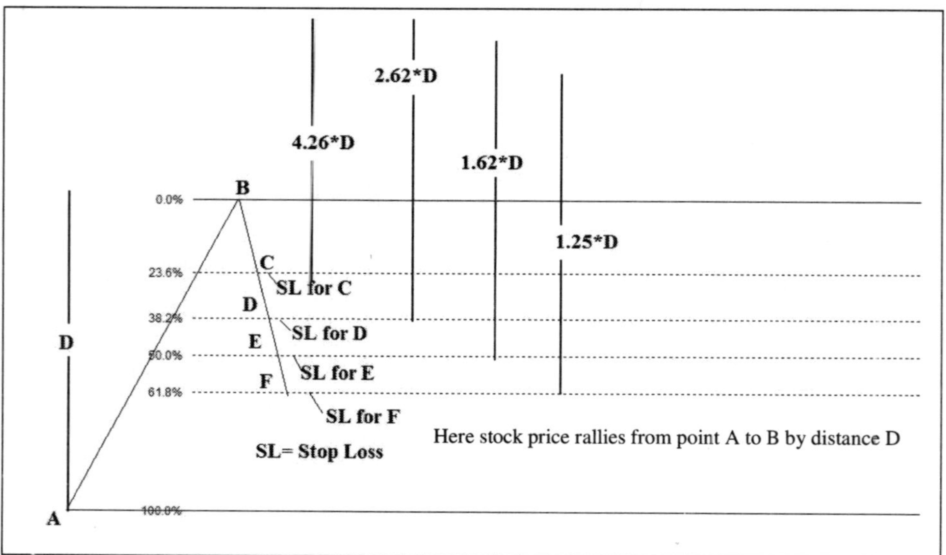

Figure 9.3: **Stop loss and target levels for buying retracements during an uptrend**

Thereafter one should work out the target. The target is determined by measuring the vertical distance from the starting point of the rally, i.e. Point A as shown in Figure 9.3, to the peak, namely Point B. This vertical distance from Point A to Point B is shown as distance D in Figure 9.3. We then measure the same distance up from the Fibonacci ratio at which the support is found and multiply this distance by:

- 4.26 times to get the target level if support is found at 23.6% retracement level as illustrated in Figure 9.3.
- 2.62 times to get the target level if support is found at 38.2% retracement level as illustrated in Figure 9.3
- 1.62 times to get the target level if support is found at 50% retracement level as illustrated in Figure 9.3
- 1.25 times to get the target level if support is found at 61.8% retracement level as illustrated in Figure 9.3

Selling Pullback Retracements in a Downtrend

Once a resistance is established at any one of the key Fibonacci ratios, namely 23.6%, 38.2%, 50%, 61.8% and 100%, a sell position can be initiated whenever prices retrace to the resistance level in a pullback rally during an ongoing downtrend. As shown in Figure 9.4, the stop loss should initially be placed above the key Fibonacci ratio level at which resistance develops.

Thereafter, one should work out the target which is defined by measuring the vertical distance from starting point of the decline, namely Point A as shown in Figure 9.4 to the bottom, namely Point B. This vertical distance from point A to Point B is shown as distance D in Figure 9.4. Then

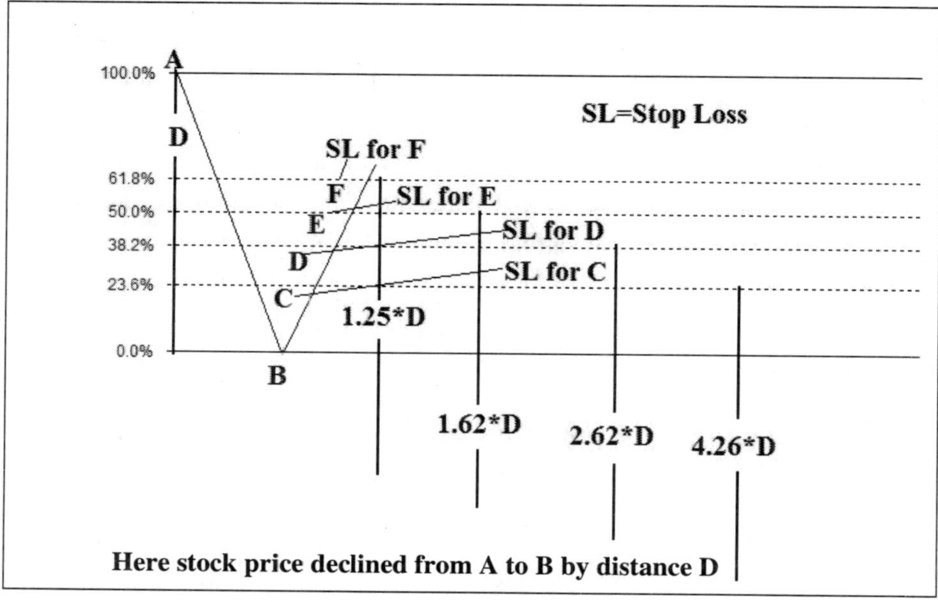

Figure 9.4: **Stop loss and target levels for selling pullback retracements in an ongoing downtrend**

measure the same distance down from the Fibonacci ratio at which the resistance was found and multiply this distance by:

- 4.26 times to get the target level if resistance is found ar 23.6% retracement level as illustrated in Figure 9.4.
- 2.62 times to get the target level if resistance is found ar 38.2% retracement level as illustrated in Figure 9.4.
- 1.62 times to get the target level if resistance is found ar 50% retracement level as illustrated in Figure 9.4.
- 1.25 times to get the target level if resistance is found ar 61.8% retracement level as illustrated in Figure 9.4.

10

Trading with Indicators

Indicators are derived from mathematical calculations of a series of data points. These data points could be stock price, volume, etc. The values so obtained are used to forecast probable price change.

In other words, indicators filter price action with the help of mathematical calculations. Some indicators are simple to derive while others entail very complex calculations.

Indicators can be used as a basis for trading, as they can generate buy-and-sell signals.

Indicators basically serve four broad functions in trading:

1. Alert

An indicator can act as an alert to chart pattern study. For example, if a head and shoulders pattern formation is in the making and the indicator suggests that the stock price is also losing its upside thrust, this would serve as an alert to watch out for a breaking of the neckline.

2. Confirm

Indicators can be used to confirm chart patterns. For example, if there is a breakout on a chart, the buy signal generated by indicators could be used to confirm the breakout.

3. Predict

Most commonly, indicators are used to predict the future direction of prices.

4. Mechanical Trading

Indicators are the backbone of mechanical trading which is discussed ahead in Chapter 11.

Most traders use indicators to accomplish points 3 and 4 listed above.

As indicators are derived from price action they are not its direct reflection. Before looking at indicators more deeply, therefore, it is important to emphasize that a trader should not ignore the price action of a security and focus solely on buy / sell signals generated by an indicator. Rather, an analysis of what the indicator is saying should be done in conjunction with the security's underlying price action. An indicator may flash a buy signal, but if the chart pattern shows a descending right angle triangle pattern formation in progress, with a series of lower top, lower bottom formations already in place, it would be a false buy signal.

There are hundreds of indicators in use today, and any number of new indicators get created every month. There is often also a needless hype associated with the word indicator; so choosing an indicator to follow can be a difficult task, at least for a beginner. This task becomes even more difficult as most indicators move in agreement and generate the same signal. So actually you need only a few indicators that can complement each other and which have stood the test of time. Which is why only a few select indicators are discussed in detail ahead in this chapter to enable you to fully grasp their intricacies.

Indicators are basically of two types:

1. Leading indicators.
2. Lagging indicators.

Leading Indicators

Leading indicators predict the change in direction of the ongoing trend in advance, i.e. they help you predict what the price will do next.

The value of leading indicators ranges between 0 and 100. Whenever a leading indicator's value is more than 70, the underlying security is considered overbought (or over owned), while whenever a leading indicator's value is lower than 30, the underlying security is considered oversold (or under owned).

Leading indicators work by measuring how overbought or oversold the underlying security is and work on the assumptions that:

- A security that is oversold is likely to bounce back; hence one should buy an oversold security.
- A security that is overbought is likely to decline; hence one should sell an overbought security.

Experience, however, suggests that there is nothing called overbought or oversold zone. Often, stock prices have a tendency of rallying further after entering a so-called overbought zone, and even stay above the overbought zone for a long time before any actual price correction is witnessed. Similarly, stock prices have a tendency of declining even more after entering an oversold zone, and stay there for a long time before any actual price pullback is witnessed.

In April 2002, for example, the stock of Jindal Iron witnessed an excellent breakout on charts at around ₹ 5.80 levels. A chart pattern study clearly suggested that the stock could turn into a multibagger from there on. We bought the stock around these levels. Thereafter, the stock became overbought, as per most leading indicators, around ₹ 9 levels. The stock, however, rallied further almost vertically to around ₹ 27 levels. At that point we exited our buy side position as the stock was trading in the so-called overbought zone. Moreover, the stock's price had tripled even within the overbought territory — from ₹ 9 to ₹ 27 levels. This forced us to assume that the stock price would now decline. In fact, the stock price never declined. Rather, it rallied vertically upwards to around ₹ 70 levels by June 2002, without any major correction in between (Jindal Iron later got merged into Jindal Vijay Nagar Steel and the merged entity is now known as JSW Steel).

Such cases are numerous and for this reason too much emphasis should not be given to overbought / oversold zones. Instead, indicators can be more profitably used to look for divergences as described ahead.

Most leading indicators move in agreement and generate the same signal at the same time. For this reason, we shall take up only one popular leading indicator, namely Relative Strength Index (RSI).

Relative Strength Index (RSI)

RSI has been around for a long time and has therefore stood the test of time. It is also perhaps the most popular among all available leading indicators.

RSI is an indicator whose value ranges between 0 and 100. The most widespread interpretation of RSI is that the security is considered overbought when RSI is above 70, and is considered oversold when RSI is below 30. As explained above, leading indicators should not be mechanically used to define overbought and oversold zones; but for identifying divergences. This would become clearer from the examples below.

Example 1

Figure 10.1 illustrates an excellent breakout in Nifty futures at 4,750 levels on 19 September 2007. At the time of this breakout, the RSI value was above 70 levels, i.e. Nifty futures were supposedly overbought. Yet, after the breakout Nifty futures rallied even higher all the way to 6,300 levels and that, too, without any major correction — and in a short span of three months. Had one avoided initiating buy side positions in light of the RSI being in the overbought zone, one definitely missed an excellent buying opportunity.

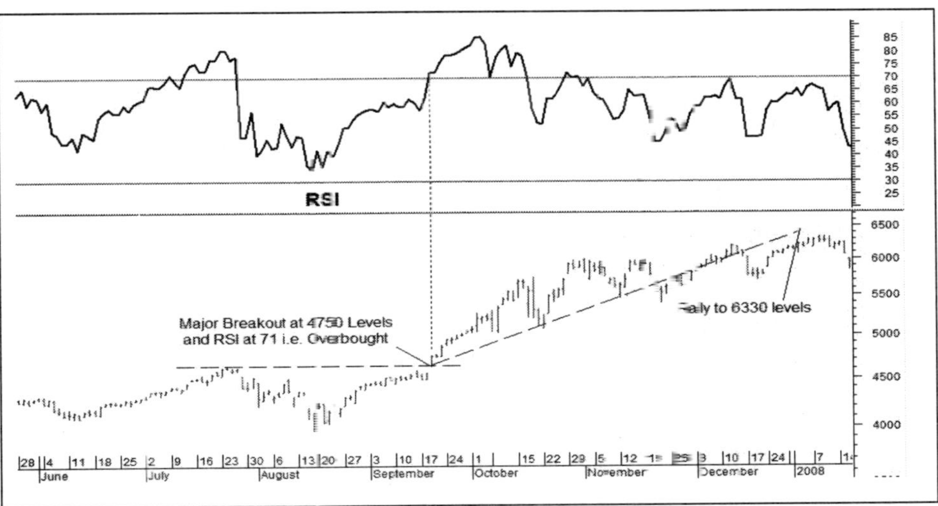

Figure 10.1: **Daily chart of Nifty futures shows Nifty rallying fast even after entering an overbought zone**

Example 2

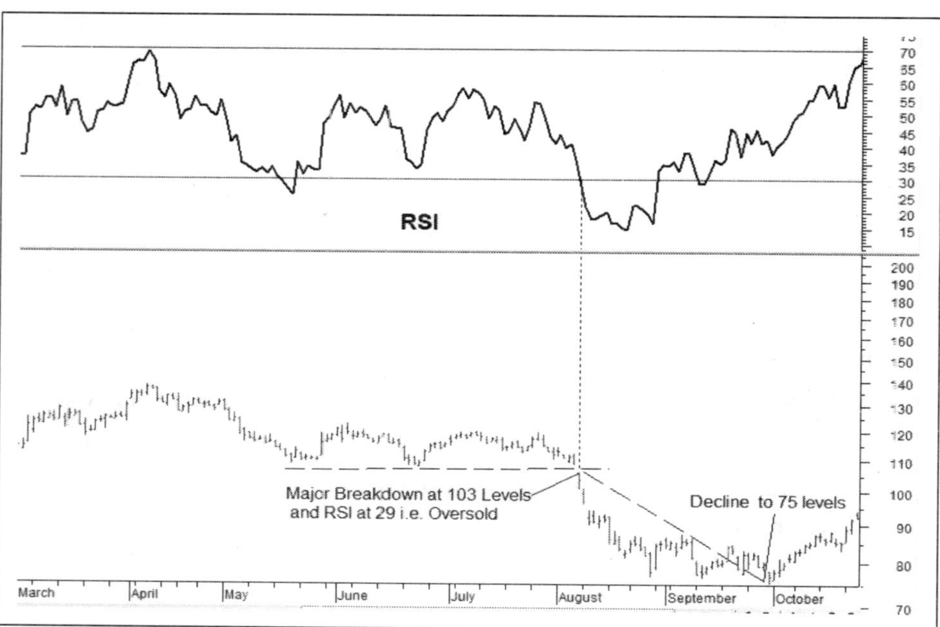

Figure 10.2: **Daily chart of Reliance Power futures shows stock price declining fast even after entering an oversold zone**

Figure 10.2 illustrates an excellent breakdown in Reliance Power futures at about ₹ 103 levels on 5 August 2011. At the time of this breakdown, the RSI value was below 30, i.e. it indicated the security to be oversold. Yet, after the breakdown Reliance Power futures declined even lower to ₹ 75 levels, and that without demonstrating any major pullback, in a short span of just one month. If one avoided initiating a sell side position in light of the RSI being in the oversold zone, then one definitely missed an excellent selling opportunity.

Trading Divergences: The Best Way to Trade RSI

The best way to trade using RSI is to look for a divergence. Divergences are of two types:

1. Positive divergence, and
2. Negative divergence.

Trading Positive Divergence

A **positive divergence** occurs when the price makes new lows but RSI fails to break its previous lows. This divergence suggests a reversal of trend from down to up.

Figure 10.3 illustrates CNXIT futures making new lows whereas the RSI fails to break its previous lows.

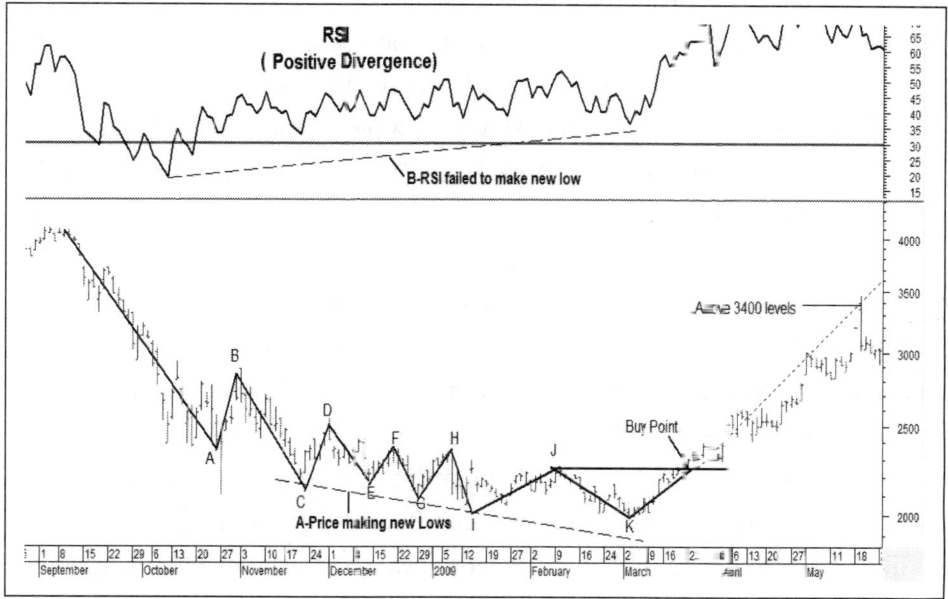

Figure 10.3: **Positive divergence on the daily chart of CNXIT futures as the futures price makes new lows (lower window) but the RSI (top window) does not do so**

As was explained in Chapter 4 (*see* Figure 4.7), one should buy when the immediate lower top, i.e. Point J, is breached without waiting for the formation of a higher bottom, provided you have a buy confirmation by way of a positive divergence on the charts. Here in Figure 10.3, Point J was breached on CNXIT futures price chart on 23 March 2009 at 2,300 levels, Thereafter CNXIT futures rallied 47% in a short span of two months.

Now that divergence has been explained, let us go back to the rationale for closing the sell side positions in Bank Nifty futures (*see* Figure 7.25A) and Nifty futures (*see* Figure 7.25B) ahead of the target levels after the completion of the broadening top pattern.

Let's understand this one by one.

Bank Nifty futures price chart demonstrated the completion of a broadening top pattern formation on 18 November 2010 at 12,422 levels (*see* Figure 7.25 A). As per trading rule of the broadening top pattern, Bank Nifty futures turned a sell at 12,422 levels on 18 November 2010 for a target of 6,637 on the downside. However, after making a low of around 7,750 on 20 December 2011, Bank Nifty futures started rallying and so the sell side target was not achieved.

At this point, positive divergence was also observed on the Bank Nifty futures price chart, in that the price was making new lows while the RSI was not. In fact, the RSI was actually making new highs then (*see* Figure 10.4). Such a positive divergence suggests initiating a buy side trade when the first higher top, higher bottom pattern formation takes place. It is clearly evident from Figure 10.4 that Bank Nifty futures made their first higher top, higher bottom formation when the level of Point L was

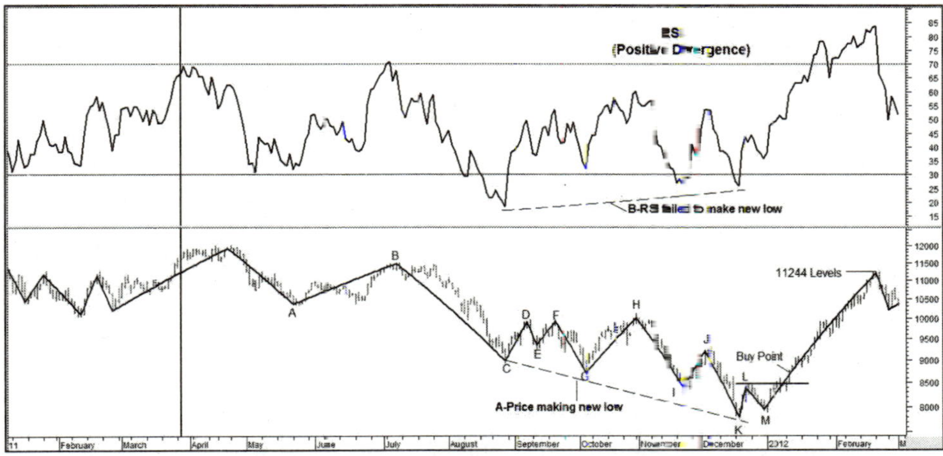

Figure 10.4: **Positive divergence suggests closing the sell side position in Bank Nifty futures**

crossed on the upside on closing basis at 8,775 levels on 10 January 2011 as the Nifty futures rose from Point M. Thus, there was clearly a reversal of trend from down to up in Bank Nifty futures, and it was a buy at 8,775 level. Those who went short in Bank Nifty futures on the completion of the broadening top pattern formation at 12,422 levels should then have closed their sell side position at this point, and simultaneously initiated a buy side position. Thereafter, the price rallied almost vertically for 2,400 points to 11,244 levels in the next 27 trading sessions.

You would recall that the Nifty futures price chart (*see* Figure 7.25 B) demonstrated the completion of a broadening top pattern formation on 16 November 2010 at 6,075 levels. As per the rule of trading broadening top patterns, Nifty futures were a sell at 6,075 levels for a target price of 3,802 levels on the downside (*see* Figure 7.25 B). However, after making a low of around 4,540 on 20 December 2011, Nifty futures started rallying. Thus, the sell side target on Nifty futures was not achieved.

At this point a positive divergence was observed in the Nifty futures price chart as the price was making new lows while the RSI failed to do so. In fact, the RSI was actually making new highs then (*see* Figure 10.5). Such a positive divergence suggests a buy side trade once the first higher top, higher bottom pattern formation is in place. It is clearly evident from Figure 10.5 that Nifty futures made their first higher top, higher bottom formation when the level of Point H was crossed on closing basis at 4,877 levels on 10 January 2011 during the up move from Point I. This clearly showed a reversal of trend from down to up and Nifty futures became a buy at 4,877 level. Hence those who went short in Nifty futures on the completion of the broadening top pattern formation at 6,075 levels must close their sell side position at this point and simultaneously initiate a buy side position. Thereafter, the price rallied almost vertically for 700 points to 5,600 levels in the next 28 trading sessions.

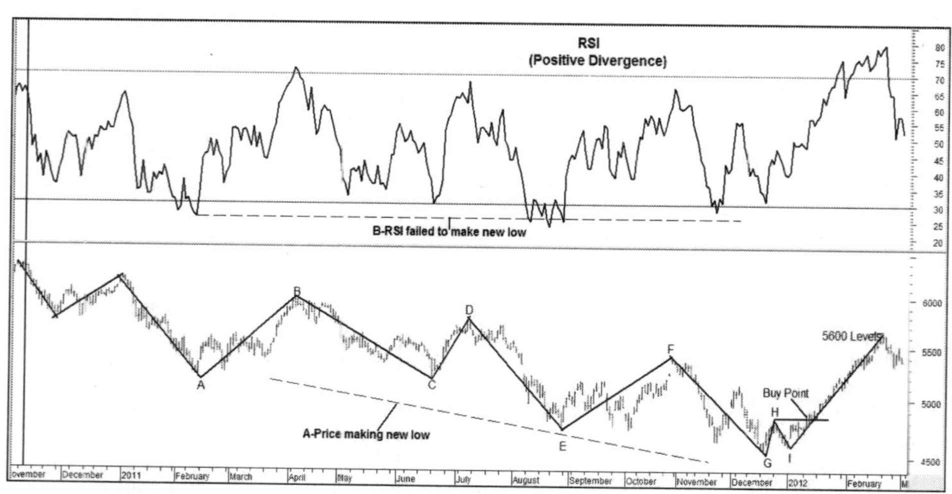

Figure 10.5: **Positive divergence suggests closing sell side position of Nifty futures initiated upon the completion of a broadening top pattern**

Trading Negative Divergence

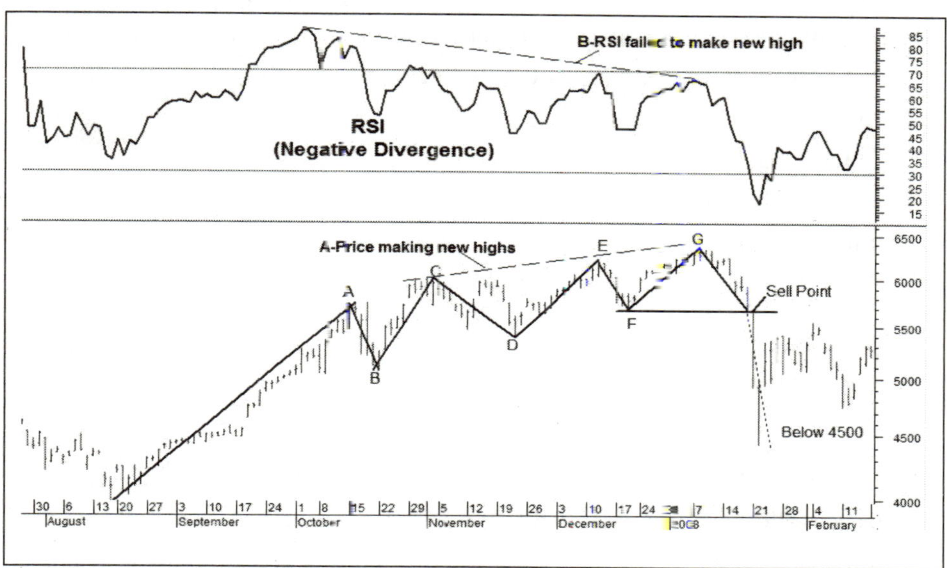

Figure 10.6: **Negative divergence on the daily chart of Nifty futures — while Nifty futures are making new highs, RSI is not**

A **negative divergence** occurs when the price makes new highs but the RSI fails to break its previous highs.

A negative divergence suggests a trend reversal from up to down.

Figure 10.6 depicts Nifty futures making new highs, while the RSI fails to break its previous highs.

It was explained in Chapter 4 (*see* Figure 4.8) that one should sell when the level of the immediately preceding higher bottom is breached, even without waiting for the formation of a lower top, provided you have a sell confirmation by way of a negative divergence on the charts. Thus, one can sell when the level of the immediately preceding higher bottom, i.e. the level of bottom F in Figure 10.6 is breached during the down move from Point G, even without waiting for the formation of a lower top once a negative divergence is evident. In this case, once the level of Point F was breached by Nifty futures on 21 January 2008 at 5,670 levels during its down move from Point G, it crashed 21% in two days with a circuit freeze on the lower side.

Lagging Indicators

Lagging indicators follow the price action and are popularly known as trend following indicators. Since these indicators follow the price, a drawback is that a significant portion of the move would generally have occurred before these indicators are able to provide any signal.

Nevertheless, trend following indicators can be used with profit in trending markets.

There are number of lagging indicators and most of them generate similar signals around the same time. For this reason, we shall take up only the widely used lagging indicators, namely moving average and MACD.

Before that, however, let's understand moving averages themselves.

Moving Average

This is one of the simpler and most popular trend following indicators.

It involves mathematical calculation regarding the average value of a security's price over a given period.

There are a number of methods for calculating moving averages, such as simple, exponential, weighted, time series, etc. The most common among these are the simple and exponential moving averages. In calculating a simple moving average, equal weightage is given to all previous prices while in calculating the exponential moving average, greater weightage is given to the more recent prices. Software packages are available to compute all such calculations.

One can use either simple or exponential moving averages but my preference is for exponential moving averages as these react relatively faster to any change in the trend's direction.

Moving Average Trading Systems

Single Moving Average Crossover Trading System

Here one buys when the price closes above the single moving average and one sells when the price closes below the single moving average.

The commonly used single moving averages are 50-day, 100-day and 200-day moving averages.

Figure 10.7 illustrates a 50-day exponential moving average (EMA) plotted on the Nifty futures chart. Buy signals are generated when the price closes above the moving average and sell signals are generated when the price closes below the moving average line.

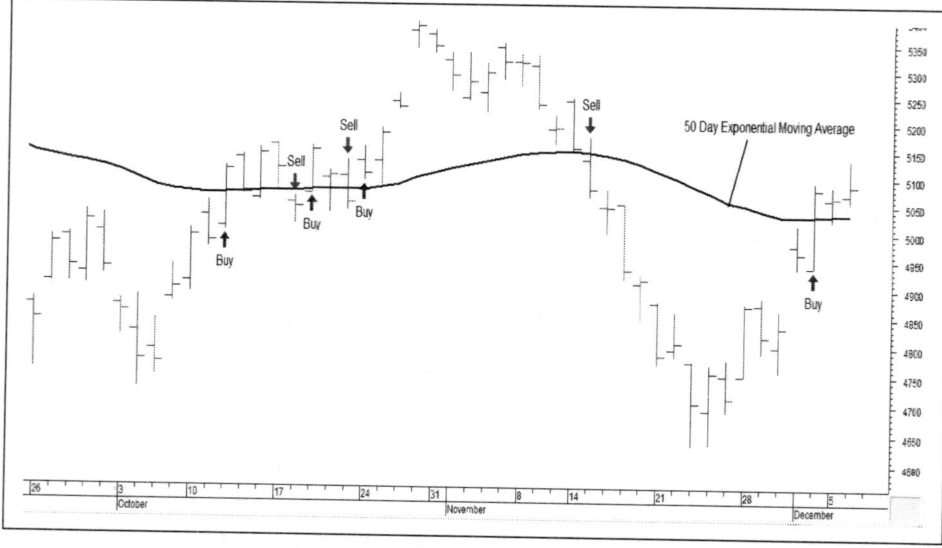

Figure 10.7: **Buy and sell signals generated by a single moving average crossover system on the daily chart of Nifty futures**

Double Moving Average Crossover Trading System

In this case, two moving averages are plotted, and:

- One buys when the shorter term moving average crosses above the longer term moving average, and
- One sells when the shorter term moving average crosses below the longer term moving average.

The commonly used double moving averages are 15-50 and 50-200.

Figure 10.8 depicts the 15-day and 50-day exponential moving averages (EMAs) plotted on the Nifty futures chart. In this system, the buy signal is generated when the 15-day moving average line crosses above the 50-day moving average line as shown by the buy arrow in Figure 10.8, while a sell signal is generated when the 15-day moving average line

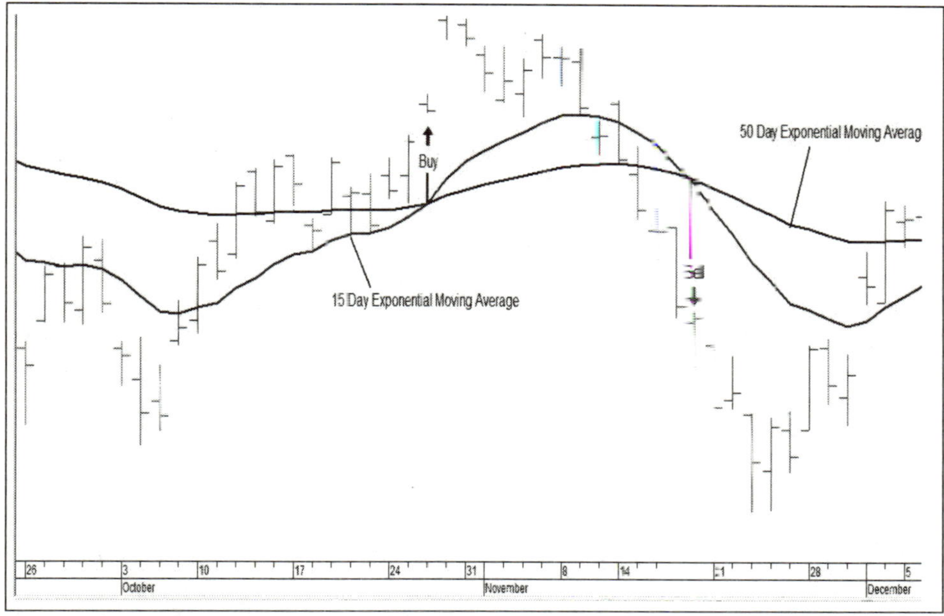

Figure 10.8: **Buy and sell signals in the Nifty futures chart with a double moving average crossover system**

crosses below the 50-day moving average line as shown by the sell arrow in Figure 10.8.

Moving averages should, however, not be used in such a manner as there is no guarantee that the price would respond automatically to 50-, 100- or 200-day moving averages. One should therefore avoid buying / selling on price crossover of widely used moving averages (50 DMA, 100 DMA, 200 DMA). This is so because it's nothing more than a crowd belief. I am saying this because the same number is not going to work on all stocks and so you don't know which moving average crossover would perform on which stock. For this one needs proper testing which is explained ahead in Chapter 11.

The best use of the moving averages is in mechanical trading.

MACD (Moving Average Convergence Divergence)

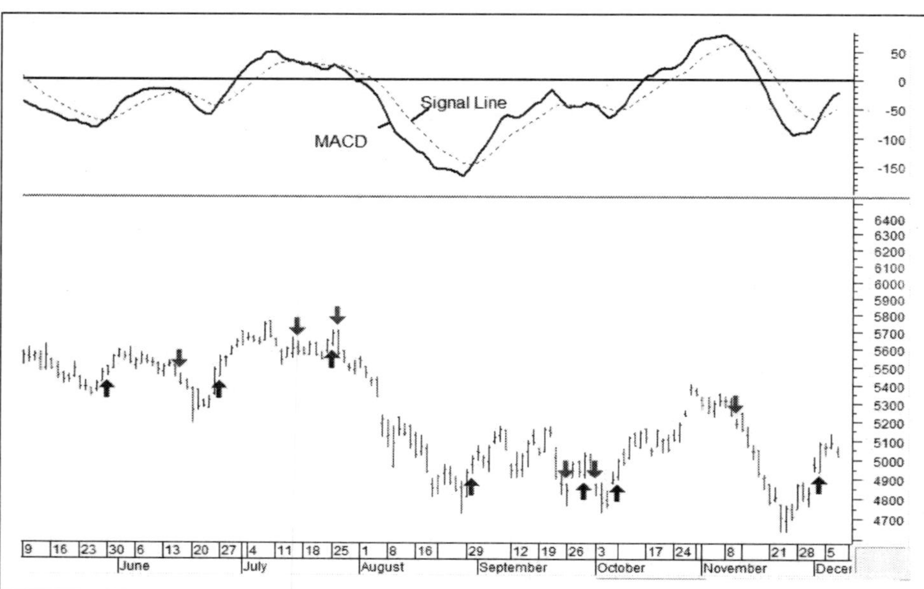

Figure 10.9: **MACD and the signal line in the daily chart of Nifty futures**

MACD is a modified version of a double moving average crossover trading system. Here the first moving average is known as MACD, which is derived by subtracting the 26-period exponential moving average from the 12-period exponential moving average. The second moving average is known as the Signal Line, which is derived by plotting a 9-period exponential moving average on first moving average, i.e. MACD.

The conventional rule is to buy when MACD rises above the signal line and sell when MACD falls below the signal line as illustrated in Figure 10.9.

I would not suggest using MACD in the conventional way because it's nothing more than buying / selling on double moving average crossover. The best way to use MACD is, again, to look for a divergence.

As we saw earlier, divergences are of two types: positive divergence and negative divergence.

Trading Positive Divergence

A **positive divergence** is formed when the price makes new lows, but the MACD fails to break its previous lows. Such a positive divergence suggests a trend reversal from down to up.

Figure 10.10 illustrates a positive divergence in the daily chart of JSW Steel with the price making new lows, even as the MACD fails to break its previous lows.

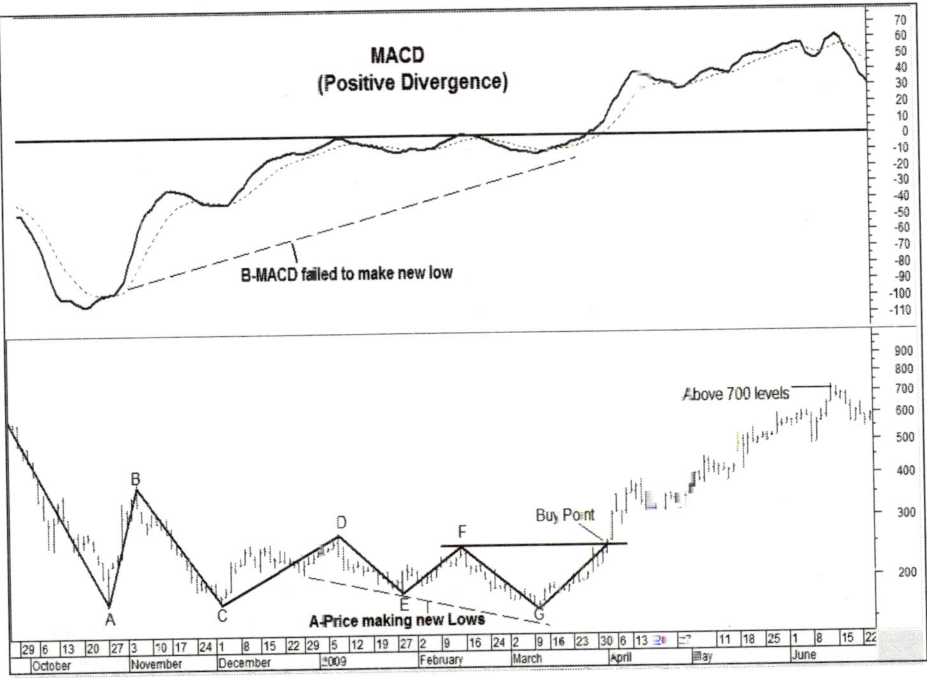

Figure 10.10: **A positive divergence on the daily chart of JSW Steel — the price is making new lows but the MACD is not**

As explained in Chapter 4 (*see* Figure 4.7A), one should buy when the immediate lower top is breached without waiting for the formation of a higher bottom, provided you have a buy confirmation by way of a positive divergence on charts. Here in Figure 10.10 one should buy as soon as the level of the immediate preceding lower top, i.e. the level of Point F is breached in the up move from Point G since a buy confirmation by way of a positive divergence is evident on the chart. The level of Point F was breached on the subsequent up move on the JSW Steel price chart at ₹ 252 levels on 1 April 2009. Thereafter, the price of JSW Steel stock rallied 200% in short span of less than two months.

Trading Negative Divergence

A **negative divergence** occurs when the price makes new highs, but the MACD fails to break through above its previous highs. Such a negative divergence suggests a reversal of the trend from up to down.

Figure 10.11 depicts a negative divergence as the price of Reliance Capital is making new highs, while MACD fails to break its previous highs.

As was explained in Chapter 4 (*see* Figure 4.8), one should sell when the level of the immediately preceding higher bottom is breached, even without waiting for the formation of a lower top, provided you have a sell confirmation by way of a negative divergence on charts. Here in Figure 10.11 one should sell when the level of the immediately preceding higher bottom, i.e. the level of bottom H is breached during the subsequent down move from Point I, even without waiting for the formation of a lower top as we have a sell confirmation by way of a negative divergence on the chart. In Figure 10.11, Point H was breached on Reliance Capital price chart at ₹ 2,300 levels on 21 January 2008. Thereafter Reliance Capital's stock price declined 53 % in a little less than two months.

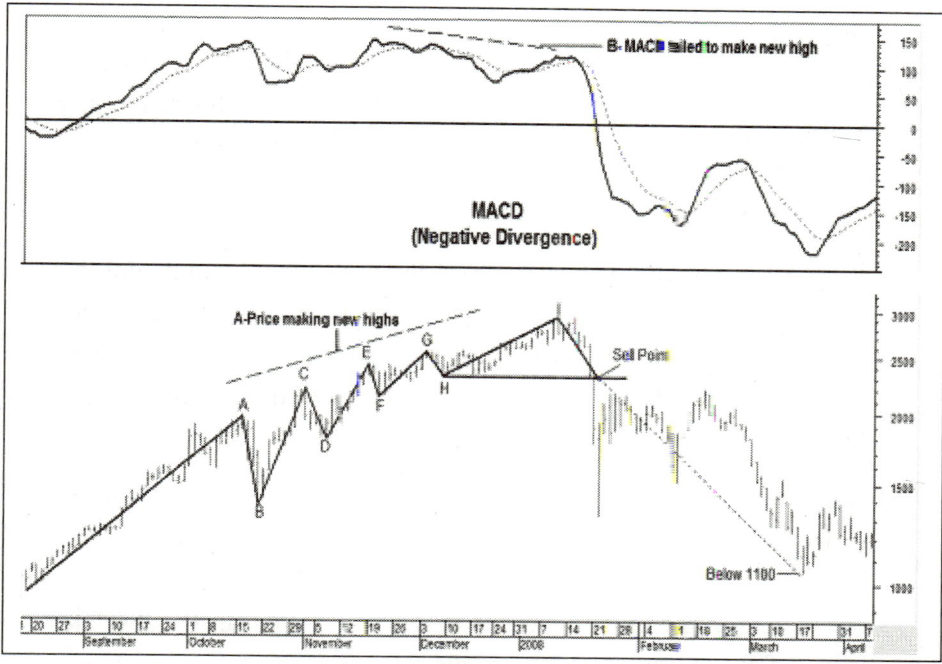

Figure 10.11: **A negative divergence in the daily chart of Reliance Capital — the price is making new highs but MACD is not**

Average True Range (ATR)

Developed by J. Welles Wilder, Average True Range (ATR) is an indicator that measures volatility. Wilder felt that a volatility formula based only on the high-low range would fail to capture actual volatility as prices often open with gaps. It is important to remember that ATR does not provide any indication on the price trend; it only measures the extent of price volatility.

ATR is based on the True Range (TR), which uses absolute price changes. True range is defined as the greatest of the following:

1. Current high minus current low;
2. Current high minus previous close (absolute value); and

3. Current low minus previous close (absolute value).

Absolute values are used to ensure the use of only positive numbers as Wilder was interested in measuring volatility of the price (by measuring the distance between two points) and not its direction:

- If the current period's high is above the prior period's high and the current period's low is below the prior period's low, then the current period's high-low range is used as the True Range, i.e. TR then equals the value of the difference between the current high and the current low.
- If the price opens with an upside gap and the current period's close is above the prior period's close, and the low is also above the prior period's low, True Range is then the current period's high minus previous period's close. In other words, in this case TR equals the absolute value of the difference between the current high and the previous close.
- If prices open with a downside gap, the current period's close is below the prior period's close and the low is below the prior period's low, True Range is then the current period's low minus previous period's close. In other words, in this case TR equals the absolute value of the difference between the current low and the previous close.

Computation of ATR

To begin with, the first TR value was simply taken as the High minus the Low by Wilder. Once you have price data of more than one day, TR value can be easily determined as explained above.

At first Wilder computed ATR as 14-period average of daily TR values for the previous 14-periods. Thereafter to smooth the data, he incorporated the formula:

Current ATR = [(Prior ATR x 13) + Current TR] / 14

In this formula, you

Multiply the previous 14-period ATR by 13.
Then add the most recent day's TR value.
Thereafter divide the total by 14.

Figure 10.12 illustrates ATR plotted on a Nifty futures chart.

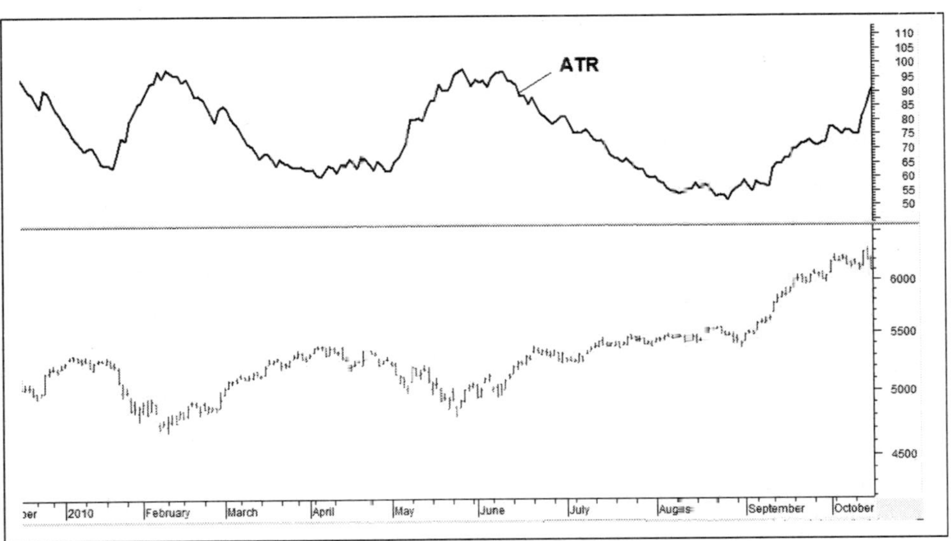

Figure 10.12: **ATR plotted on the daily chart of Nifty futures**

Using ATR

ATR is not a directional indicator, such as MACD or RSI. Rather ATR reflects volatility as absolute level, i.e. ATR is not shown as a percentage of the current close. This means low priced stocks will have lower ATR values as compared to high price stocks.

ATR is a unique volatility indicator that reflects the degree of interest or disinterest in a move. Strong moves, in either direction, are often accompanied by large true ranges. Lacklustre moves in either direction, on the other hand, are often accompanied by relatively narrow true ranges.

ATR can thus be used to authenticate the enthusiasm behind a breakout or a breakdown.

A bullish breakout with an increase in ATR would reflect strong buying interest.

Correspondingly, a bearish breakdown with an increase in ATR would reflect strong selling pressure.

Experience suggests that since it is not a directional indicator, ATR should not be used independently for taking any buying / selling decisions. In fact, ATR should always be used in combination with other indicators to arrive at better buying and selling signals. For example, ATR could be used along with moving averages which is explained in the next chapter on mechanical trading.

11

Mechanical Trading Strategies

To grasp the idea of mechanical trading, we need to first understand the subject of trading systems.

A mechanical trading system can be defined as a distinct set of trading rules which encapsulate all buying and selling decisions and which generates trading signals.

Trading systems are basically of two types; discretionary trading systems and non-discretionary trading systems.

Discretionary Trading Systems

Here buying and selling decisions are determined by the technical analysis of chart patterns, breakouts, support and resistance, etc. The trader or investor concerned exercises some discretion in making trades as he or she is not going to buy / sell on each and every trading signal or breakout.

Non-Discretionary Trading Systems

These are systems in which all entries and exits are determined mathematically or statistically. Here, the trading rules are well defined and you buy / sell on each and every trading signal.

Back Testing of Trading Systems

Mechanical trading involves discovering the best trading rules for selected securities. This requires countless hours of testing on past price and volume data to verify various trading rules and strategies in order to capture the maximum number of profit making trading rules of the past. As the testing is done on past price and volume data, it's known as back testing.

Back testing is the backbone of mechanical trading as it highlights the performance of the trading system purely in terms of profitability. Hence back testing is done before any hard earned money is put into a trading system to check three important aspects of the system's profitability, namely:

1. First, the trading system should be profitable.
2. Second, the trading system should be profitable on a consistent basis.
3. Finally, the consistency in profitability should be sustainable.

Back testing summarises the trade capability of a system by using the following parameters:

1. Total number of trades;
2. Number of profitable trades;
3. Number of unprofitable trades;
4. Total profit;
5. Average profit;
6. Highest profit;
7. Lowest profit;
8. Average loss;
9. Highest loss;
10. Lowest loss; and
11. Total loss.

Thereafter, you need to evaluate the above trade summary to check the efficacy of the trading system as follows.

First, you should assess the total number of trades generated by the trading system. This number should not be too large; the trading system should not be generating buying and selling signals every now and then. As a thumb rule:

- A good day trading system would generate 6 to 10 trading signals a day, while
- A good short term trading system would generate a single trade signal daily.

Second, you need to work out the ratio of the number of profitable trades to unprofitable ones. You should use the trading system only if this ratio is greater than one; else, the trading system should simply be rejected.

Third, you need to assess the figures for the highest profit, the lowest profit, the average profit, and the total profit generated by the trading system, as you need to make sure that a majority of the profit is not accumulated simply due to one or two winning trades. This is easily done by comparing the total profit *vis-a-vis* the highest profit from any single trade. More specifically, you need to determine if the system is generating profit on a consistent basis and whether the generated profits are sustainable. You should follow a trading system only when it's generating profit on consistent and sustainable basis; else, the system should be rejected.

Fourth, you need to assess the highest single trade loss, the lowest single trade loss, the average loss per trade, and the total loss generated by the trading system because you need to make sure that a majority of the loss is not accumulated due to only one or two losing trades. This is easily done by comparing the total loss *vis-a-vis* the highest single trade loss generated by the trading system. More specifically, you need to ensure that the system is not generating losses on a regular basis. You should only follow a trading system when:

- A major portion of the loss is not accumulated due to only one or two losing trades.
- Ratio of the average profit per trade to average loss per trade is at least greater than one.

It's very important to do this entire analysis before you put any of your hard earned money into a trading system. It's only through the above trade summary that one comes to know about the practical performance of a trading system.

Advantages of Mechanical Trading

1. It eliminates emotional trading. Mechanical trading systems are totally mechanical in nature and exclude the undue influence of emotions, which hinder the performance of most traders. Human emotion is one of the most complex and hard to control areas of trading. No trader or investor has been able to conquer the market without first adequately controlling his or her emotions.

2. Eliminates trading pitfalls, such as overtrading, buying before the breakout, and missing trading signals.

3. Risk control is another big advantage as the maximum risk is defined well in advance.

We shall now consider two mechanical trading strategies which I currently employ in my personal trading across both equities and commodities.

Moving Average Plus / Minus ATR Strategy

Most market participants buy when a popular moving average — say, 50 DMA, 100 DMA or 200 DMA as the case may be — is taken off on the upside. Correspondingly, they sell when a popular moving average is taken out on the downside.

Experience suggests that this is not the right way of trading as the same moving average is not going to be profitable on all stocks and at all times. To know which moving average would work profitably on which security, one again needs to perform back testing. With back testing, one can easily find an optimum moving average which generates the maximum profit on its stock price cross over.

In a single moving average cross over trading system, the strategy is to buy when the stock price closes above the selected moving average, and sell when the stock price closes below the selected moving average. Many market participants trade on this system. However, the volatility of stock markets often results in simultaneous buying and selling signals when one trades in this way. These simultaneous buying and selling signals ultimately result in substantial loss.

To overcome these simultaneous buying / selling signals, one can make use of ATR (which was discussed in Chapter 10), along with moving averages. ATR lends a hand in reducing the number of buying or selling signals which would otherwise be generated due to the volatile nature of the markets.

Basically in a moving average plus / minus ATR strategy, we add the value of the ATR to the moving average on the one hand and simultaneously subtract the value of the ATR from the moving average on other. By doing so, we get an upper band (moving average plus ATR) and a lower band (moving minus ATR) as shown in Figure 11.1.

The strategy then is to buy when the price closes above the upper band on the selected time frame.

Correspondingly, one sells when the stock price closes below the lower band on the selected time frame.

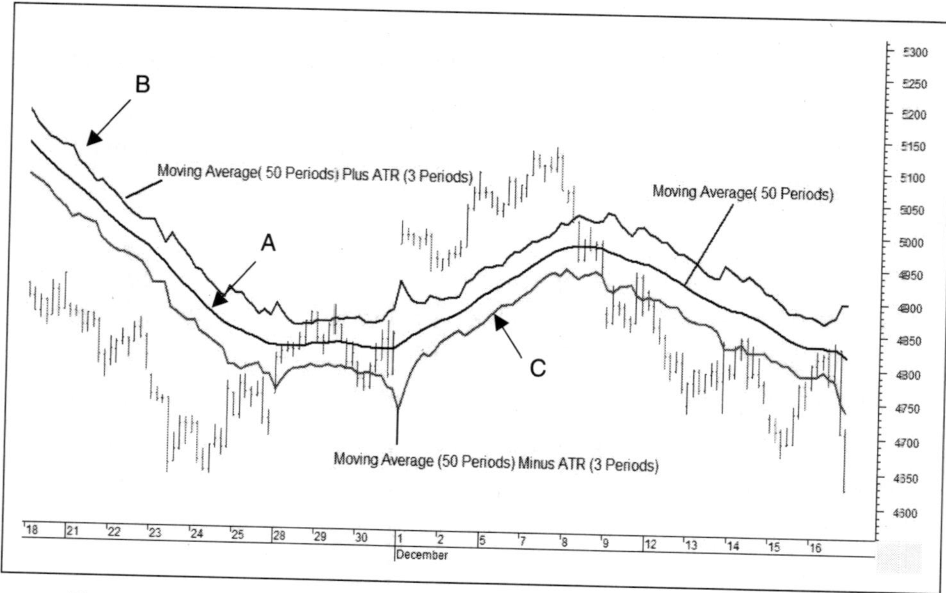

Figure 11.1: **60-minute Nifty futures chart with 50-period Moving Average and plus / minus ATR bands**

In other words, the system enters a long position when the price closes above the upper band. Thereafter, the position is closed when the price closes below the lower band. Correspondingly, the system enters a short position when the price closes below the lower band. Thereafter, the position is closed when the price closes above the upper band.

By employing back testing facility, one can identify the optimum moving average and ATR parameters. Experience suggests that for short term trading one could back test for optimum moving average parameters ranging between 20 and 50 periods and for optimum ATR parameters for value ranging from 3 to 7 periods.

Figure 11.1 illustrates a 60- minute Nifty futures chart where:

- Line A is a 50-period moving average.
- Line B is a 50-period moving average plus (+) a 3-period ATR.

- Line C is a 50-period moving average minus (-) a 3 period ATR.

In this system:

- One buys when the price closes above the upper band, namely above Line B.
- One sells when the price closes below the lower band, namely below Line C.

Experience suggests that this system works best on hourly time frame charts (60-minute charts). This system is a backbone of my personal mechanical trading desk.

Breakout from a Highest High Value (HHV) / Lowest Low Value (LLV) Strategy

In this system you buy when the price moves above the highest high value (HHV) and, correspondingly, you sell when the price breaks below the lowest low value (LLV).

Thus, you buy when the price moves above the highest high value, and you keep on holding your buy side position until and unless the price moves below the lowest low value. Once the price moves below the lowest low value, you close your buy side position and enter a sell side position. The sell side position is then held till the price again moves above its highest high value.

Now arises the big question: what are these highest high and the lowest low values. To determine these values, one needs to do back testing for the security concerned.

In the other words, the key question is: which time period to use for identifying HHV and LLV? This can be determined by back testing for different time periods.

As we are concentrating on short term trading, this system works best on hourly time frame charts, i.e. 60-minute charts. In other words, we are taking one period as being equal to 60 minutes.

Experience suggests that one should back test this strategy of breakout from HHV / LLV for 7 to 28 time periods. Any period less than 7 time periods generates an unnecessarily large number of loss making trades. I have also experienced that any period larger than 28 on the hourly time frame is useless because many profitable trades, each giving 4%-6% profit, are missed which otherwise would have been easily captured.

This system is a backbone of my personal mechanical trading desk.

A Final Word on Mechanical Trading

- If followed with discipline and patience, mechanical trading has the potential to multiply one's money @40% per annum.
- As per unofficial data, mechanical traders are the second highest paid professionals after doctors in the US.
- One should not forget that all trading, including mechanical trading is like a business and losses are part of any business and should be treated as a business expense.
- If you want to succeed big in mechanical trading, then you need to apply your own mind and develop and refine your own mechanical trading strategies.

12

Algorithmic Trading

Algorithmic trading is the most highly developed form of trading. To understand algorithmic trading better, consider robotic surgery. Here, the surgeon uses a computer controlled robot to perform a surgical procedure. In robotic surgery, the surgical strategies and procedures developed by medical science are encapsulated in the robot's software.

Similarly, algorithmic trading is the most highly developed form of trading where everything is pre-programmed in order to enhance the trader's capabilities.

Basically, technical trading is of three types:

1. **Discretionary Trading:** Here buying and selling decisions are determined by the technical analysis of chart patterns, breakouts, support and resistance, etc. The trader or investor concerned exercises discretion in making trades as one doesn't buy or sell on each and every trading signal. The trader decides what buy and sell signals to take and thereafter buying and selling orders are placed manually into the stock exchange.

2. **Mechanical Trading:** Here all entries and exits are defined by a distinct set of trading rules. Unlike discretionary trading, in mechanical trading the trader or investor concerned would buy / sell on each and every breakout or trading signal. While both buying and selling signals are computer generated but both buying and selling orders are manually placed into the stock exchange.

3. **Algorithmic Trading:** This is one step ahead of mechanical trading in the sense that not only are both buying and selling signals computer generated, but both buying and selling orders are also automatically placed by a computer into the stock exchange.

Accordingly, algorithmic trading can be defined as a distinct set of trading rules in which both buying and selling signals are generated by computers along with automatic placement of both buying and selling orders into the stock exchange.

Algorithmic trading is essentially of two types:

1. Low frequency algorithmic trading; and
2. High frequency algorithmic trading.

Low Frequency Algorithmic Trading

Low frequency algorithmic trading is one step forward from mechanical trading. Low frequency algorithmic trading is so designed that along with automatic generation of both buying and selling signals, buying and selling orders are also placed automatically into the stock exchange.

Personally, I favour lower frequency algorithmic trading because:

First, it eliminates chance of any human error in the execution of trade.

Second, it makes trading multiple assets across multiple exchanges straightforward. This is so because it's difficult to manually put in numerous buying and selling orders especially when simultaneous buying and selling signals are being generated across various assets and across various exchanges.

High Frequency Algorithmic Trading (HFT)

In high frequency algorithmic trading buying and selling signals are not generated on the basis of technical analysis. And, most important, the number of buying and selling signals is so high that they cannot be manually placed into the stock exchange. This is so because high frequency algorithmic trading is employed in:

1. **Arbitrage.** It's basically the buying of a security in one stock exchange and selling it in another stock exchange for a higher price. More precisely, it can be defined as the practice of taking advantage of a price difference between two or more exchanges.

2. **Capturing price mismatches which occur for a fraction of second in the same stock exchange.** Such price mismatches occur in cash, futures and options segment of the market. Typically, such price mismatches occur for a fraction of second and are sought to be captured by a high frequency algorithmic trader well before any naked human eye is able to spot the mismatch.

Thus, high frequency algorithmic trading is used to quickly spot a profitable trading opportunity followed by a quick execution of the trade before anybody else can do so.

Most market participants make use of high frequency algorithmic trading in arbitrage and in capturing price mismatch on the same exchange in today's hyper-competitive trading environment.

I have limited my explanation on high frequency algorithmic trading as high frequency algorithmic trading has nothing to do with technical analysis.

TAKING LIGHT
FROM
EACH OTHER

University of Central Florida
Contemporary Poetry Series

By the Same Author

Naked as the Glass (poems)
Journey Toward Poetry (essays)
A Celebration of Cats (anthology)

and six books on animal welfare

Cover Calligraphy
"All the waters contain the moon"
Zen poem.
Original calligraphy by Alan Watts,
as a gift to the author, 1958.

TAKING LIGHT FROM EACH OTHER

Poems by

JEAN BURDEN

University Press of Florida
Gainesville Tallahassee Tampa Boca Raton
Pensacola Orlando Miami Jacksonville

Library of Congress Cataloging-in-Publication Data

Burden, Jean.
Taking light from each other : poems / by Jean Burden.
p. cm. — (University of Central Florida contemporary poetry series)
ISBN 0-8130-1113-2 (cloth : alk. paper). — ISBN 0-8130-1114-0 (pbk. : alk. paper)
I. Title. II. Series: Contemporary poetry series (Orlando, Fla.)
PS3552.U7T35 1992
811′.54—dc20 91-26166
CIP

The University Press of Florida is the scholarly publishing agency for the State University System of Florida, comprised of Florida A&M University, Florida Atlantic University, Florida International University, Florida State University, University of Central Florida, University of Florida, University of North Florida, University of South Florida, University of West Florida.

Orders for books should be addressed to
University Press of Florida
15 Northwest 15th Street
Gainesville, Florida 32611

ACKNOWLEDGMENTS

Thanks are due to the following magazines in which these poems first appeared:

The American Scholar: "Insomnia"
The Beloit Poetry Journal: "Costume Play," "The Cemetery"
The Bennington Review: "Cataracts," "Suicide"
Blue Unicorn: "The Saints and I," "The Gift"
Chicago Tribune Magazine: "Graveyard in Illinois," "On Being Told That Animals Live in Absolute Time," "Hummingbird," "In Other People's Houses," "Between These Weathers"
Colorado Quarterly: "Fairy Tale," "On Being Asked to Join a Communal Tub, Mt. Tamalpais"
The Georgia Review: "News of a Death," "The Dance," "Against the Night," "Between Seasons"
The Hudson Review: "Connection"
Kayak: "You Ask," "Signs, Cardinal and Mutable"
Kentucky Poetry Review: "After the Memoirs, the Usual Interview"
Landfall: "Recurring Dream"
Michigan Quarterly Review: "Autograph Party"
Milkweed Chronicle: "Theme and Variations," "Hospital"
New Jersey Poetry Journal: "The Given"
The New York Times: "Evangel," "Rubbing Stone"
Outposts: "Taking Light from Each Other"
Ploughshares: "Return to an Island"
Poet & Critic: "Sleepwalker," "Free Association"
Poetry: "Premonition in the Midst of Plenty," "On Coming Upon an Old Snapshot of Peter DeVries"
Poetry Miscellany: "Lost Word"
Salmagundi: "Photograph of My Mother at Eighteen," "Portrait of My Father at Four," "Poem for Eric Barker"
Saturday Review: "Charwoman at St. Patrick's," "For Hildegarde Who Received for Christmas a Moon-Window in a Wall"

Shenandoah: "Speech for a Small Room"
The Smith: "Lost: Antique Gold Bracelet (Family Heirloom)"
The Southern Review: "For a Yellow Cat at Midnight"
The Texas Quarterly: "Poem for a Birthday"

Eight of these poems have appeared in the annual anthologies for best poems of the year by Borestone Mountain Poetry Awards. Six have appeared in the annual *Anthology of Magazine Verse,* edited by Alan Pater.

Grateful thanks are extended to The MacDowell Colony, where many of these poems were written.

In Memory of
Hildegarde Flanner
and
Raymond Roseliep

Contents

I made a list of things I have
to remember and a list
of things I want to forget,
but I see they are the same list . . .

—Linda Pastan
"Lists" in *PM/AM*

Taking Light from Each Other

I

Connection

(for Hildegarde Flanner)

We are talking of Hopkins and Joyce,
of cicadas and tree
frogs. You from your hilltop
500 miles away explain
in your delicately explicit way
the difference in their night speech.
I stretch languidly between
the sleeping cats and smile
at the faint indignation in your voice.
"Anyone can hear it," you say.
"All one has to do is listen."
Then suddenly we hear a sound—
not kin to frog or insect—a squeak,
a whisper, a lilliputian squawk.
"What was that?" you ask, alarmed—
you who once bashed two rattlesnakes to death
in less than a minute,
and thought it no great feat.
"Probably only a snide comment from
some faulty silicon chip," I say—
I the expert, who knows so much about such things.
"Or the CIA?" I venture, warming up,
thinking of le Carré and all those other spooks.
"They don't tap poets' phones," you say severely,
though anyone can tell you're not quite sure.
Crackle, squeak, chirrup, snap.
We lose a word. It could have been important.
Is there between two people, no matter
how connected, always a third?

There is no time to wonder.
"Are you there?" you ask. "Can you hear me?"
And back across the fragile line,
speech thinned to a hiss,
comes the stranger's answer: *Yes,*
oh yes, oh yes.

Premonition in the Midst of Plenty

It was a day of loose words,
like shale,
with many stumblings.
The sun came out,
undecided
I wandered the fields,
looking for landmarks,
but the rocks had strayed
like sheep; the moss
was on the wrong
side of the trees.
I ransacked the house
searching for what I had been
faithful to,
but the floors tilted.
I dialed authorities
for the day's mantra, the season
and the hour.
I heard nothing but Urdu.
Now it is dark.
A wind rises with the moon. The cats
fatten their tails.
The walls rattle with rumors.
None of the terms are negotiable.

Signs, Cardinal and Mutable

Always at the edge of dark
and certain the time is brief
at best, I look for signs:
for bricks in pathways
adding up to seven;
a caterpillar crawling to my palm
as though it were a leaf;
the leaf itself, blown
to my lap from empty air.
Nor am I too blessed
to ignore a bird
that taps three times
against the pane; the track
of foxes in a ring of snow;
the book that falls open
at a page where long ago
a vanished hand had underscored a word
with *yes*.
Careful of heaven,
I see omens in a stone, signed
with four circles:
earth, water, fire, air;
portents in clouds that shift
under my stare from
whale to Everest
to lyre.
Once a magnolia bloom fell
like a star at my feet—
unbruised and open.
The whole day
was an archangel's gift.

For Hildegarde Who Received for Christmas a Moon-Window in a Wall

He let the tree in.
It was a gift few would have loved enough to make.
The wall itself
had been the first offering.
But enclosure was not enough.
(When is it ever enough?)
As though he had plunged his fist through the stones
he drew a circle about space
and let in the round air.
He brought before her eyes
a young maple,
gaillardia the color of sun,
and a sloping hill.
Being his own wizard,
he gave her an eye in the center of her sight;
and at night he gave her low stars,
and tree frogs
leaping through the stone hoop.

Cataracts

"Some things I see more clearly than before . . ."

The necklace of coral
I wear around my neck,
can you see the pendant is an old man
carrying a rolled umbrella?
Can you count the pearls?
The Venetian glass decanters
twinkle like nebulae
against the light,
but what about the grapes—
is each one a cluster or alone?
Does the plum tree blur?
The mountains still curve
against the east like a huge
Spanish comb,
but what of the spider
and the inchworm?
Boulders, you say, even at high noon
are huddled sheep.
No matter, let them graze.
The fern is still feathered, the pansy
velvet to your poet's eye.
At night, you tell me with a child's awe,
you can look up with single sight
and count four fringed
and blazing moons.

The Given

There is a poem in here
somewhere. It displaces
doorbell and telephone
and the voices
of strangers asking for light,
neighbors at the door
offering persimmons.
Enemies and scholars
have been locked out;
the room is emptied
of dissertations and numbers.
Far away, horns argue
in the streets. Nothing
comes closer than the memory
of hands.
What is absent is not
the poem, nor is it
a synonym for silence.
The poem is what a spider
weaves out of the emptiness
in the last light.
I undo the spider's web,
then slowly, strand by hair,
reinvent
its secret threads. That
is the poem.

Suicide

(for L.N.)

August was the month she died,
the day guessed at, the hour
unknown. Omissions like these
bothered the police. It would have helped,
they said, if she had left a note,
spelling out statistics for the blotter:
"I died at 4:23 P.M. peacefully.
There was no murderer but myself."
If she had mentioned
where she bought the rubber hose,
and how she fooled the nurses,
the case could have been closed, neatly,
with a snap.

The doctors fussed. She was going home
in a week. What was her hurry?
Her analyst, his face older than Zeus's,
denied his guilt:
"All we can be sure of is—
she was ambushed by freedom.
Life leaks out of all of us,
a breath at a time."

Husband and son collected clothing,
purse, books, canvases—
it was such a good sign, they had thought,
she had gone back to painting—
and wondered when, precisely,
in the four days between disappearance and discovery
she had left the motor running in the dark wood,
and where at that moment
they were.

The stonecutter was not held up;
he needed only years—
the beginning and the last—
while we who loved her
were diminished and angry,
not understanding why we were not enough,
why nothing was enough.

The princess had vanished into air
while we sickened and grew old.

Death did not stop her dying.
Like a leaf that falls
eternally from a height we cannot see
to a ground that sinks
forever out of reach,
she slips past us, an ever-present fugitive,
elusive as light,
bequeathing us death
but not of our own choosing.

Theme and Variations

(for Mark Strand)

These are the words that leap
from the page: *gathered, field,*
cold, nameless, sleep;

all words for counting time:
north, weather, silence,
dark, winter, keep;

words to pierce the eye:
portent, dust, water,
nothing, window,
weep.

News of a Death

"It is not down in any map; true places never are."
—Melville

Perhaps I mourn
because there is so little
left to mourn,
as though it had happened
a long way off—in Tibet,
let's say, or Mozambique—
with strangers carrying torches
and incense.

(Who said, "Disbelief brings
its own geography"?)

Nowhere near as the grave
you dug for Beckett
under the rosebush;
or your black expensive robe
still hanging in my closet;
not as near as the two silver
cups on the shelf, empty
of wine ("I love fine liquor
and cheap music," you used to say,
misquoting Noel Coward, as you
misquoted everyone);
far from the celadon lamps
blooming as brightly as before
in the paneled room;
far from the wedding ring
we bought together in a tourist town,
buried now under a litany
of faux pearls.

(The place recedes as it comes close.
I search for your death
as for my own tears.)

The pine tree you planted
when it barely reached your knees
towers above its dark
and puzzling roots,
shading my house.
It has transcended us both,
finding its own shape—forgiving
and silent—like the shell
we brought back from Ocho Rios
so many lives ago, once loud
with the god's voice
and fury.

You Ask

You ask what lasts.
I used to know: stones, the pull
and suck of tides, trees
rooted in ore.
(Even when trees fell they fell to earth
and earth endured.)
Now I am less sure.
Things do not stay
where they are put.
Atoms and planets spin.
Suns burn out. What lasts?
I turn in the wood
toward eyes
that glow like small moons
close to the ground, too wide apart
for a cat. Something
turns its head—
the moons are quenched.
I walk toward a dark cabin
carrying two flames in my mind,
pressing the weeds down.
What lasts?
The turning day, falling water
over stones, the sweet disorder
of leaves,
moons that come and go,
wings.

"Against the Night"

(for Father Raymond Roseliep)

From this uncertain vantage point of age
and pain, I think of how you lived for years
with your plain pine coffin in the spare room,
bought and paid for, at the ready.
Even from one as well prepared as I,
this brought a small reproach: Was the poet-
priest perhaps a trifle morbid? "Not at all,"
you said. "Some damn fool might have gone in
for bronze. Besides, it makes a dandy file
for manuscripts and poems." And so it was,
and for my letters, thick with love,
and for Ivan, the wanderer, a bed
for curling tail to nose.

Three years ago this month, the rocket burst
inside your skull, and you fell headlong
into night or dazzle—who will know?
"Be in advance of all parting," Rilke wrote.
You took him at his word. At ease with dying
as with delight, you chose the plot,
dictated copy for the granite stone,
and bought the box, pulling the future
toward you, like a creature of the sea
suddenly in love with air, like a wild bird
blind with light.

II

The Dance

At seven
I danced like Pavlova,
or at the very least,
Isadora Duncan.
My soul was not in some ghostly cavity
but fixed securely
in my patent leather feet.
When the big bands played
at the Edgewater Beach Hotel
and the dinner guests tried waltzes
or the foxtrot,
my father and I
showed them how.

At the first summons of the alto sax,
he rose and bowed,
and I was on my feet *instanto*,
bobbing in reply. He offered me his arm;
we found the floor; the other dancers
took us in.

At the level of his silver buckle,
I never missed a beat.
My pleated skirt lifted like a tutu.
The others watched us: We were the Castles;
Valentino with Agnes Ayres;

we were prince and princess,
Marilyn Miller and Monsieur Beaucaire.

And when at the last eight
bars, *pianissimo*,
he leaned down,
lifting me lightly from the floor,
he took upon himself
his only child—
balancing her slight
imponderable weight.

The Saints and I

Along with *Little Women,*
The Myths of Greece and Rome,
and Schliemann's tales
of how he dug up Troy,
I read and re-read
A Child's Book of Saints
with Catherine on the cover
in a fit of joy.

Before I reached eleven,
I was much at home in hell.
I feasted on crusts and water;
longed to shave my hair;
wished for thistles under-
neath my thin chemise;
told my button-rosary
up and down the stair.

The burden of my wrongs
grew heavier with age.
I knew Sebastian's arrows,
Joan's faggots, Peter's cross.
Sure of martyrdom, if lucky,
I dragged myself to twelve,
ecstatic in Barbara's tower,
sybarite of loss.

The Cemetery

(for Rah)

We were sixteen
and hell-bent for Truth.
In the past that shifts
under my gaze,
it was always snowing,
like a paperweight turned over.
Mufflered and mittened,
galoshes slapping against our legs,
we weaved among the friendly graves,
while the short twilight raced us
to evening,
and the lake cracked and groaned
just out of sight.
We threw snowballs at God,
recited Teasdale and Millay,
picked up stones, debated the Trinity,
read epitaphs, made up our own,
felt our bones grow longer in our skins.
Our breaths turned ectoplasm in the cold;
hand in hand,
we stomped home in darkness. Later
in the warm room,
we chattered about nothing. Light-
years from death,
we never told
about the snow's colors on the
prismed ground, nor ever mentioned
where we'd been.

Photograph of My Mother at Eighteen

She did not know me then,
though perhaps some part of me
was sprouting in her secret
field.
She looked—how can I say?—
like Jessica
whose part she played
on commencement day,
whose lines she spoke so often
to her child, pretending to be
Shylock's daughter.

Her serious eyes were fixed
on some point in middle distance
no one else could see.
(They were a color hard to name—violet
when I knew them.)
Her nose was thin and straight,
the heavy dark hair
tied back with ribbons.
(She turned gray at 30; I never knew
her any other way.)

She was wistful even then,
as though virtue
had wrung from the slight frame
an early price.
(Whenever I surprised her in repose,
she looked as though she could not bear
the heavy pride she wore.)

I found the white dress
in tissue paper in the attic trunk.
Even at twelve
I could not fasten the waist.

Straight-backed, full-breasted,
lithe as a whip,
she menstruated at nine, she told me,
read Ovid for pleasure,
worked in the garden on her knees,
baked thirteen kinds of bread,
sang me to sleep with "La Bohème."
At 91 she almost outlived me.
Her eyes were as bright as finches'.
She weighed less than a child.
"Let me go," she said. It was her last command.
I carry her lightly in my bones.

Graveyard in Illinois

Because strangers had planted your ashes
(neatly boxed, sent by parcel post),
I had to follow after. I had to try to find the place,
doing the last thing for you that I could,
tucking you in, I guess you'd say,
like a mother, even as you had long been mine.

But in all that grove of planted trees
I could not find your bed.
The stones were old. I kicked the leaves
from names like Kittredge, Hamilton, Parnell,
while a raw wind blew around my feet
in a coincidence of mood and time.

If you had really been there
you would have shown me where to look.
If you—the undiluted essence of you—
not some wispy ghost,
had been anywhere in that landscape by Corot,
you would have outbeamed a kind of radiance,
and the new stone would have gleamed
from the brown earth
pulling me around.

But you escaped me
in the end (what else could I expect?)
and I am caught forever in an unfinished poem
finding you nowhere—
and everywhere.

Portrait of My Father at Four

1.

In the days it hung above the mantel
in my parents' house
I used to pretend
he was the prince of Bavaria,
or, at the least, some small lord
who sat for Gainsborough
in a draughty hall.
That would explain the vestments
of blue velvet and lace;
the fair hair, the color of oats,
curling about his face,
and the eyes—
sulky, I called them,
dark as hazelnuts.
Under brows feathered and shaped
like my own,
he gazed straight ahead as though
none of us was there—
too solemn for my father,
but fitting for an heir
unwilling to ascend a throne.

2.

I have lived half a lifetime
past his early leaving.
I have carried his likeness from house
to house.
It hangs where on waking
I can surprise the sun
on the pale hair,
and watch the disdain of kings
drain from his stare.
Who are you? I dare
to ask. Neither in light
nor shadow is the answer plain,
though I dismiss both prince
and Fauntleroy.
In a strange twist of kinship
he is, one moment, eternal parent,
the next,
my child I never saw.
And on some days in the cloudy
room, this square of gold frames
something more: mandala,
ageless as a dreaming god,
icon
forever four.

III

Sleepwalker

The summer after he went away
she began to leave her bed—
eyes shut, hands outstretched like wands—
to move into the midnight hall,
reaching for a banister of air.
As though it were high noon, and the mission
urgent but secret, she drifted down the stair
like a small white moth, but sure
of the going down, and what was waiting
for her there.
Between the table and the velvet
chair, she made her narrow way,
sweeping aside the dark
until she found the spot between
the ticking clock and hunting knife. With eyes
still closed she took from the mantel
something only her touch could see,
then moved slowly back, bearing
at votive height some unseen treasure,
magic lamp, or perhaps only the night
wind, who could tell?
Tomorrow, before sleep, she will remember
nothing, but if the tether
loosens and the dream is right,
she will walk again, up and down
the rungs of her life,
carrying its riddles in careful hands,
from one place to another.

Recurring Dream

For years she dreamed her teeth
were falling out.
How could anyone as young as she
bite into an almond like a squirrel
only to have a mouth
suddenly full of molars
and blood? ("If the dream persists,"
said the doctor, "you might try
growing up.")

Then she dreamed her hair was chalk.
At night a long-branched tree
reached through the window
of her room, its leaves white
with moon. ("Women like you
are always vain. Why can't you stand alone?")

She dreamed a cat fell open
in her arms, stiff as a split
log. She was slipping on a subway
platform, headed for the third rail.
With her mother at the wheel,
she was falling over a cliff
in a slow parabola of doom.
("If I were you,
I'd have it out with her,"
the doctor mused. And then he said,
"Before you land, take notes.")

Fairy Tale

When her lover would not rescue her,
being preoccupied with perils of his own,
she asked for her father.
He came at once, riding on the usual white stallion,
and his spear was long
and deadly.
He lifted her to his saddle with one arm,
as though she were a child.
All the gates were down.
The dragon in their path
melted like butter.
Safely across the moat
he spoke to the huge doors,
and they opened inward at his shout.
When they stood in the courtyard,
alone at last,
she could not reach to the horse's withers.
The wall behind them
was barred with light.
"Daughter," he said, "is there more
you want of me?
By morning I must be far from here.
I leave you, snug as a babe,
wrapped round by stone.
Do not call for me.
The wind is from Asia,
and I have perils of my own."

Charwoman at St. Patrick's

From the door, a city block away,
she is a priestess
intent on some ritual of her own,
blessing the chancel marble
with water and a rod.
Or if I look again
she is a Javanese dancer,
leaning to left and right
in long, slow gestures
of an old ballet.

If I move toward her
will she change to some grotesque
out of Daumier,
an old crone aslant upon her staff;
or merely an Irish Martha,
furious and tired;
a harpy raking stone?

Neither the shadows, innocent
or guilty,
nor the streaming sun,
tell us who we are.
A nave away
I watch her dance my dream—
clearer than waking,
nearer by far.

On Coming Upon an Old Snapshot of Peter DeVries

I found you pasted on the flyleaf
of your first book,
awkward as a scarecrow,
hollow chested, your face so thin
the nose looked broad as a fist.
You were posed outside *Poetry*'s old office
on East Erie. Associate Editor.
Was it '38 or '39?
You sold taffy apples on the side
to grocery stores and schools;
collected coins from candy vending
jars all over town. It was a good racket,
you said, and helped to pay the rent.
On days you shuffled poems
at the rolltop desk,
you sometimes spent your lunch hour
acting heavies at a nearby
station. Once you played a wounded gorilla
with noble voice and no rehearsal.
On Sunday mornings you read funnies
to the kids
over WAAF.

Your sleeves were always a little
too short; you liked double-breasted suits.
You said the first snow
each winter made you ache
with childhood, remembering Lowell
and all the recitations by the grade school desk.

Once, in an expansive mood,
you recited "Peter Quince at the Clavier"
(all 66 lines and no fluffs),
and we dropped everything and fell in love
with Wallace Stevens.
None of us predicted the humorist
of belles lettres, election to the Institute
of Arts and Letters,
or your photograph
in *Time*.
But now that we think about it,
you were only half with us, even then,
and leagues away
long before you went.

Evangel

As though the streets were all downhill,
he lunges against the crowds,
clutching the Book,
his glare
a pointed lance,
bearing no banner but his rage.

Police ignore him; shoppers stare.
Stenographers, eleven stories up,
turn to the window at his shout,
hearing their names.

Prophet or knight
or avatar,
this is his kingdom, plainly marked.
Who anointed him, or from what stone
he drew his sword,
are questions lost within his cry.

Slayer of dragons,
hawker of heaven,
he hurls against our pride
the only litany he knows.
What souls he saves we cannot guess;
perhaps his own.

On Being Told That Animals Live in Absolute Time

What kind of time they live in
only they know.
On plains, perhaps, in jungle
wilderness, or where bush and thorn
nourish the wildebeest and doe.
But here in this public park
is it always for the first time
the impala leaps against the grill?
Or the panther
crawls into the matching dark?
Does the bear
rattle his iron cage
only in the Eternal Now?
And is it always new
when the leopard coughs his rage?
Without yesterday or tomorrow
there is no need of hope.
Only today—for the first time (they tell us)—
the flamingo flies against the net,
the sky is roofed
above the antelope.

For a Yellow Cat at Midnight

As though drifted inland
in some dark current of your own,
you settle against my side,
cumbrous as clay or a warm stone,
and I wake to find you there.

Why at night, small lion,
are you so much heavier than by day?
Only this afternoon
you slept, upside down, in a lap
already full of books and child,
and you were a tawny feather,
a fluff of sun.

Now pulled hard to the earth's center,
as though to a final place
(lion, are we older by a night?),
we wait for sleep,
held fast by separate stars,
ponderous with what we do not know,
caught in a common dark.

Camera Study

In the town of Bourton-on-the-Water
(the Venice of the Cotswolds),
by the Windrush River,
a white
tomcat
dozed on the high circle
of a fence pole,
folded within himself like a pillow.
Hearing me stalk him
through the jungle of his dream,
he slowly stretched alive,
and posed,
tall as a jug of cream,
one paw lifted to salute or shrive,
as I clicked
clicked
clicked
hello.

Hummingbird

He dangled in air, level
with my eyes, making a difficult
choice,
then lighted on a twig the color
of himself, two feet from my chair.
The whir drained from his wings;
he was small as an acorn,
smaller than my thumb.
Did I summon him,
or did he come,
driven by weather to this sheltered place?

He dared me with his coral eye,
measuring my menace
against the gale outside the wall.
Whether I shared his world,
or he mine,
was not the question.
We were bound
as separate leaves upon a vine;

marked time, kept truce
until the mountain blackened and the wind
let the oleanders go:
a bird, brief haiku
of a bird, and I—
judged less fearful
than an element—
sipping each other's presence
like the dew.

IV

Insomnia

It is like no other waking.
The darkness thins.
I turn in it, slowly,
like a seal rolling over in its watery bed.
What appointment do I keep,
                                        night after night,
that I must surface
from my sleep
to this unwelcome, arid
                                    place?

A white night, they call it—
well named as lime,
as tusks of beast or feathers of a gull;
O white as salt,
as burnished skull.

It is a time
            I lose by day,
a fifth season
I neither want
nor choose.
Stranded on a reef, I take
                                    from the bleached night
what sustenance I can.

I count invisible shells,
I stalk the dead—
father, mother, lover, child—
who stand around me
                                        on this shore,
their faces drawn in chalk.
The world strikes four.

Foam thickens to opal,
opal to emerald.
                    The tide crawls inland.
I exhale the stars,
turn upside down,
and in the green wake of waking
drown.

In Other People's Houses

In other people's houses
I pick up shells from coffee tables,
examine book titles,
take down fat volumes on calligraphy or Zen,
and thin ones by poets;
examine photographs, stones, Ming trees
and small Buddhas;
read anything in print,
such as bulletin boards,
fine writing on a
Sister Corita poster,
or a market list:
    (veal, watercress, toilet paper, Lux).
In general,
I ignore furniture unless
it is very bad
or very old;
paintings (unless Oriental);
flower arrangements (except dried grasses);
and anything on four legs,
unless
it is a cat.
If left alone,
my eye finds silver,
brass, and sometimes pewter,
and will select a window
if it frames water or a tree.
In other people's houses
I move between
clear and clouded surfaces.
I make do
with what I love.

Lost: Antique Gold Bracelet (Family Heirloom)

If I had given it a name
(Clara, Clara, did you claim it for your own?),
I could call it home through the dark
spaces between us,
whistle it down from a branch
where it might have caught
like a thin trinket
of moon.
If, waking or in dream,
I could picture it
(hinge, link, mesh and clasp),
I might glimpse again
its circle of memory and light,
like a rind of fruit
in lemon blossoms,
or a slice of honeycomb
blurred by bees.
If I had made it
a totem against harm,
I might see it glitter
like a wild canary
in the summer trees, tamed
to my grasp.
If I had given it a name,
lustrous as my love,
I could call it,
call it back,
homeward to my grieving arm.

Lost Word

I do not believe in a God
who bothers Himself in the trivia
of this planet, but
Lord, could you find me this word?
I know it as well as my name,
but it is running backwards into darkness
as I lurch after it.
It stands for the small mammal
that ate raspberry parfait
at the back door in Big Sur; the huge one
that climbed through Eric's window,
and clawed at his cats;
the old one that made a shambles of his kitchen.
I say *possum, skunk,*
porcupine, knowing it is not any of these.
The word, Lord! You are supposed to be good
at words. Remember the Word? It is midnight
and I yearn for the elusive thing. I sleep
and waken. It is coming closer. It skitters by
avoiding my eyes. I scurry from attic to cellar
of my mind. It is not there.
Weasel, squirrel, badger, rat.
I am not asking to see the dark side of the moon, God.
Only one word. Will you give it to me with Your light?
I roll to one side. The beast
turns its black triangle of a face
full on me. Ah, *raccoon.*

Autograph Party

On a warm day in a cold month
I signed my given name
(*Jean*, for a Scotch girl I never knew)
one hundred and three times
for people who had come
on foot, by bus, by car,
or because they lived in the neighborhood
and a party was a party—
all for a book and a name.
Every time I wrote it,
it spoke a different sound.
And as the afternoon fizzed
with champagne, and people kissed
in several small reunions
they had not anticipated,
I signed and signed on the bleached page
while the calligraphy blurred
as though seen under water,
and all the pens went dry.

The Gift

(for Cristy)

You gave me the socks
off your feet—
dark blue, striped in red and white,
with embroidered clocks of cats.
"Of course you must have them,"
you said, propping up ankles
on the staid restaurant table
and stripping to pink toes.
The waitress, demure
in Japanese kimono,
looked down at her sandals
and almost spilled the tea.
I wrapped them in a napkin
and stuffed them in my Gucci bag.
We squeaked up Park Avenue,
you in your sockless feet
and leather boots,
I embarrassingly
over-shod.
I never gave you anything
as right as that
except once—a fossil polished
by the sea.
The socks cost 49¢
at the five-and-dime,
you said.
Nothing comes out even.
The stone was free.

Free Association

(for Hildegarde)

"The world is a bed."
—Donald Hall

You mentioned a birthday cake, burning with five candles, being carried up to you through the orchard in the twilight.

You were not five, or even fifty, but eighty-four, and you knew I knew it.

Why then did I remember the painter in New York who paid the rent by baking sculptured cakes: a football, an ice skate, a cello? Name it and she plunged into butter cream up to her elbows.

And that reminded me of the famous West Side bakery that specialized in pornographic cakes. "What do you think of that?" I asked.

"Not really!" you gasped, though it is hard to shock you even on long distance.

I began to explain about the *poitrine* in pink icing with "Breast Wishes" written across the cleavage. "But that is only the beginning," I warned.

"Of course," you said. "Kama Sutra and all that. Well," your voice dropped low, "I've never seen pornographic pastry, my dear, but I once saw some pretty lewd furniture."

Furniture? I had been hoisted on my own confection. I meekly asked for more.

"It was a small stool in front of the fireplace of a rich man's house here in the valley, and all around the seat was carved a frieze of—you will not believe this—penises!"

"In various stages of erection?" I wanted to know instantly.

"No, hanging down," you replied, with what I took to be real regret. "*Such* poor taste."

On Being Asked to Join a Communal Tub, Mt. Tamalpais

Wacky, bearded gent,
friend of my childhood,
you howl with laughter
at my doubt, and tell me
your mother at eighty
just learned to play the drums.
The tub holds seventeen—plenty
of room, you say, for me
so slight you could lift me in one hand.

The invitation is tempting,
as though you had proposed
seduction in a bed
big enough for a clutch of mermaids,
impersonal as a pond,
and innocent
as what the fish do under it.

I imagine saying *yes*.

The water will be warm as a womb's,
warmer than the night air.
There will be music, you promise,
and fragrance of eucalyptus
like that of a tomcat on prowl.

I remember bathing
with a cousin when he was four
and I was seven.

Later, curious and fearful,
I glimpsed my father naked
through an open door.
Who looks down
looks into.

As though I were a critic of tubs,
I say, "Well . . ."

Who does not long for absolution,
some local Ganges
without the lepers,
a ritual of passage arranged
for mixed choir and guitars?

Still I hesitate and wonder why.
Only a few nights before,
companioned by a troll,
I stepped into a dark river, ringed
with trees, and swam through carp
gliding swift and shallow,
through pebbles rushing from melted snow,
toward stars blurred and intimate.

Mountain host, forgive me.
I am unresigned
to waters measured and tender,
tested by an elbow. Reflection
has a double meaning
and three eyes. *No.*

Hospital

In this place I wear
my bones on the outside;
you can see through them
like straws
to the veins and arteries
bulging with secrets.
I rattle when I move,
but nobody notices.
My teeth gleam in the dark
like chessmen. My head
is a moon.
My heart sounds like
Big Ben;
at night they muffle the clapper,
but it tells me its hours
whenever I ask.
I am shadow and phosphorus
like the tree's profile
on the wall, flocked with birds,
all skeleton and song.

Poem for a Birthday

I do not find myself
in mirrors
or the pond's face,
but in the bark of trees
rough to the palm;
in the gray unpolished
pebble with a glint of light
beckoning from the path.

Something of me comes back
in the stroking of a cat's fur
along the spine.
Even a minnow flicks its tail
in the cold water
with my full consent.

When I pick wild goldenrod
and phlox—pink to lavender—
sun and sunset meet
in an instant,
and both
tell me
where I am.

I am not in anyone's eyes
except by chance.

I find my sign
in the leaf's palmistry
and the matching shimmer
of my mind.

I stumble on myself
in the tensed
surviving
winter root.

Between Seasons

Sometimes, between seasons
of the calendar or soul,
all we can do
is wait.
It is not as though
nothing were happening.
Appointments are kept,
the rain falls as promised,
garden chairs are stored
against the cold, persimmons
swell on the thinning trees.

We speak to our animals;
they are waiting, too.
We polish the brass candle-
sticks, the rosewood chairs.
Custard cools on the sill.

At night, if we are quiet,
ghosts settle under the eaves.
They say, *it is almost time.*
Not knowing whether we look
to death or birth,
we lean toward light
as toward another day,
pulling down through oak and pine:
lantern; perhaps moon, round
as another world;
perhaps star.

After the Memoirs, the Usual Interview

Did you begin at the beginning?

Where *did* it begin? With a wreath on the door of my great-grandfather's house, or earlier than that? Tombstones and fairy rings, they both point the way.

Did you tell the truth?

Sometimes. As often as I dared. Honesty is never as graceful as pretense. Sometimes I preferred to dance. It was never important. It was not falsehood.

Have you told us everything?

Only as much as I thought you could bear. You will understand by the time you reach the death of my child and the parade of lovers, one by one, gardenia after orchid after violets.

Who is the main character?

An interesting question. I had always thought it was I. Or perhaps my father whose death colored my life like a stain. But it turned out quite differently. You will see. (I am most like her, which is also disturbing.)

Is it a book about sorrow or happiness?

A little of both, but you will learn to redefine happiness. (You already know about loss.) This is a book of occult definitions: war, friendship, animals, innocence.

It sounds a little tedious—all those abstractions.

It is not, I promise you. Sometimes you will even laugh. The lights blink on and off. The line goes dead, then a voice asks, "Are you there?" Don't overlook the scene in the cemetery.

Were you "funeralizing" someone?

No, trading conundrums with God, and making up my own epitaph. After all, I was almost seventeen.

What did it say? Some romantic razzle-dazzle, I presume?

Read the book.

V

Taking Light from Each Other

We leave the mountains
framed in glass
darkening in violet snow.
We turn from the lake
and the cold swans
and move toward each other
in a strange familiar place.

Is it for this we came
so far,
fleeing entanglements,
only to be caught by these frail reeds?

Taking light from each other,
we marry on a rented bed,
naked as children,
biting into the dimming day
as into a fruit.

Even as we love, the world
is constantly passing away.
(At home I would be winding my father's watch
against another day. How could he have died
younger than I am now?)

It is time to gather space into this shrunken room.
We let in lake and sky;
we clutch the mountain that endures,
fading as though for the last time,
and hold each other as we fall to darkness,
prescient of birth,
remembering what it is
to die.

Rubbing Stone

Endurance is a stone's first name.
I give you a stone.
Not something to stroke like a cat,
nor polish idly like a silver blade;
not a trinket for your touch—
an ivory fan,
or ruby, faceted and bright—
but a stone, smooth and heavy,
found on a beach—a talisman.
Harder than gold or wood long dead,
it lies in your hand, keeping
its own shape,
symbol of things inviolate and pure.
It is not a stone to skip,
though it is flat and knows joy,
but something to wish upon, to hold.
Though all else between us
blows apart,
this gift endures,
signed with the signature of shells,
shaped to the hollow of a heart.

Speech for a Small Room

Having laid aside all but the armor of air,
asprawl on the sheets,
looking somehow smaller than the branched tree
you are,
you turn to me as toward your own solitude,
and speech spills from my hands.

In this momentary marriage,
my fingers, phrasing endearments
of their own,
trace upon your limbs
what woman knows with her first tears,
what the dumb cry.

And when in answer
light moves from your body
like shimmer from leaves,
nothing in love is left untouched,
no canticle unsaid.

Costume Play

Not all of what you doffed
hangs over the chair,
waiting to be jerked to life again.

Shirt and trousers loll
above the empty shoes,
while I with love uncover
skin, bone, coiled nerve,
peel off your bright will
like foil,
toss anger to the floor.

Afterwards
when innocence is old,
and time beats in the wrist again,
you rise, put on
your skeleton,
your skin,
your cold clothes; reach for your
will,
and button to the chin
your frayed hostility.

Between These Weathers

Neither bound
nor set free,
I wobble on your wrist
like some crazy, drunken thing,
not knowing up from down,
nor friend from prey.

Why am I here, I say?
I, more wing
than claw,
peck at this tether,
yet hunger for your hand
both flesh and metaphor.

The sun says wait,
the night says fly.
Between these weathers and these hopes
I hesitate.
The earth turns green and golden.
The dark sky
opens like a door.

Return to an Island

I was middle-aged
before I learned
not even place is constant.

Moths surrender flight each morning,
like the huge ones we found
dead against the screen.
Madmen even cage the kling-kling bird.

Places drift.

Where had everything gone?
Boulder, mountain, meadow, beach
wore time's integument
like mist. Poinciana blurred.
Palms, once a silhouette of summer,
ran down the hill
tangled with oleanders.
Sugarcane higher than corn
covered a wild familiar field.
Bees menaced the path we used to walk.

(Once we stole a conch shell
from this shore. It roared
with a voice like Poseidon's
until I took it home.
I placed it next to a sculptured fish.
It lay there a year or more
mute as onyx.)

Even now I do not understand
how places move without moving,
how what is done
becomes undone. But I record it here
for travelers who are lost,
for lovers looking for themselves
in landscapes they never saw before,
once known
and knowing.

Poem for Eric Barker

The manner of your going
was like the long-legged water bird you loved
suddenly lifting itself from the pebbled bank
of the Big Sur
and disappearing through the alders
with a ghostly flash of wings.

When I sort out the places
that claim your presence
I see you posed, naked and exulting,
on the diving rock of that same river,
arms above your head,
crowing
like a white-haired
Pan;

and the day we picked up beer cans
from the shore
with you swearing, "Fuck the barbarians!"
Later we waded upstream to gather watercress
and swim. You recited Graves and Auden.
I remember you wore a wide-brimmed straw hat
someone had left behind, and nothing else.
We slept on the warm stones.

In your one-room house,
just big enough for you and the mice,
you played Vivaldi or Bach. Whenever
I hear "The Four Seasons" I remember
how the music drifted out from the casement windows
to greet me,

past the loud bees in the
nasturtiums.
The bed was piled with books,
and the enormous dictionary
open on the stand.
We drank coffee there, and
played with Dylan and Caitlin—
names I had given them when they were kittens.
You cried when Caitlin died.

Once we roasted marshmallows
in the fireplace of an old house
while bats
flew overhead. That night you read me
a new poem about Madelynne.
I heard them all, and about
the young girls you laid so tenderly,
and forgot as soon as you had put them
in a poem.
But Madelynne, the red-haired dancer
"with the faith of a firewalker,"
Madelynne you never forgot.

Nor shall I forget you, Eric—
the sight, touch, smell of you—
warm and musty with pipe tobacco and sage
and crushed leaves.
You are my thumb in the eye
of all the stuffed shirts in the world.
You are my wild sea on the other side of
the breakwater,
and my reminder of pure, single flight
like that of the cormorants we watched together
from the hill.

When I need you, you are there,
or by the river, patiently building
stone towers
until they topple.
"Twenty-three! Did you see that?
A record!"
And then you start rebuilding,
stone upon stone,
carefully feeling for the invisible balance
and center,
while the sun pours its golden honey
on your hands,
and the kingfishers scream.

Photograph by Carolyn Kozo

Jean Burden graduated from the University of Chicago, where she studied under Thornton Wilder. Her first group of poems was published in *Poetry*. She has lived in Southern California since 1946, dividing her time between a career in public relations, free-lance writing, and poetry. She has over a thousand articles in print, from *The Atlantic* to *Mademoiselle* to *Prairie Schooner* to *Woman's Day*. She has taught poetry at local colleges, and today conducts two master classes from her home. She has lectured and read her poems across the country—from Harvard and Brandeis to UCLA and University of Washington. She recorded her poems for the Library of Congress, and has been Poetry Editor of *Yankee* magazine since 1955. A poetry series in her name was established by California State University, Los Angeles, in 1986, featuring such luminaries as Howard Nemerov, Mark Strand, Maxine Kumin, and Lucille Clifton, among others.

University of Central Florida Contemporary Poetry Series

Diane Averill, *Branches Doubled Over with Fruit*
George Bogin, *In a Surf of Strangers*
Van K. Brock, *The Hard Essential Landscape*
Jean Burden, *Taking Light from Each Other*
Lynn Butler, *Planting the Voice*
Daryl Ngee Chinn, *Soft Parts of the Back*
Rebecca McClanahan Devet, *Mother Tongue*
Rebecca McClanahan Devet, *Mrs. Houdini*
Gerald Duff, *Calling Collect*
Malcolm Glass, *Bone Love*
Barbara L. Greenberg, *The Never-Not Sonnets*
Susan Hartman, *Dumb Show*
Lola Haskins, *Forty-four Ambitions for the Piano*
Lola Haskins, *Planting the Children*
William Hathaway, *Looking into the Heart of Light*
Michael Hettich, *A Small Boat*
Roald Hoffmann, *Gaps and Verges*
Roald Hoffmann, *The Metamict State*
Hannah Kahn, *Time, Wait*
Michael McFee, *Plain Air*
Richard Michelson, *Tap Dancing for the Relatives*
Judith Minty, *Dancing the Fault*
David Posner, *The Sandpipers*
Nicholas Rinaldi, *We Have Lost Our Fathers*
CarolAnn Russell, *The Red Envelope*
Robert Siegel, *In a Pig's Eye*
Edmund Skellings, *Face Value*
Edmund Skellings, *Heart Attacks*
Ron Smith, *Running Again in Hollywood Cemetery*
Katherine Soniat, *Cracking Eggs*
Dan Stap, *Letter at the End of Winter*